Christopher Johnson was born in 1931 and educated at Winchester College and Magdalen College, Oxford, where he received a first-class honours degree in philosophy, politics and economics. He worked as a journalist on *The Times* and on the *Financial Times*, where he was successively Paris correspondent, diplomatic correspondent, foreign editor, managing editor, managing director of the Business Enterprises Division, and a director of the company. He became economic adviser to Lloyds Bank in 1977, group economic adviser in 1981, and chief economic adviser in September 1986. He is the editor of *Lloyds Bank Annual Review* and of the bank's other publications.

Christopher Johnson is Visiting Professor of Economics at Surrey University, and a member of the Council of the Royal Economic Society. He is a specialist adviser to the Treasury Select Committee of the House of Commons. His other books include *Anatomy of UK Finance* (1977), and *North Sea Energy Wealth* (1979).

CHRISTOPHER JOHNSON

Measuring the Economy

PENGUIN BOOKS

PENGUIN BOOKS

Published by the Penguin Group
27 Wrights Lane, London W8 5TZ, England
Viking Penguin Inc., 375 Hudson Street, New York, New York 10014, USA
Penguin Books Australia Ltd, Ringwood, Victoria, Australia
Penguin Books Canada Ltd, 2801 John Street, Markham, Ontario, Canada L3R 1B4
Penguin Books (NZ) Ltd, 182–190 Wairau Road, Auckland 10, New Zealand

Penguin Books Ltd, Registered Offices: Harmondsworth, Middlesex, England

First published in Pelican Books 1988
Reprinted in Penguin Books 1990
1 3 5 7 9 10 8 6 4 2

Printed by Clays Ltd, St Ives plc
Filmset in Monophoto Plantin

Contents

List of Figures   vii
List of Tables   xi
Abbreviations   xv
Author's Preface   1

Introduction   5
The political use of statistics · Pitfalls for the unwary ·
What price forecasts? · Notes

1 Economic Growth   15
The UK's growth record · Output-based GDP · Index
of output of the production industries · Expenditure-
based GDP · Income-based GDP · Forecasting GDP ·
Cyclical indicators of the UK economy

2 Personal Income and Saving   40
Personal income and expenditure · Consumers' expenditure · Retail sales · Distributive trades survey · The
economic theory of consumption and saving

3 Industry and Commerce   60
Industrial and commercial companies · Capital account
and financial surplus · Fixed capital expenditure ·
Stockbuilding · CBI industrial trends survey · The
theory of profits and investment

4 Labour Statistics   81
The definition of unemployment · How the unemploy-
ment statistics were reduced · Unemployment and

employment · Earnings, productivity and labour costs · The economics of unemployment, pay and productivity

5   Inflation   105
The Retail Prices Index · The history of the RPI · Method of compilation of the RPI · Strengths and weaknesses of the RPI · Owner-occupation and the RPI · What is in the RPI basket? · Short-term behaviour and the RPI · The Tax and Price Index (TPI) · Producer prices · Other inflation indices · Economic influences

6   The Balance of Payments   137
The trade figures · The changing pattern of visible trade · Capital account and reserves · Exchange rates · The economics of the balance of payments

7   Money, Banking and Finance   162
The meaning of money · The publication of money and banking statistics · The public-sector borrowing requirement (PSBR) · Interest rates · The theory of money and banking

Conclusions   199

Appendix: Main official macro-economic press
          notices and publication days   209

References   211

Index   225

Figures

1. Gross domestic product, 1948–86: average measure (annual) at 1980 factor cost (*source:* Blue Book 1987, table 15.11)   19

2. Shares of GDP (output), 1980 (*source: Industry Statistics*, CSO Occasional Paper 20; CSO Press notice (87)43, 19 May 1987)   23

3. Manufacturing output, 1948–86 (*source: Economic Trends*, Annual Supplement, table 80)   26

4. Factor income distribution, 1980–86 (*source: Economic Trends*, April 1987, pp. 80, 84, 85,87)   33

5. Personal-income analysis, 1986 (*source:* Blue Book 1987, tables 4.1, 4.9)   46

6. The flow of personal sector saving, 1986 (*source:* Blue Book 1987, tables 4.1, 4.9, 4.10; *Financial Statistics Explanatory Handbook* 1987, p. 95)   47

7. Life assurance and pension funds: income and expenditure analysis, 1986 (*source:* Fig. 6)   47

8. Changing shares in saving (*source: UK National Accounts* 1986, tables 4.1, 4.4, 4.5)   48

9. Shares of consumers' expenditure and retail sales, 1986 (*source: consumers' expenditure: Monthly Digest of Statistics*, April 1987, table 1.5; *retail sales:* DTI Press notice 313, 8 June 1987)   54

10. Gross trading profits, 1980–86, industrial and commercial companies (net of stock appreciation) (*source:* Blue Book 1987, table 5.4)   65

11. Industrial and commercial companies' use of savings, 1980–86 (*source:* Blue Book 1987, tables 5.4, 5.6)   68

12. Industrial and commercial companies' flow of funds, 1980–86 (*source:* Press notice CSO (87)59, 29 June 1987)   70

13. Shares of capital expenditure by sector and by asset, 1986 (*source: by sector: Financial Statistics,* May 1987, table 1.2; *by asset: Monthly Digest of Statistics,* April 1987, table 1.7)   72

14. Shares of capital expenditure by industry, 1986 (*source: Monthly Digest of Statistics,* April 1987, tables 1.7–1.9; *British Business,* 26 June 1987)   73

15. Unemployment in the UK, 1971–86 (September) (*source: Economic Trends,* Annual Supplement, tables 102, 103; *Employment Gazette,* July 1985, p. 275; *Unemployment Unit Briefing,* October 1986)   89

16. Economic status of the UK population: Great Britain, spring 1986 (*source:* Labour Force Survey)   92

17. Population of working age, Great Britain, March1979 to March 1987 (*source: Employment Gazette*)   94

18. The Retail Prices Index, 1962–86   108

19. The RPI with and without mortgage costs, 1985–7   118

20. Consumption changes, 1975–85 (*source: UK National Accounts,* 1986, tables 4.8, 4.9)   125

21. The changing composition of the current account, 1974–86 (*source: Monthly Review of External Trade Statistics, Annual Supplement,* 1987, pp. 7, 17, 19)   141

22. Commodity analysis of visible trade, overseas trade statistics basis, 1976 and 1986 (*source: Monthly Review of External Trade Statistics, Annual Supplement,* 1987, p. 72)   147

23. Area analysis of visible trade, overseas trade statistics basis, 1976 and 1986 (*source: Monthly Review*

of External Trade Statistics, *Annual Supplement*, 1987, p. 73)   148

24. UK reserves: end-1975 to mid-1987 (*source: Financial Statistics*, table 10.3)   153

25. Exchange rates, monthly, 1977–87   157

26. M0, M1 and M3: monthly levels and targets   165

27. Private and public sector borrowing as percentage of GDP, 1980–86 (*source: Economic Trends*, June 1987, tables 56, 64; *Financial Statistics*, June 1987, tables 7.6, 7.7)   168

28. Shares in personal sector liquid assets, 1976–86 (*source: Bank of England Quarterly Bulletin*, May 1987)   181

29. Shares of mortgages outstanding, 1979–86 (*source: Bank of England Quarterly Bulletin*, May 1987)   182

30. Base rate, 1976–86   193

Tables

1. The national aggregates, 1986 (*source:* Blue Book 1987, table 1.1)   18

2. How GDP(E), GDP(I) and GDP(O) diverge (*source:* Press notice CSO (87)46, 20 May 1987)   21

3. GDP(O) growth: contribution of sectors, 1980–86 (*source:* Blue Book 1987, table 1.5)   25

4. Production industries: relative growth, 1980–86 (*source:* Press release CSO (87)73, 13 August 1987)   29

5. Coal, oil and gas, and GDP(O): percentage rates of change, 1981–6 (*source:* Blue Book 1987, table 2.4)   30

6. GDP, total domestic expenditure and total final expenditure, 1986 (*source:* Blue Book 1987, tables 1.2, 15.1)   33

7. Growth of personal income and expenditure, 1980–86 (*source:* Blue Book 1987, tables 4.1, 4.9)   42

8. Two derivations of personal saving, 1986 (*source:* Blue Book 1987, tables 4.1, 4.2, 4.3)   43

9. Personal and household sector accounts, 1986 (*source:* Blue Book 1987, tables 4.1, 4.9)   45

10. Reliability of personal sector statistics (*source:* UK National Accounts: Sources and Methods, p. 62)   50

11. Short-term changes in consumption and retail sales, 1986–7 (*source:* Press notice CSO (87)39,

30 April 1987; DTI Press notice 313, 8 June
1987; *British Business*, 24 April 1987)   52

12. Consumption and saving trends, 1980–86
    (*source:* Blue Book 1987, tables 4.1, 4.6, 4.9;
    DTI Press notice 313, 8 June 1987)   54

13. Industrial and commercial company profit
    trends: percentage changes, 1980–86 (*source:*
    Blue Book 1987, table 5.4)   63

14. Company appropriation account 1986 (*source:*
    Blue Book 1987, tables 5.4, 5.7)   67

15. Trends in fixed capital spending, 1980–86
    (*source:* DTI Press notice, 18 June 1987;
    Monthly Digest of Statistics, April 1987, table 1.7)   74

16. Stockbuilding trends, 1979–86 (*source:* DTI
    Press notice 87/348, 23 June 1987)   76

17. Criteria for being unemployed and alternative de-
    finitions of unemployment (*source:* Labour Force
    Survey 1986)   83

18. Unemployment by age, sex and duration, April
    1987 (*source: Employment Gazette*, July 1987,
    table 2.5)   84

19. The UK unemployment percentage, December
    1986 (*source: Employment Gazette*, July 1987,
    tables 1.1, 2.1)   87

20. Changes in the method of compiling the unem-
    ployment statistics, 1979–86 (*source: Employment
    Gazette*, October 1986, p. 422; *Unemployment
    Bulletin*, no. 20, summer 1986, pp. 14–15, and
    statistical supplement, May 1986, p. 6)   90

21. The effect of special employment measures: num-
    bers off the unemployment count, March 1987
    (*source: Charter for Jobs Economic Report*, May
    1987, table 1)   92

22. Changes in employment and unemployment in
    Great Britain, 1979–87 (*source: Employment
    Gazette*, Historical Supplement no. 1, and
    'Labour force outlook for Great Britain', May
    1987; Department of Employment Press notice
    156/87, 16 July 1987)   95

23. Average earnings in Great Britain, 1981–6 (*source: Economic Trends*, April 1987, tables 40, 42; *Employment Gazette*, July 1987, table 5.1)   100

24. Earnings, productivity and labour costs, 1980–87 (*source: Economic Trends*, April 1987, tables 34, 40; Department of Employment Press notice 156/87, 16 July 1987)   101

25. Changes in RPI weights between 1986 and 1987 (*source: Employment Gazette*, April 1987)   110

26. Analysing RPI increases over time (*source:* Department of Employment Press notice 40/87; *Employment Gazette*, March 1987, p. 119, table 1; *Monthly Digest of Statistics*, January 1987, table 18.1)   112

27. Calculating the RPI (*source:* Department of Employment Press notice 40/87)   113

28. Averaging the RPI, 1986 (*source: Economic Trends*, January 1987, table 4.2)   114

29. The price of owner-occupation, 1977–87 (*source: Building Societies Fact Book*; *Monthly Digest of Statistics*; *Employment Gazette*)   117

30. Weight of owner-occupation expenditure, 1985 (*source: UK National Accounts*, 1986, table 4.8; *BSA Bulletin*, April 1987, tables 12 and 13; *Methodological Issues Affecting the Retail Prices Index*, Cmnd 9848, July 1986; Vanessa Fry and Panos Pashardes, *The RPI and the Cost of Living*, Institute for Fiscal Studies, May 1986)   120

31. The RPI and other inflation indices, 1975–86 (*source:* Press notices; *UK National Accounts*, 1986, table 1.16; *Economic Trends*, table 42)   130

32. The changing trade figures for 1985 (*source:* DTI/CSO Press notices)   144

33. The UK current account, 1986 (*source; UK Balance of Payments 1987* (Pink Book))   145

34. Visible UK trade trends, 1977–87 (*source: Monthly Review of External Trade Statistics*

Annual Supplement, 1987, p. 12; *Economic Trends*, April 1987, p. 79)   149

35.   The capital account, 1986 (*source:* Press notice CSO (87)50, 4 June 1987)   152

36.   Exchange rates, 1976–87 (*source: Monthly Review of External Trade Statistics, Annual Supplement*, 1987, p. 87)   156

37.   The components of M1, M3, M4 and M5, 1979–86 (*source:* Bank of England banking statistics, June 1987; *Financial Statistics*)   172

38.   Monetary targets and results, 1976–87 (*source:* Bank of England)   173

39.   The credit counterparts of changes to M4, 1983, 1986 (*source:* Bank of England banking statistics)   175

40.   Banks' sterling lending to the UK private sector, October 1986 to June 1987 (*source:* Banking statistics; Bank of England Press notice; Monthly statement of the London and Scottish Banks; Banking Information Service)   177

41.   Building societies' flow of funds, 1982 and 1986 (*source:* Building Societies Association Press notice, July 1987; *Financial Statistics*, June 1987, tables 7.6, 7.7)   180

42.   Analysis of loans and advances to UK residents, 1983–7 (*source:* Bank of England and CLSB Press notices)   183

43.   Consumer credit, 1986 (*source: Financial Statistics*, August 1987, table 9.3; DTI Press notice, 3 October 1987, table 2)   185

44.   The public sector borrowing requirement, 1986/7 (*source:* CSO/Treasury Press notice, CSO (87)67, 16 July 1987; *Financial Statistics*, June 1987, table 1.2)   189

Abbreviations

BoE   Bank of England
BOP   Balance of payments
BT   British Telecom
capex   Capital expenditure
CBI   Confederation of British Industry
CED   Consumers' expenditure deflator
CGBR   Central government borrowing requirement
c.i.f.   Carriage, insurance and freight
CLSB   City of London and Scottish Banks
CSO   Central Statistical Office
DoE   Department of the Environment
DTI   Department of Trade and Industry
EC   European Community
EMS   European Monetary System
ERI   Effective rate index
FES   Family Expenditure Survey
GDFCF   Gross domestic fixed capital formation
GDP   Gross domestic product
GNP   Gross national product
GTP   Gross trading profit
ICC   Industrial and commercial company
ILO   International Labour Organization
IMF   International Monetary Fund
IPD   Interest, profits and dividends
LABR   Local authority borrowing requirement
LAPF   Life assurance and pension funds
LHS   Left-hand scale
MTFS   Medium-term financial strategy

NAFA Net acquisition of financial assets

NBR Net borrowing requirement

OECD Organization for Economic Cooperation and Development

OFI Other financial institution

OPEC Organization of Petroleum Exporting Countries

OTS Overseas trade statistics

PCBR Public corporations' borrowing requirement

PDI Personal disposable income

PLC Public limited company

PNB private non-profit-making body

PSBR Public sector borrowing requirement

PSFD Public sector financial deficit

PSL Private sector liquidity

RNDI Real national disposable income

RPDI Real personal disposable income

RPI Retail Prices Index

RPIAC Retail Prices Index Advisory Committee

SIC Standard Industrial Classification

SNAPS Ships, North Sea installations, aircraft, precious stones and silver

TDE Total domestic expenditure

TFE Total final expenditure

TPI Tax and Price Index

UIB Unincorporated business

VAT Value-added tax

YTS Youth Training Scheme

Author's Preface

The idea of this book arose casually over the coffee after lunch with Andrew Franklin, the senior business editor of Penguin Books. He noticed the list of monthly economic indicators on the back page of *Lloyds Bank Economic Bulletin*, and asked whether I had thought of writing a book on these indicators, and on how to interpret them. Acting on the theory that one should respond to a known demand rather than generate an unwanted supply, I promptly accepted.

As I developed the idea, it seemed to provide a way of integrating into a coherent whole some of the material that I had been writing every month since January 1979 in the *Bulletin*. Some sections of the book have already appeared in different versions of the *Bulletin*. I here express my gratitude to Lloyds Bank for giving me the freedom to develop my comments on economic policy in this publication, and the resources to write a book associated with it. Particular personal thanks are due to colleagues in the bank: Nicholas Cobb, statistician; Patrick Foley, deputy chief economic adviser; Marcia Howard, my secretary; David Thornhill, graphics artist; and John Young, economic adviser for the UK. I should also like to acknowledge the help of a number of experts who read the various chapters, while making it clear that any remaining errors are my own: Ray Ash, Peter Bull, David Flaxen, Richard Layard, Michael Lockyer, Don Sellwood, E. W. Shepherd and John Walton. I should also like to thank the members of the Treasury Select Committee in the House of Commons, and its chairman, Terence

Higgins, for appointing me as their specialist adviser. This gave me the opportunity to express through the committee's publications my own comments on official financial policy, and on some of the statistical concepts involved, to discuss them with committee members and staff, and to hear at first hand the evidence of ministers and officials summoned by the committee. Some of the ideas put to the committee re-appear in a different form in this book.

The plan of each chapter differs somewhat according to the nature of the material, but in each case the aim is the same. I start by explaining why an indicator is important, by looking at its impact on the economy and on financial markets. I define the meaning of the statistical concept, and explain how the figures are compiled. I say something about the past history of the indicator, and illustrate how it has moved in previous years. Where appropriate, I assess and criticize the particular statistics used as indicators, and sug-gest improvements. At a more political level, I observe the way in which governments have turned key statistics to their own use, sometimes against the better judgement of profes-sional statisticians. The figures for economic growth, unem-ployment and public borrowing have all been presented or defined in such a way as to favour the government case. Finally, I give a brief mention of some of the economic theor-ies that are used to explain and predict the behaviour of the indicators.

The references at the end of the book are mainly official sources. They give the Press notices covered in each chapter, which are also listed in the Appendix. They show how government departments and the Bank of England were think-ing about the main indicators and their behaviour. They also include issues of *Lloyds Bank Economic Bulletin* and *Lloyds Bank Review*. There has been no space to do more than hint at the diversity of similar material from economists in the universities and in business. There are also references to help the reader find his or her way around the government statistical sources. Footnotes are not given in the text, but readers should be able to follow up sources from the ref-erences at the end. When sources are given at the foot of tables and figures, this means that they are derived from the sources, rather than being reproduced from them directly. The prime source is the Press notices. Most Press-notice material is later published in hard-copy publications, but not all. It is of permanent value in showing what figures were originally announced, before being revised, since these are the figures that influence financial markets and that need to be used in any study of the impact of news based on them. The hard-copy publications show the revised, but suppress the original, figures.

I have resisted the temptation to make international comparisons between the British way of doing statistics and those of other countries, and between the UK statistics themselves and those of the UK's main rivals. I am anything but insular in my approach, but this would have made the book unmanageably long.

This book is meant for school and university students of economics, professional economists, politicians, civil servants, statisticians, financial-market analysts and bank managers, among others. Economists should therefore bear in mind that much has been simplified for the intelligent lay person with a head for figures. Others should be reassured that all economic and statistical concepts are explained, so that familiarity with the subject, while desirable, is not essential. Readers of Lloyds Bank publications, or the financial press, should have few problems. The book is not just about statistics, but about the states of affairs which they describe. I am a firm believer in making statistics come alive by showing their relevance to economic and financial policy issues. To measure the economy is also to measure the performance of the government and the private sector. So the book should appeal even to those whose main concerns are wider than statistical sources and methods.

Christopher Johnson
Lloyds Bank Economics Department
September 1987

Introduction

'Here, then, are a few suggestions for getting the headline figures into some sort of perspective . . . Never trust a single month's figures . . . Be suspicious of seasonal adjustment . . . Remember the broad context of all the numbers you read.'

Anthony Harris, *Financial Times*, 25 July 1987

Almost every day a new economic statistic is announced. An important sector of the information industry has grown up around these statistics, predicting, analysing and disputing them. Financial analysts and traders in the City can add on or wipe off billions of pounds from the value of shares and currencies by their reaction to these economic indicators. Politicians attempt to interpret them so as to favour government or opposition, particularly in the run-up to elections. Employers and trade unions fasten upon such key numbers as the inflation rate as an essential input into pay negotiations.

Most of the indicators are announced by means of Press notices, which are distributed by messenger in central London to a handful of agencies, newspapers, broadcasting stations and City firms. A precise embargo time must be observed to the nearest second, so that no one gets an unfair advantage in the financial markets. Most members of even the informed public never see these Press notices, but have to rely on the incomplete and selective versions of them which come out on wire services, radio and television, and the next day's papers. The public can buy most of the same information in government statistical publications, but by the time they appear, the following month's indicators in Press-release form have already made them out of date. In view of the importance of Press notices, it would be an undesirable restriction on the freedom of information if they were available only to the Press and one or two 'insiders'. Some of them can now be obtained from government departments on subscription, following a recommendation by the Rayner Committee in 1980. There is no reason why they should not similarly be made instantly available to anyone at home or in the office with the appropriate screen and telecommunications equipment.

This book sets out to explain those economic indicators that are announced in Press notices, most of them once a month, some once a quarter. It includes also such key financial-market variables as interest rates and exchange rates, which both influence and are in turn influenced by the economic indicators. It therefore tends to focus on the short-term changes in the economy, while putting them in a long-term perspective. It does not attempt to cover the wealth of economic and financial statistics which appear in government publications that are not officially considered to be of sufficient short-term significance to merit Press releases.

Financial markets are often criticized for 'short-termism', which could be defined as over-reacting to short-term changes in economic performance, and not thinking enough about the long term. The facile answer to the charge is that if everyone else in the market reacts in a certain way to a short-term signal, then you may lose money by not doing the same. The more serious answer is that short-term changes may be the best indicator we have when trying to forecast the longer term. If the short-term change is erratic and unrepresentative of the trend, the official Press notice may try to make this clear, and markets will usually be prevented from rushing herd-like in the wrong direction – provided that they trust the official explanation.

The political use of statistics

The reliability of official statistics used in political debate has itself become a political issue in the case of some of the more controversial indicators, such as unemployment and inflation. The publication of statistics is one of the government's tasks. It might therefore seem as if the government could use its monopoly in this field as a political advantage, distorting, postponing and suppressing figures that put its own economic performance in an unfavourable light, and exaggerating, leaking in advance, and publicizing figures that seem to be to its credit. This is indeed apt to happen in totalitarian regimes.

In a democratic society, the objectivity and openness of official statistics should be beyond reproach. Like all democratic ideals, this one is only imperfectly realized in the UK and many other Western democracies. It was a great step forward when the then Prime Minister, Winston Churchill, established the Central Statistical Office in 1941, under its first director, Professor Harry Campion. He was succeeded by Professor Claus Moser, who presided over a major expansion of official statistics, particularly in other government departments. This reflected the passion for statistics of Harold Wilson, who became Prime Minister in 1964, and it followed the recommendations of the Estimates Committee in 1966. Unfortunately the compilation and publication of all official statistics was not centralized in the CSO, as is done in most other countries. Fortunately, the existence of a Government Statistical Service, under the same director as the CSO, gives some guarantee of professional ethics among those responsible for official statistics in other departments, even though they may be responsible to politically appointed ministers.

The CSO is directly responsible for less than half the main Press notices, and in some cases has joint responsibility with other departments. As a department in the Cabinet Office, it is technically responsible to the Prime Minister, although in practice it works closely with the Treasury, and is in the same building. Other departments which publish key indicators in Press-notice form are the Treasury, the Bank of England, the Department of Trade and Industry and the Department of Employment. Other, more specialized indicators are published by other departments, but we are concerned here with only the macro-economic indicators, not those for particular sectors of the economy such as health, housing and transport.

It would have been better had the CSO been given a greater degree of independence and central control of statistics, so as to avoid accusations that particular departments massage economic indicators in a way that suits their policy objectives. Governments have preferred to operate on the principle that the department responsible for collecting statistical information should define, publish and answer for the indicators based on it. This argument could have been countered by making the CSO responsible for collecting the information as well as for publishing the statistics. Once a more decentralized structure had been established, it was never likely that the great Whitehall departments, conscious that information gives power, would readily surrender it in this way to the CSO. Indeed, as long as the CSO is a department of the Cabinet Office, centralization of statistics could be open to the criticism that it puts even more power in the hands of the Prime Minister, at the expense of departmental ministers. A greater degree of independence for the CSO would be required to offset the dangers of centralization under the present arrangements. The point is not that, for example, the Department of Employment deliberately keeps redefining 'unemployment' so as to minimize the published figures (see page 88). The department's statisticians may well have been doing no more than seek a true and fair definition comparable with that used by other countries. The point is that the department will always be open to the accusation that it is massaging the statistics to suit its own ends, as long as it is responsible for them. Such accusations might be avoided by transferring responsibility for the figures to an independent Central Statistical Office, whose objectivity was beyond reproach. The CSO would still have to rely on other departments to administer the collection of statistics, but it could be given more say in how this is done.

The review of government statistical services by Sir Derek Rayner in 1980, whose main task was to economize on their cost, was a blow to the democratic concept of statistics as a public good rather than a political tool. 'The primary duty for the CSO is to serve central government requirements . . . We have found the Office too heavily committed to serving the public at large,' said his report. Within the limits imposed by the Rayner cuts, and their primary responsibility to ministers, the members of the Government Statistical Service have nevertheless done their best to serve the public interest according to their own professional standards.

Pitfalls for the unwary

Even when there is no dispute that indicators are intended to be objective, they can still be wrong or misleading, for a number of reasons.

Seasonality. When retail sales go up in the months just before Christmas, no one is misled into thinking that the trend has suddenly started rising. Part of the rise can be attributed to seasonal factors. Many statistical series are therefore seasonally adjusted. This is a complex statistical procedure. It consists in analysing how much of the change in the figures in the same month or quarter of previous years was due to seasonal factors and how much to other trends. The seasonal factors can then be isolated, and added to or subtracted from the unadjusted figures to give the seasonally adjusted figures. In some months, for example, unemployment may be rising on an unadjusted basis, and falling on a seasonally adjusted basis, or vice versa. There is danger that unscrupulous commentators will pick whichever figure suits them best from month to month.

Revisions. Some, but not all, statistics are revised in the light of later information. Some Press notices specifically publish revised figures a few months after the original figures. Particularly in the short term, some revisions may show that the trend indicated by the unrevised original figures would have been quite different had the revised figures been known at the time. Some analysts attempt to predict revisions, or cast doubt on an indicator when it is originally published, on the grounds that the revised version will show something different and more accurate.

It is seldom possible to be confident that revisions are anything other than random. If they show a consistent pattern, then the official statisticians should be able to spot it, and incorporate it into their estimating technique so as to get the figures right first time. For example, estimates of part of the black economy are now built into the national income figures, even though they do not purport to record the whole of it (see page 20).

Data sources. Some statistics are unreliable because they come from sources which cover only part of what is being measured, and may also supply inaccurate information. The government is generally in a better position to get accurate data about its own activities, such as the public-sector borrowing requirement, than about those of the private sector. Most British businesses regard filling in government forms as a chore to be delegated to as low a level as possible, and it is often not feasible to send forms to more than the largest companies, or to a sample.

In the case of the personal sector, data can sometimes be inferred only as the residual which remains when data for the other sectors have been deducted from the total. In the case of the balance of payments, the invisibles account is notoriously difficult to estimate (see page 143). It is often revised, but even after revision there is little confidence that the figures are accurate. Balance-of-payments figures are revised, more often than not in a more favourable direction, sometimes years after the event. Some of the balance-of-payments crises of past years would never have happened had it been known at the time that the true figures were not as bad as those first announced.

Changes in definition. The way in which an indicator is defined often changes over the months and years. Statisticians try to improve their definitions so that they are measuring what they want to measure. The definition of unemployment, for example, has been changed on numerous occasions over the last few years. This definition has been narrowed down to such an extent that it excludes over 400,000 people who would have been included under earlier definitions. The latest definition may or may not be more accurate than its predecessors. It certainly makes it more difficult to compare like with like when looking at a trend over the years, even though the statisticians may provide runs of figures on the old and new definitions for a limited period. There is something to be said for sticking to a definition, however imperfect, so as to facilitate the study of trends over a period of time. But definitions change as the use to which statistics are put changes, and this depends on government policy.

Turning-points. Because economic trends go up and down, the latest figure in a series can be made to look good or bad according to which earlier figure it is compared with. Take as an example a two-year recession, shown in the table below. In the first year the amounts produced each quarter are 100, 98, 96, 94, in the second year 94, 96, 98, 100. How should the second year's figures be presented? The first quarter shows no change from the previous quarter, but a 6 per cent drop compared with the same quarter of the previous year. The second quarter shows a 2.1 per cent increase on the previous quarter (8.8 per cent at an annual rate), but a 2 per cent fall on the same quarter of the previous year. The third quarter shows a 2.1 per cent increase both on the previous quarter and on the same quarter of the previous year.

Quarters	1	2	3	4	Average
Year 1	100	98	96	94	97
Year 2	94	96	98	100	97
Year 2 change (%) *over:*					
One quarter	0.0	+2.1	+2.1	+2.1	1.6
Four quarters	−6.0	−2.0	+2.1	+6.4	0.0

The fourth quarter shows again a 2.1 per cent increase on the previous quarter, but a 6.4 per cent increase compared with the same quarter of the previous year. Growth through the year to the fourth quarter looks good. Yet if the quarterly figures for each of the two years are averaged, they come to exactly the same figure of 97. There has on this measure been no growth at all from one year to the next.

This simple example illustrates two points. First, the same figure can be made to tell two quite different stories, according to what it is compared with. Second, the comparison of one statistic with another, whichever that is, often fails to tell the full story. Press notices do generally give a recent series of figures, but these are seldom reproduced in press comments. A graph may tell the story better.

A good example of the importance of turning-points was provided by the dispute between government and opposition in the run-up to the June 1987 election about the recent record of economic growth. The government claimed, quite correctly, that economic growth had averaged 2.7 per cent a year over the five years 1982–6. The opposition argued, equally correctly, that growth had averaged only 1.5 per cent a year over the seven years 1980–86, if the 1980–81 recession, with a 3.6 per cent fall in economic output, was included. (These figures have already been, and will no doubt for years continue to be, subsequently revised.)

What price forecasts?

The importance of the economic indicators is such that considerable research is carried out by financial analysts to try to forecast what the next Press notice will show. Financial markets form expectations in advance of each announcement, based on some kind of average of analysts' figures. Inside information seldom leaks out of Whitehall, at least on macro-economic figures, unless ministers have some reason for leaking, such as a desire to soften the blow of bad news. If the figures are close to expectations, markets remain unaffected by the announcement. If they are very different, markets can be expected to react. Money can be made by following analysts who diverge from the consensus: if they are usually right, follow their advice; if they are usually wrong, follow the opposite of their advice.

Even short-term indicators can sometimes be successfully predicted by the use of econometric models based on some theory of how the economy works. Equal success is claimed by those who use charts and other methods based entirely on the previous behaviour of the series of figures being predicted, without bringing in the causal impact of other variables, as do the econometric models. In both cases, it is difficult to allow for short-term monthly disturbances, which may throw off course models that could be relatively successful for annual or quarterly forecasts. Patient factual research can sometimes discover what such apparently random factors are, even in advance of an announcement. For example, the inflation analyst who buys his own vegetables and spots that there is a glut and a fall in the price of seasonal foods, in a month when they are normally expensive and in short supply, may steal a march on the competition. Variations in the price of seasonal foods are an important short-term influence on the Retail Prices Index (RPI).

As well as describing and defining each of the main indicators, the book will outline the main economic factors which determine them, as well as citing some of the more erratic short-term factors which can cause them to depart from trends. They have been grouped under seven main headings: economic growth; personal spending; industry and commerce; labour; inflation; the balance of payments; and money and finance. The scope is limited to the United Kingdom. Even though the economic indicators of other countries, notably the USA, are almost as important to the UK economy as our own, differences between the statistical methods of the various countries are such that each requires and deserves a separate book.

In some foreign-exchange dealing rooms, whenever an important economic indicator comes up on the ticker-tape, a bell rings to tell the dealers that it is an important piece of news to which they have to react. As with Pavlov's dogs, the reaction is instinctive, thanks to assiduous conditioning.

Some scope is allowed to human initiative, since the dealers still have to work out whether it is a buy or a sell signal. The herd instinct ensures, however, that they all react in the same way. This book is designed to set out a slightly more sophisticated approach to the magic numbers which can make our fortunes or mar our lives.

Notes

1. I state here, but do not repeat throughout the book, that when I write, for example, that the rate of inflation was 8.1 per cent in 1980–86, I mean that, taking 1979 as the starting, 'base', year, inflation averaged 8.1 per cent (compound) during the years 1980–86. The alternative convention, used by the Treasury among others, is to take the first of the two years quoted as the base year, rather than the year preceding it. I also use 1986/7 to mean the financial year from April 1986 to March 1987, and 1986–7 to mean the period composed of the two years 1986 and 1987.

2. The statistics used in this book were the latest published during June–September 1986. In some cases, the 1987 Blue Book and Pink Book (*UK National Accounts* and *UK Balance of Payments*) have been used. In others, figures from Press notices and other sources have been used, which date from some weeks before these two prime sources. They may therefore have been revised by the time the Blue and Pink Books appeared, and may not be fully consistent with them. However, some of the figures in the Blue and Pink Books may already have been revised by the time this book appears. The statistics should thus be taken as being reasonably, but not totally, up to date, and as exemplifying the main points of the book. Those who want the up-to-date figures are encouraged to consult the latest available version of the sources quoted.

1

Economic Growth

> 'There was mixed news for the government in official statistics published yesterday. First-quarter figures showed growth continuing in the economy. But money supply accelerated last month, which is likely to add to Bank of England caution on interest rates.'
>
> David Smith, *The Times*, 21 May 1987

The rate of growth of the economy is the most important single indication of a country's economic performance. Mrs Thatcher and her ministers tried to break with tradition when they came to office in 1979 by arguing that it was the role of government to control inflation, and the role of the private sector to promote economic growth. After 1981, when the economy grew for five years at an average rate of $2\frac{3}{4}$ per cent, the government nevertheless claimed that the credit was due to the success of its policies. The growth rate is used to compare the UK's progress with that of other economies, and differences of a fraction of 1 per cent may affect positions in the league tables, even though they may be less than the average error in each country's statistics. Strictly speaking, it is the per head growth of the economy which should be used as an indicator of the rise in human welfare. (Consumption or personal income per head more accurately reflect living standards.) In many countries population growth absorbs much of the economic growth, and welfare may rise little, or fall, on a per-head basis. In the UK, population grew by 25 per cent to 56 million in the forty years to 1971. Since then the population has been virtually static, so for the period since 1971 expressing economic growth on a per-head basis is little different from measuring it in the aggregate, as is generally done.

The government has in fact moved half-way in its official pronouncements towards recognizing economic growth ex-plicitly as an objective. It has in recent years been using the increase in money GDP (gross domestic product – see below), a measure of the economy in current money terms that combines inflation and real economic growth. However, while the government wants to maximize real economic growth, it is at the same time trying to slow down the rate of increase of money GDP. The Treasury said in its *Financial Statement and Budget Report 1987–88* (paragraph 2.02): 'Monetary and fiscal policies are designed to reduce the growth of money GDP, so bringing down inflation. They are complemented by policies to encourage enterprise, ef-ficiency and flexibility. These policies improve the division of money GDP growth between output growth and infla-tion, and help the creation of jobs.' Clearly the objective of reducing nominal economic growth can be reconciled with the presumed objective of stable or increasing real economic growth only by means of a squeeze on inflation.

It was not until the early 1930s that economists began to give satisfactory definitions of the 'economy' whose growth was to be measured. There are three main ways of looking at economic activity, which correspond to three different ways of estimating its size:

1. As the *total output* of goods and services, referred to as gross domestic product, or GDP. This does not mean simply the total sales value of all goods and services pro-duced, because many of them are intermediate, and used in the production of other goods, so it would be double-counting to include them and the finished products of which they are a part. GDP is therefore defined as total 'value added', or what each of the producers adds to their inputs. For the economy as a whole, the inputs are imports. Imports are by definition excluded from GDP, while ex-ports are included.

2. As the *total income* derived from producing the output by the 'factors' of production; as employment incomes of labour, as profits of capital, and as rent of land and property. This is by definition equal to the value of the factors' output at 'factor cost' – what it costs to pay them. It does not include transfer incomes such as welfare benefits, or interest payments, which are not counted as value-added. This is called the income measure of GDP.

3. As the *expenditure* on total output, excluding spending by UK residents on imports and including spending by foreigners on UK exports. It is measured initially at market prices, including indirect taxes, such as value-added tax, which are part of prices, and excluding subsidies, which reduce prices. This, the expenditure measure of GDP, should be equal to the income or output measure, when the 'factor-cost adjustment', indirect taxes minus subsidies, has been subtracted from it.

It is natural to measure output in terms of the volume of goods and services produced. Income and expenditure, however, are most easily measured in money of the day, at current prices. They can then be expressed in volume terms by 'deflating' each year's figures by the increase in prices since a 'base' year. This gives income and expenditure in constant prices, which can then be used to measure changes in volume. Apart from the government's use of money GDP, which is in current prices, GDP changes are usually expressed in constant prices, or in real as opposed to nominal terms.

The three measures of GDP are called, for short, GDP(O), GDP(I) and GDP(E), output-, income- and expenditure-based GDP. Although they are by definition equal, they always differ somewhat in practice, because each of them is estimated by a different statistical method, none of them perfect. They are averaged to give the average estimate, GDP(A). However, GDP(O) can be estimated at an earlier stage than the others, and is the best short-term indicator of economic growth. Some other countries more

Table 1. The national aggregates, 1986 (current prices)

	£ billion
GNP at market prices (expenditure)	379.6
Less net property income from abroad	−4.7
GDP at market prices (expenditure)	374.9
Less factor-cost adjustment	−55.8
GDP at factor cost (expenditure)	319.1
Add residual error	6.9
GDP at factor cost (income)	326.0

Source: Blue Book 1987, table 1.1.

commonly use GNP, gross national product, which adds net property income from abroad to GDP. This comprises the return on British investment abroad, less the return on foreign investment in the UK, and is thus national in the sense of belonging to UK residents, but not domestic, because not derived from production in the UK.

Table 1 shows the arithmetical relationship between some of these national aggregates. It can be seen that GNP exceeds GDP by about £5 billion, or just over 1 per cent. There was also a residual error of £6 billion, the difference between GDP(E) and GDP(I), which would not exist in a world of perfect statistics.

The UK's growth record

Official GDP figures for the UK began to be calculated during the 1939–45 war. The present published series goes back to 1946 on an annual basis and to 1955 on a quarterly basis for GDP(E) and GDP(I), and back to 1948 (annual) and 1958 (quarterly) for GDP(O). The Royal Economic Society has made estimates of GDP going back to 1855. All GDP figures are first published in quarterly form, later annually. Monthly figures are published for the output of the 'production industries' (see page 27). This is a major

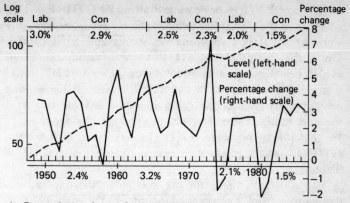

1. Gross domestic product, 1948–86: average measure (annual) at 1980 factor cost (*source:* Blue Book 1987, table 15.11)

constituent of GDP(O), and gives a good indication of the likely quarterly trend, so we deal with it in this chapter.

GDP(A) has increased by an average of 2.4 per cent a year at constant prices from 1949 to 1986, multiplying by 2.45 times in real terms. GDP per head has increased at an average of 2.1 per cent, multiplying by 2.15 times, because population has increased at 0.3 per cent a year. This is broken into shorter periods in Figure 1. Those at the bottom of the graph are decades (e.g. 1950–59). The 1960s were the best, with a 3.2 per cent growth rate. Growth fell to 2.1 per cent in the 70s, and 1.5 per cent in the first seven years of the 80s (this improves to 2.7 per cent if the recession of 1980–81 is omitted, see page 12). The record by administration of different parties (see the top of the graph), shows a relentless decline from 3 per cent in the last three years of the post-war Labour governments to half that figure for Mrs Thatcher's government. Such long-run trends may be attributed to economic rather than political factors, and may in any case be reversible. Governments cannot be held responsible for everything that happens in the economy, particularly the situation which they inherit from their predecessors.

The three GDP measures have diverged from each other in the 1980s. GDP(O) and GDP(I) have tended to show faster growth. They have moved ahead of GDP(E). This suggests that expenditure is inadequately recorded, possibly some of industry's spending on stocks and fixed capital. Until the early 1980s, GDP(I) was falling short of GDP(E), leaving a residual error. The official statisticians have attempted to estimate the size of the 'hidden economy' by taking this difference between the two as a measure of undeclared income, and trying to bridge the gap. In the 1980s, however, GDP(I) has been higher than GDP(E), so the residual error is in the other direction (see Table 1).

The allowance made for tax evasion in the national accounts rose from 2 per cent of incomes in the early 1970s to 3 per cent in the mid-1970s. It fell to $1\frac{1}{2}$ per cent in 1980 and about 1 per cent from 1982. Since self-employment incomes, thought to be one of the main areas of tax evasion, have risen, the evasion allowance should have risen. Yet the new tendency for income to exceed expenditure rather than falling short of it points the other way. In fact, it is likely that both income and expenditure are being under-recorded. Estimates of the size of the 'black economy', ranging up to $7\frac{1}{2}$ per cent of recorded GDP, greatly exceed any figures derived only from the difference between various ways of measuring GDP. Some estimates of the 'black economy' also include transfer payments, such as interest, which would not count as part of GDP because, by definition, they are not value-added (see page 17).

Table 2 shows how sharply the GDP measures can diverge in the short term, even after seasonal adjustment. In 1986 GDP(E) rose nearly 1 per cent less over the year to the fourth quarter than GDP(I). Yet in the first quarter it rose by nearly 2 per cent, twice as fast as GDP(I) and nearly five times as fast as GDP(O). It then fell by 0.5 per cent in the second quarter, while the other two rose by 1.2 per cent. Such divergences make it difficult in practice to use money GDP to steer policy, because there may be contradictory readings on three different dials.

Table 2. How GDP(E), GDP(I) and GDP(O) diverge (1986: Percentage changes at constant factor cost, seasonally adjusted)

	Quarters				Year average
	1	2	3	4	
GDP (Average)					
On previous: quarter	1.1	0.7	0.7	1.0	0.8
year	2.5	1.8	2.7	3.4	2.6
GDP (Expenditure)					
On previous: quarter	1.9	−0.5	0.2	1.3	0.3
year	2.6	1.7	2.0	2.9	2.3
GDP (Income)					
On previous: quarter	0.9	1.2	0.7	0.9	0.9
year	2.6	1.5	2.6	3.8	2.6
GDP (Output)					
On previous: quarter	0.4	1.2	1.3	0.6	0.9
year	2.3	2.3	3.5	3.5	2.8

Source: Press notice CSO (87)46, 20 May 1987.

Output-based GDP

The first indication of how GDP is moving is the quarterly Press release from the Central Statistical Office (CSO) giving a preliminary estimate of GDP(O). It comes out about seven weeks after the end of the quarter, and about a month before the fuller provisional estimates of the three different measures of GDP. It is seasonally adjusted, and at constant prices – those of 1980 at the time of writing. Quarterly and annual figures for the three types of GDP, and the average estimate derived from them, are also given in index form.

In the preliminary estimate, the only figure for the most recent quarter is that for GDP(O). It is regarded as the most reliable indicator of short-term trends. In recent years it has shown more rapid growth than GDP(E), the expenditure measure. It is therefore likely to be revised upwards later by less than GDP(E) as more information becomes available. It is thus also a more accurate guide to the true position of the economy in the longer run. The change in GDP(O) is subject to a mean upwards revision of 0.2 percentage points in the fuller GDP estimates a month after the preliminary GDP(O) estimate. Because this mean revision covers a range of −0.2 to +0.4, it can occasionally be downwards rather than upwards. This pattern of revisions has held good since September 1983. It would surely have been better to have added the 0.2 to preliminary estimates of GDP(O) from, say, the end of 1985. The average quarterly increase in GDP(O) during 1986 was 0.7 points in the preliminary estimate, which went up to 0.9 after the first revisions a month later. A mere 0.2 points sounds insignificant, but it is currently worth some £750 million in a year. These revisions are linked with the downwards bias of the index of production (see page 28).

The change in the index of GDP(O) is estimated by taking each sector of the economy in turn, and working out the change in the volume of its output. This is done sometimes by means of physical measurements of tonnage of products such as steel or oil, although of course one tonne of microchips has a greater value than one tonne of concrete. Sometimes it is done by looking at the change in current value of output, where there is a diversity of products, and deflating it by the price change for that industry. In theory, both inputs and outputs should be deflated to give the change in the volume of value added, which is what GDP is. But this is seldom possible in practice. It is particularly difficult to measure output of non-marketed public services such as health and education. Labour inputs are used as a proxy for outputs, and the assumption is generally made that labour productivity remains unchanged, which is unlikely to be the case in practice.

Because each industry is changing its output at a different rate, the weight given to each is important. The weight is the proportion of a part to the whole. At the time of writing, the weights are based on value added in 1980, which also marked the introduction of the new Standard Industrial Classification, SIC (1980), in place of the old system of Minimum List Headings (MLH).

Figure 2 shows the weights of the ten main SIC divisions in GDP(O), at 1980 volumes and prices. These do not cor-

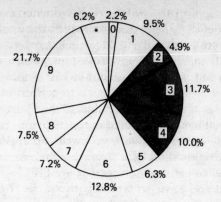

KEY 0 Agriculture, forestry and fishing
   1 Energy and water-supply industries
   2 Extraction of minerals and ores other than fuels; manufacture of metals, mineral products and chemicals
   3 Metal goods, engineering and vehicles industries
   4 Other manufacturing industries
   5 Construction
   6 Distribution, hotels and catering; repairs
   7 Transport and communication
   8 Banking, finance, insurance, business services and leasing
   9 Other services
   * Ownership of dwellings
NOTE: The shaded area comprises manufacturing industry.

2. Shares of GDP (output), 1980 (*source: Industry Statistics*, CSO Occasional Paper 20; CSO Press notice (87)43, 19 May 1987)

respond neatly to the old primary, secondary and tertiary categories. Something like a 'primary' sector consists of agriculture, at 2.2 per cent, and energy and water, 9.5 per cent, a total of 11.7 per cent (but energy now includes oil refining, which could be seen as 'secondary'). North Sea oil and gas was 4.4, coal and coke 1.5 of the 9.5 per cent. That was at the high oil price of 1980. In 1986, at two-thirds of the sterling oil price of 1980, after a volume increase in output of about 50 per cent, the contribution of the North Sea to GDP remained about the same as in 1980. Divisions 2, 3 and 4 are the manufacturing sector, accounting for 27 per cent of the economy. With the addition of division 1, energy and water supply, they are termed the production industries. Construction, division 5, can be added to the manufacturing sector to form a 'secondary' sector, making up one-third of the total. (It includes mineral extraction, which is, strictly, 'primary'.) This leaves the various service industries, adding up to 55 per cent of the economy, once termed the 'tertiary' sector. Just over 6 percentage points of the 55 are for ownership of dwellings, for national output includes the services which home-owners derive from owner-occupation. In the national accounts there is a figure for the rent which they are 'deemed' to pay themselves (see page 119).

Financial and business services amount to 11.6 per cent, but 4.1 per cent of this consists of net interest charged to other sectors. Because of the statistical convention that interest is a transfer payment and not value added, there has to be a corresponding negative 'adjustment for financial services', so their share then falls to 7.5 per cent after the deduction of net interest.

There is enormous disparity between the growth rates of different sectors of the economy, as Table 3 shows. The 'primary' sector grew most rapidly in the first half of the 1980s, followed by the 'tertiary' sector and then the 'secondary' sector. By applying the 1980 weights growth rate of each sector, we can see what their contribution is to GDP growth. Over the five years to 1986 agricultural output rose by nearly one-fifth, one and a third times as fast as GDP, thanks to the encouragement given by the EEC Common Agricultural Policy, and higher crop yields. The resulting surpluses mean that such a growth rate is unlikely to continue. Energy and water, with growth of 25 per cent, have also made a disproportionate contribution to GDP growth; oil and gas have gone up by 50 per cent, and the rest of this sector, which includes coal, very little. Again, the future trend for the energy industries is one of decline, as the potential output of the North Sea diminishes.

Manufacturing, on the contrary, has contributed less to GDP growth than its share of total output. Its 1986 output was only 5 per cent higher than in 1980 (see Table 3), so it accounted for only 8 per cent of total GDP growth, less

Table 3. GDP(O) growth: contribution of sectors, 1980–86

	Percentage change to 1986		1980 weight in total output (%)	Contribution to change in output		Percentage shares of (5)
	From 1985	From 1980		From 1985	From 1980	
	(1)	(2)	(3)	(4)[1]	(5)[2]	(6)
Agriculture	0.0	18.8	2.2	0.0	0.4	2.9
Energy and water	4.4	25.4	9.5	0.4	2.4	17.3
Manufacturing	0.9	4.7	26.6	0.2	1.2	8.6
Construction	2.3	2.1	6.3	0.1	0.1	0.7
Services	3.9	17.7	55.4	2.2	9.8	70.5
Total	3.0	14.0	100.0	3.0	14.0	100.0

1. = (1) × (3).
2. = (2) × (3).
Source: Blue Book 1987, table 1.5.

than a third of its output share. As an illustration of how sensitive statistics are to the base year of calculation, manufacturing did even worse from a 1979 base (see Figure 3). Its output fell by no less than 8.7 per cent in volume in the recession year of 1980, when high interest rates and the rising pound caused widespread cutbacks. By 1986, manufacturing had recovered by over 11 per cent from the trough of its recession in 1981–2, but was still 5 per cent below its 1979 peak, which was reached again only in 1987. However, manufacturing output in 1987 was still 6 per cent below its highest peak in the second quarter of 1974. The graph of percentage changes (see Figure 3) shows that manufacturing output tends to rise and fall in sharp cycles of about four years, but the peaks have been lower since 1973, and the cyclical movement has been less.

The low growth of manufacturing is sometimes seen as a consequence of the high growth of North Sea oil, because the high exchange rate, partly caused by the latter, had a depressing effect on manufacturing export performance. However, government policy could have offset the exchange-rate rise to some extent, no doubt at some cost in

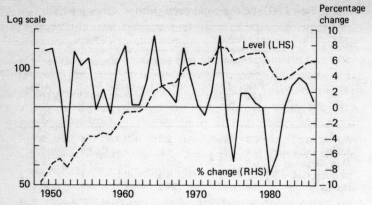

3. Manufacturing output, 1948–86 (*source: Economic Trends,* Annual Supplement, table 80)

terms of higher inflation, but with beneficial effects on manufacturing output and employment. The fall in the exchange rate which the government has allowed to occur in the wake of the drop in oil prices in 1986 is partly reversing the earlier decline in manufacturing-output growth, as UK exports again become more competitive. Manufacturing is thus expected to grow faster, while the energy sector moves into decline. Manufacturing may not, however, be able to grow fast enough to offset the negative growth of North Sea oil and gas, and its dampening effect on total GDP growth.

Services have expanded far more rapidly than manufacturing, across a broad front, including tourism, transport, telecommunications, finance, and computer and other services for business. With a 55 per cent weight in the economy, they have accounted for 70 per cent of the growth. They were less affected by the exchange rate and by the 1980–81 recession.

There is some loss of accuracy in the GDP(O) estimates, because it is not possible to re-weight the various industrial sectors each year for lack of up-to-date information. This would mean recalculating each sector's share of total output each year. In general, the effect of annual re-weighting should be to reduce the total growth rate. Goods which rise least in price should have the largest volume output increase, because the lower price stimulates demand. So relatively large output increases would have their weight reduced, as their value share went down with their relative price. (If value-added rose because inputs went up less than outputs, then the value share would be maintained.) The opposite is true for goods whose price rises most. This does not always occur in practice, because demand and output do not always respond fully to price, and may even move in the reverse direction because of other influences, such as income levels.

Thus North Sea output rose, even though oil prices had risen sharply in 1979–81. The weight of North Sea oil also rose because production, as well as prices, had risen. The main result of re-basing GDP on 1980 weights and prices, which was done in 1983, was that the weight of rapidly growing North Sea production almost trebled compared with the previous estimates based on 1975 oil prices. The result of the re-weighting was that the change in GDP(A) between 1978 and 1982 was found to be 0.7 per cent higher than before; other revisions added 0.9 per cent. So GDP(A) fell only 0.2 per cent, rather than 1.8 per cent, during these four years. When, GDP(O) is next re-based (in 1988), on 1985 prices, the weight of North Sea oil will rise because sterling oil prices will have risen by about 40 per cent from 1980. Because there is little change in input costs, the price increase shows up as a rise in value added. The 23 per cent fall in the dollar price of oil was more than offset by the 55 per cent fall in the pound against the dollar. A re-basing on 1986 prices would give a lower weight to oil, because the sterling oil price fell by 52 per cent. An 11 per cent rise in the pound reduced the 45 per cent fall in the dollar oil price by still more in sterling terms.

Index of output of the production industries

This monthly indicator from the CSO goes into greater detail at more frequent intervals than the quarterly

GDP(O) indicator, which is based on it. It also comes out with a seven-week time-lag. The production industries (see Figure 2) make up 36 per cent of GDP, comprising energy, water, and manufacturing. Energy and water are just over one-quarter of the production industries in terms of 1980 output shares. The production industries can also be sub-divided by market sector. Again, in 1980 shares, investment and consumer goods were each one-quarter of total output, and intermediate goods one-half.

The index of output of the production industries is compiled from 330 separate indicators from different sectors of industry. Most are obtained monthly, but about one-sixth are available only quarterly. Construction-industry output indices can also be got only quarterly. All the figures are seasonally adjusted, then combined into broader categories, then into the four standard industrial classification divisions (1, 2, 3, and 4) which make up the production industries (see page 23).

Towards the end of 1985, it was becoming clear from a comparison of the index of production and the CBI industrial trends survey that there was a downwards bias in the published monthly figures. The monthly figures are obtained from a smaller number of larger firms than the quarterly figures, and tend to be adjusted upwards on the basis of more complete quarterly information. For March 1987, the most recent monthly figures were adjusted upwards by 1.5 per cent. As time goes by, the adjustment is removed by revisions, and thus disappears after six months. However, some downward bias remains even after the adjustment. The reasons for this are not fully understood. The CBI industrial trends survey (see page 77) is used to estimate the size of the adjustment.

Table 4 shows wide disparities in the rates of growth of the various production industries. Energy has grown fastest, as we have seen. The next most rapidly growing sector since 1980 was chemicals, whose output rose by 20 per cent over the five years to 1986, accounting for the more rapid rise in output of intermediate goods than that of investment or consumer goods. By contrast, production of minerals other than

Table 4. Production industries: relative growth, 1980–86

	Percentage change to 1986		1980 weight in total output (%)	Contribution to change in output	
	From 1985	From 1980		From 1985	From 1980
	(1)	(2)	(3)	(4)[1]	(5)[2]
Chemicals	1.6	20.8	6.8	0.1	1.4
Engineering	−1.1	2.9	32.5	−0.4	0.9
Food, drink, tobacco	1.5	2.5	9.9	0.1	0.2
Metals	−2.2	10.9	2.5	−0.1	0.3
Minerals	2.5	−3.1	4.1	0.1	−0.1
Textiles, etc.	1.8	3.7	5.2	0.1	0.2
Timber, paper, etc.	5.0	4.0	12.6	0.6	0.5
Manufacturing total	0.9	4.7	73.6	0.7	3.5
Energy	4.4	25.4	26.4	1.2	6.7
Production total	1.9	10.2	100.0	1.9	10.2

1. = (1) × (3).
2. = (2) × (3).
Source: Press release CSO (87)73, 13 August 1987.

North Sea oil and gas fell by 3 per cent during the same five years. The engineering sector, including vehicles, which accounts for one-third of manufacturing, grew by only 2.9 per cent in 1981–6, with a fall of 1 per cent in 1986, four years into the recovery from the 1980–81 recession.

The contributions of both coal and North Sea oil and gas to the growth of production-industry output and GDP(O) are often highlighted as a source of volatility. The index of output of the production industries gives a quarterly figure for oil and gas extraction. This, and the index of coal production, are also published monthly in the *Monthly Digest of Statistics*. The coal strike in 1984, and the slow recovery from it, have distorted the underlying trend of GDP. So, to a lesser extent, has the change in the trend of North Sea output from above average for the rest of GDP to merely average in 1985 and 1986. The effect of these two important sectors on GDP is shown in Table 5.

Table 5. Coal, oil and gas, and GDP(O): percentage rates of change, 1981–6[1]

	Contribution to GDP growth by		GDP without		Total GDP(O)
	Coal	Oil and gas	Coal	Oil and gas	
1981	−0.04	0.4	−1.6	−2.1	−1.6
1982	−0.06	0.6	1.8	1.1	1.7
1983	−0.06	0.4	3.3	2.9	3.2
1984	−0.9	0.3	4.1	3.1	3.3
1985	0.5	1.0	3.2	3.0	3.7
1986	0.3	0.08	2.8	3.0	3.0

1. In order to avoid exaggerating the importance of the sharp changes in coal output in 1984 and 1985, they have been assigned a weight of 0.5 per cent in the latter year, in line with the volume of coal output in the previous year, rather than the 1980 weight of 1.5 per cent.
Source: Blue Book 1987, table 2.4.

Before the strike, the gradual decline in the coal industry since 1980 by about 4 per cent a year was taking about 0.06 percentage points off GDP growth each year, since the 1980 weight of coal in GDP was only 1.5 per cent. When coal production fell by 60 per cent in 1985, the result was to take 0.9 per cent off GDP growth. Most of the loss was restored over the two years 1985 and 1986, when coal added 0.5 and 0.3 per cent to GDP growth. The whole shape of the economic cycle was thus changed by sharp fluctuations in only 1½ per cent of the economy. The growth rate of GDP(O) actually peaked at 3.7 per cent in 1985. If the coal strike had not happened, it would have peaked at 4.1 per cent in 1984, showing a deceleration thereafter. The coal strike, whatever its other costs and benefits, thus incidentally helped the government in its claim that the recovery had been steady and stable. Even in 1986, two years after the strike, the recovery from it pushed the UK's growth up from 2.8 to 3.0 per cent.

North Sea oil and gas have had a less distorting impact on GDP growth than coal in the 1980s, after the very rapid growth of the second half of the 1970s. With increases of 10 per cent or so in oil and gas production in the first four years of the decade, the growth of GDP was about $\frac{1}{2}$ per cent higher than otherwise. By 1985 and 1986 there was little difference between the rate of growth of oil and gas and that of the rest of the economy, so GDP was unaffected. After 1987, North Sea output may decline, and the Treasury assumes in its *Financial Statement and Budget Report 1987–88* that it will reduce GDP growth by one-quarter of 1 per cent a year for three years after 1987/8. Oil and gas production remained on a high plateau in 1985 and 1986, and only in 1987 did a decline begin.

Expenditure-based GDP

A comprehensive Press release giving full details of the four different measures of GDP and its constituents is published about twelve weeks after the end of the quarter which it covers, just over a month later than the preliminary estimate of GDP(O). It is then republished, with some revisions, in the issue of *Economic Trends* dated four months after the last month of the quarter covered (January, April, July and October). In both are to be found the first estimates of GDP(I), GDP(E) and GDP(A) for the quarter, as well as a revised version of the preliminary GDP(O) figures. The summary at the front of this Press notice gives all the main estimates of GDP in index form. It also shows the gross national disposable income at 1980 market prices. This is a good measure of economic welfare, because it adjusts the change in exports by the change in the terms of trade (see page 151), which is the ratio between export and import prices, as well as including net property income from abroad, like GNP. A fall in UK export prices relative to import prices, such as occurred in 1986 owing to the fall in the oil price, therefore depresses the growth of real national disposable income (RNDI) below that of GDP. In that year GDP(A) rose by 2.6 per cent, RNDI by only 2.2 per cent. Because of the fall in terms of trade, the UK was able to pay for fewer imports with its exports, with obvious effects on living standards. The GDP deflator, an index of home costs, is also given (see page 133).

Tables at the back of the GDP Press notice give GDP(E) and its components at both current and constant prices, and consumers' expenditure in detail. GDP(I), showing the distribution of incomes of the factors of production, is given in current-price form, and GDP(O) and its main constituents in index form. A final table shows GDP(A) in current and constant prices, at market prices and factor cost, and in pounds and in indices.

The split of GDP(E) into its main components is shown in Table 6. Private consumption of goods and services is just over three-fifths of total expenditure on the GDP, public consumption of goods and services, such as education and health, just over one-fifth. Public, or general government, consumption refers to the purchase of inputs by central and local government; it is the private sector which 'consumes' the output of services, even though they are generally free of charge. This leaves one-sixth for fixed-capital investment and stocks.

Only a fraction of 1 per cent of GDP, included in capital investment, was stockbuilding in 1986, a small but sharply fluctuating quantity; the rest was gross domestic fixed capital formation, or expenditure on investment goods (see page 71). These three items are seldom equal to GDP(E), because of trade in goods and services, the balance of which was slightly negative in 1986. Exports were just over 26 per cent of GDP, imports 27 per cent. (See page 145.) The sum of the two kinds of consumption, plus investment, is called 'total domestic expenditure', or 'domestic demand'. TDE plus exports is called 'total final expenditure', or TFE. Domestic expenditure thus equals GDP(E), with the trade balance taken out, but TFE is about one-quarter larger than GDP, because both imports and exports are included.

While these concepts are useful in economic analysis, they figure little in public discussion of indicators. Domestic demand becomes more significant when its growth diverges from that of GDP because of major changes in the trade balance, such as the USA, Japan and the Federal Republic of Germany have experienced in recent years.

Table 6. GDP, total domestic expenditure (TDE) and total final expenditure (TFE), 1986 (at current market prices)

		Percentage of		
	£ billions	GDP[1]	TDE[2]	TFE[3]
1. Consumers' expenditure	234.2	62.5	61.9	49.2
2. Public consumption	79.4	21.2	21.0	16.7
3. Investment (including stocks)	64.8	17.3	17.1	13.6
4. Exports of goods and services	97.8	26.1	—	20.5
5. Imports of goods and services	101.3	−27.0	—	—

1. GDP = 1 + 2 + 3 + 4 − 5 = £374.9 billion.
2. TDE = 1 + 2 + 3 = £378.4 billion.
3. TFE = 1 + 2 + 3 + 4 = £476.2 billion.
Source: Blue Book 1987, tables 1.2, 15.1.

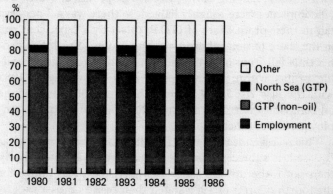

4. Factor income distribution, 1980–86 (*source: Economic Trends*, April 1987, pp. 80, 84, 85, 87)

Income-based GDP

A quite different picture is given by the split of GDP(I) into factor incomes (see Figure 4). Employment incomes, the share of employees, fell from 68 per cent of the total in 1981 to 64 per cent in 1985. This is due partly to the fall in the numbers employed, corresponding to the rise in unemployment, and partly to the fact that average earnings, while rising faster than inflation, have risen less than profits. Most of the employees' loss of share went into gross trading profits, the share of employers, in the public as well as the private sector. Their share, in effect the return on capital, went up from 14 to 18 per cent of the total. While the share of North Sea oil profits rose only from 5 to 6 per cent, that of all other gross trading profits (GTP in the figure) rose more sharply, from 9 to 12 per cent, with the North Sea still accounting for one-third of total gross trading profits. The 'other' 18 per cent of factor income consisted of rent, which is divided between companies, other landlords and owner-occupiers, and income from self-employment, which has risen as a partial offset to unemployment (see page 94).

There was a marked change between 1985 and 1986, owing to the halving of oil prices. The profits of North Sea oil companies were roughly halved, so there was a 3 per cent fall in their profit share of GDP, offset by a 2 per cent rise in the share of non-oil gross trading profits. North Sea profits thus fell from one-third to one-sixth of total gross trading profits within one year, but were recovering in 1987 with the new rise in oil prices. The lost profit share of the oil companies went not only to other companies, but to employees and to other incomes.

The average measure of GDP, like the others on which it is based, is subject to later revisions, which are more likely than not to be upwards. For example, the Press notice for the fourth quarter of 1986 stated that, based on past experience, the $3\frac{1}{4}$ per cent increase in constant price GDP(A) over the year to that quarter might eventually fall into a range of 3–5 per cent, with a 66 per cent probability. This implies that it could be revised downwards by up to $\frac{1}{4}$ per cent, but could equally well be revised upwards by up to $1\frac{3}{4}$ per cent, with a most likely central value of 4 per cent, an increase of $\frac{3}{4}$ per cent, or nearly a quarter, in the original estimate. Since the 1970s, the average revision of GDP growth rates after five years has been plus 0.8 per cent, compared with the same quarter of the previous year (see page 22). Two-thirds of the revisions have been upwards, and one-third downwards, but the latter were mostly in the exceptional 1974–5 period of high and variable inflation and recession. GDP is always more difficult to measure when unusually rapid changes are taking place, particularly in inflation rates.

Forecasting GDP

To forecast GDP, it is necessary first to explain it. There are three main approaches. The first is to construct an econometric model of the whole economy, in which numerous equations embody theories about the behaviour of each part. The second is to seek a simple, single-equation model of GDP, explaining GDP by means of a small number of independent variables, such as interest rates and the budget deficit. The third is to extrapolate the past trend of GDP itself, allowing for short-term disturbances, medium-term cyclical fluctuations and long-term changes in the rate of growth.

GDP tends to be less stable each quarter than each year, even after seasonal adjustment, which allows for the fact that, for example, the construction industry is hit by winter weather. In 1986, the average quarterly change in GDP(A) was 0.8 per cent, yet the actual quarterly changes on the various measures ranged between 1.9 and −0.5 per cent. Some forecasters observe the detailed changes in sectors of the economy during each quarter, including exceptional events such as strikes, so that they can at least have the advantage of forecasting GDP(O) before the official figure is published, even if after the end of the quarter to which it relates.

For the four years to 1986, the yearly growth of GDP(A) averaged 3.2 per cent, and varied between 2.6 and 3.7 per cent. Most forecasts for the next few years lie in a narrow range between 2 and 3 per cent, so that rival forecasters are reduced to differing over fractions of 1 per cent. Such differences can be made to look bigger by translating them into current pounds, since 1 per cent of GDP at current market prices is nearly £4 billion.

Any extrapolation of the current trend is highly sensitive to the base year chosen. Up to the end of 1986, base year 1979 gave a trend of 1.5 per cent, 1980 2.1 per cent, 1981

2.7 per cent and 1982 3.0 per cent. Any of these could be regarded as a plausible medium-term forecast for the next five years.

Most econometric models used for forecasting implicitly aim at $GDP(E)$, since they forecast the main components of expenditure, such as consumption and investment, separately, then add them together. An adjustment then has to be made to shift the forecast from market prices to factor cost, and from the expenditure to the average estimate, if the two have recently been diverging. Such statistical procedures can sometimes make more difference to a forecast than disagreements about economic fundamentals. Models based on expenditure or demand are often called 'Keynesian', which refers to the structure of the model rather than to any particular theories which it embodies.

Attempts have been made to use supply-side models, which are implicitly based on $GDP(O)$. They use production functions based on the total output achieved by the input of land, labour and capital factors as a consequence of the relative returns on them. Others have tried to develop monetarist models, in which GDP rises in line with the money stock deflated by price increases. Neither approach has had satisfactory results in the UK.

Cyclical indicators of the UK economy

One method of forecasting turning-points, if not exact figures, in the economy is to take the monthly cyclical indicators published by the Central Statistical Office three weeks after the end of the month. These turning-points are in the rates of growth of indicators rather than in the indicators themselves. They take place when the growth of an indicator moves above or below its long-term trend value. The components of the indicators are published in full in *Economic Trends* each February, May, August and November. There are four composite indicators, each composed of other, better-known economic indicators, as follows:

1. The longer leading index, which shows turning-points about a year ahead. Components:

Three-month bank-bill interest rates.

The financial surplus or deficit of industrial and commercial
companies, deflated by the GDP deflator.

Total dwellings started (new building).

FT-Actuaries 500 share index.

CBI industrial trends survey; change in optimism.

There is evidence to show that interest rates affect GDP
with a time-lag in an inverse direction, both through their
direct effect on investment, and through their indirect effect
on the trade balance via the exchange rate. The last two
indicators may appear to reveal more about how people
expect the future to develop than about how it will actually
develop. Yet business confidence can itself be a plus factor.
As Julie Andrews sang in *The Sound of Music*: 'I have confidence in confidence alone.' These 'psychological' indicators
do in fact give reasonably good predictions, as well as reveal
expectations about the future.

2. The shorter leading index, which shows turning-points
about six months ahead. Components:

Credit by finance houses, etc.

New-car registrations.

CBI industrial trends survey; change in new orders, and expected change in stocks of materials.

Gross trading profits of companies, excluding stock appreciation and oil and gas, divided by GDP deflator.

3. The coincident indicator, showing current turning-points.
Components:

GDP (E), (O), and (I).

Retail-sales volume.

Output of production industries.

CBI industrial trends survey; capacity utilization and
change in stocks of materials.

4. The lagging indicator, showing turning-points about a
year afterwards. Components:

Unemployment.

Employment in manufacturing industry.

Investment in plant and machinery by manufacturing in-
  dustry.
Engineering industries, volume of orders.
Stocks and work in progress in manufacturing industry.

The lagging indicator is more useful in confirming forecasts
of employment and activity, particularly in manufacturing,
on the basis of turning-points in the coincident indicator.
Firms lay off workers and cancel investment plans only some
time after turning-points in activity. It also helps to confirm
the coincident indicator for previous periods when it is still
uncertain because of data revisions.

The cyclical indicators are based on statistics with the
long-term trend removed, and therefore they show only
movements above or below trend. They are in the form of
index numbers which move up and down around an average
representing the trend. The indices are on a base of January
1980. They are often subsequently revised, because not all
the component series are available in the first month of
publication of the composite indicators (and some are themselves subject to revision) and it is difficult to estimate a
trend incorporating the most recent figures.

The indicators are claimed by the Central Statistical Office
to have a good track record in showing turning-points. They
require considerable interpretation, in view of revisions and
variations in their lead and lag times before and after peaks and
troughs in the economy. For example, in April 1987 the longer
leading indicator showed a strong peak in the previous month,
suggesting a peak in economic activity in about March 1988.
Yet the shorter leading indicator for the same month also
showed a peak in March 1987, suggesting that the economy
would peak in October 1987. In both cases, the Press-notice
commentary explained that the March 1987 figures might not
be a valid peak, and this later proved to be the case. The longer
leading indicator had been boosted mainly by a surge in share
prices, which had fallen back in April, and could and did
revive. The fall in the shorter leading indicator in April could
have been due to the absence of the consumer-credit data,
which might have offset the fall had they been known.

The indicators are not in fact as widely used as they might be by economic analysts, partly because the rather qualitative forecasting technique which they embody has lost favour compared with more quantitative econometric methods.

2

Personal Income and Saving

'In recent months, high street sales figures have moved
erratically and have frequently frustrated the expectations of retailers and City economists.'

Ralph Atkins, *Financial Times*, 21 July 1987

GDP is the indicator which covers the whole economy. Personal income covers the largest sector within the economy. It
is also a better guide to living standards than total GDP. It is
that part of GDP(I), the income measure of GDP, which
comprises incomes from employment and self-employment.
It also includes transfer payments, such as social-security
benefits and bank interest, which are not part of GDP because they are not value-added. Personal income after deduction of tax is termed personal disposable income (PDI). Some
PDI is saved, and the rest is spent on consumption. Consumers' expenditure on goods and services makes up over three-
fifths of GDP(E), the expenditure measure of GDP. Early
estimates of consumers' expenditure and retail sales show the
state of health of a large part of the economy. Changes in
PDI and in the proportion of it that is saved show how
changes in consumers' expenditure come about. PDI is deflated by consumer price increases to give real personal disposable income (RPDI), the main determinant of the
volume of consumers' expenditure.

Figures for PDI, consumers' expenditure and personal
saving go back to 1946, and the index of retail sales to 1955.
The concepts of personal income and saving do not mean
quite what common sense would lead us to suppose. Personal

income is the income of the personal sector. The personal sector is wider than persons. It also includes unincorporated businesses (UIBs), most farms and small shops, for example; private non-profit-making bodies (PNBs); and life assurance and pension funds (LAPFs). So personal income means the income of these entities as well as 'personal income' in the normal sense.

In recent years, the CSO has published figures for the 'household' sector, which is different from the personal sector. It excludes LAPFs, and PNBs, and attempts to exclude UIBs. However, it is impossible to separate the personal and the business income of most proprietors of UIBs, since they are small family businesses, such as farms and shops. Both types of income are included in self-employed income. A deduction is made for the capital consumption (depreciation) and the stock appreciation of U I Bs, and this is accounted for as part of the saving of the personal sector, but not the household sector. The assumption is made that UIBs save just enough to replace their capital and stocks at existing real levels; they may in fact spend more or less than this, but there is no way of knowing. The self-employed are in any case known to under-record income so as to evade tax to a greater extent than other economic agents (see page 20). The household and personal-sector accounts are thus subject to wide margins of error. The main distinctions between the two sectors are given on page 45.

Personal income and expenditure

The Central Statistical Office publishes a Press notice about twelve weeks after the end of each quarter, giving amounts and rates of change for personal income, expenditure and saving. Table 7, derived from it, shows rates of change from 1979 to 1986. Personal income and income taxes both rose by 9.7 per cent a year, implying no change in the burden of tax as a percentage of income. (Real pay rises have added back to tax revenue what rate cuts and the indexation of allowances have removed.) Social-security contributions by employers and employees rose faster than taxes, by nearly

Table 7. Growth of personal income and expenditure, 1980–86 annual percentage increase

Total personal income	9.7
Of which:	
Wages, salaries, forces pay	8.9
Employers' contributions	8.2
Current grants	13.3
Other personal income	10.3
UK taxes on income	9.7
Social-security contributions, etc.	11.9
Personal disposable income	9.5
Real personal disposable income	1.7
Consumers' expenditure	10.2
Real consumers' expenditure	2.2
Memorandum items	
Household income	10.5
Household disposable income	10.2

Source: Blue Book 1987, tables 4.1, 4.9.

12 per cent a year, so PDI rose by a fraction less than personal income, by 9.5 per cent a year, or 1.7 per cent in real terms after making allowance for inflation. The ratio of income saved, the saving ratio, fell during the period, so consumers' expenditure was able to rise by 10.2 per cent a year in value and by 2.2 per cent in volume.

The kind of income rising fastest was current government social-security grants, a reflection of the rise in unemployment. Wages and salaries rose by nearly 9 per cent, current grants by over 13 per cent a year. (Employment numbers changed little, so there was not much difference between the rate of growth of total earnings and that of earnings per head. The rise in unemployment was correlated with an increase in the population of working age (see page 95.) Employers' social-security and occupational pension contributions are counted as personal income too. Other personal income, including self-employment incomes of UIBs and receipts of LAPFs, rose faster than wages and salaries, by 10.3 per cent a year. The income of households rose nearly

Table 8. Two derivations of personal saving, 1986

	£ billion	Percentage of PDI
Personal disposable income	257.5	
Less consumers' expenditure	− 234.2	
= Personal saving (A)	23.3	9.1
Less capital expenditure	− 18.7	
Plus net capital transfers	0.1	
= Financial surplus	4.7	1.8
Financial asset purchases	50.4	
Less borrowings	− 31.6	
= Net acquisition of assets	18.8	7.3
Plus capital expenditure	18.7	
Less net capital transfers	− 0.1	
= Personal saving (B)	37.4	14.5
Less residual error	− 14.1	
= Personal saving (A)	23.3	

Source: Blue Book 1987, tables 4.1, 4.2, 4.3.

1 percentage point faster than that of the whole personal sector, by 10.5 per cent a year.

Personal saving is what is left of PDI after consumers' expenditure. There are several ways of estimating it (see Table 8). It does not mean the same as saving in the sense of accumulation of financial assets. Personal saving includes, and is used to finance, expenditure on new dwellings, and on investment by UIBs and PNBs. What is then left is the personal sector's financial surplus (or deficit), which corresponds to financial saving net of borrowing. The table shows first how the personal sector financial surplus is derived from personal income in the national accounts. It can also be derived from the financial accounts, as the surplus of financial assets purchased over borrowings, or the net acquisition of financial assets (NAFA). This method generally gives a higher figure, which exceeds the national accounts figure by a few per cent. A residual error, or 'balancing item', has to be shown to reconcile the figures, amounting to £14 billion in the example shown.

However it is derived, personal sector saving differs considerably from the saving of households, because of the inclusion of the LAPFs in the personal but not in the household sector. Household sector accounts go back only to 1975, and began to be published in 1981. They include items which do not figure in the personal sector accounts, such as transactions between households and LAPFs, on the grounds that they take place within the personal sector.

Table 9 shows just how different the personal and household sector accounts are. The personal sector counts as personal income employers' national insurance and pension contributions, the investment income of LAPFs, and imputed rent, a measure of the value of owner-occupied housing services. None of these can be regarded as income of the household sector. The household sector counts occupational pension payments as income, which the personal sector does not, because they are paid within the sector. It also counts rent, dividends and interest receipts as gross, rather than net of similar payments, as does the personal sector. This increased their size by a factor of ten in 1985, for example.

Both accounts regard employees national-insurance contributions as a deduction in arriving at personal disposable income. Likewise, employers' contributions are deducted in the account of the personal sector, but not in that of the household sector, because it does not include them as income in the first place. Employees' occupational pension contributions, however, are deducted in the account of the household sector, but not in that of the personal sector, because this transaction takes place within the personal sector as it is defined. The upshot is that disposable income is smaller for the household than for the personal sector. Household consumption expenditure is also less than personal, because it excludes imputed rent, the administration costs of the LAPFs, and final expenditure by PNBs. There are other expenditures shown only in the household sector's account; interest payments, and life-assurance premiums. The remain-

Table 9. Personal- and household-sector accounts, 1986 (£ billion)

	Personal sector	Household sector
Wages and salaries	182.6	182.6
Employers' contributions:		
Social security	13.3	
Occupational pension	13.6	
Current grants	50.5	50.2
Other personal income:		
Occupational pensions		23.8
Investment income of pension funds	17.4	
Self-employment	34.3	28.7
Imputed rent	13.6	
Rent, dividends, interest	−0.9	20.9
Transfers	2.3	
Total income	326.7	306.2
Deductions:		
Taxes on income	41.2	44.7
Social-security contributions:		
Employers' contributions	13.6	
Employees' contributions	12.5	12.5
Employees' occupational-pension contributions		5.1
Transfers	1.9	
Taxes and employees' contributions as percentage of income	16.4%	18.7%
Disposable income	257.5	243.9
Expenditure:		
Consumption	234.2	210.0
Interest paid		17.7
Life-assurance premiums		12.7
Transfers		3.8
Balance (saving)	23.3	−0.3
Percentage of disposable income	9.0%	−0.1%

Source: Blue Book 1987, tables 4.1, 4.9.

ing balance of the personal sector, its 'saving', is 9.1 per cent of disposable income. That of the household sector, which can be seen as discretionary or uncommitted saving, became slightly negative in 1986, and was minus 0.1 per

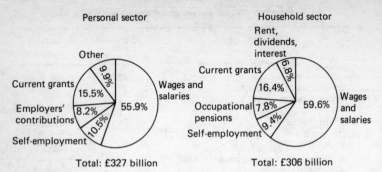

Total: £327 billion   Total: £306 billion

5. Personal income analysis, 1986 (*source:* Blue Book 1987, tables 4.1, 4.9)

cent of disposable income. All recent years show a similar disparity.

The comparison can also be seen in Figure 5, analysing the components of personal and household sector income. In both cases, wages and salaries are the main source of income, 56 or 60 per cent, and current grants from the government the next, 15 or 16 per cent. While employers' contributions are 8 per cent of personal income, occupational pensions are about the same proportion of household income. Another 7 per cent of household income is rent, dividends and interest, while over 10 per cent of personal income comes from other sources, mainly investment income of LAPFs and imputed rent.

The difference between the personal and household sectors can be better understood from Figure 6, showing the flows in and out of and between the two parts of the personal sector, LAPFs and the rest: households, UIBs and PNBs. From outside the personal sector, the LAPFs get investment income and employers' contributions. From the households within the personal sector, they get employees' contributions and premiums, including single-premium bonds, and in return they pay pensions and lump sums. The outflow from the LAPFs to outside the personal sector consists of their investment and their administration costs. On the right of the chart, it can be seen that 'personal' saving consists

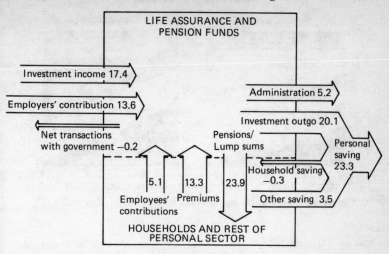

6. The flow of personal-sector saving, 1986 (*source:* Blue Book 1987, tables 4.1, 4.9, 4.10; *Financial Statistics Explanatory Handbook* 1987, p. 95)

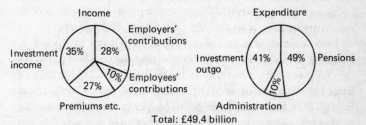

7. Life assurance and pension funds: income and expenditure analysis, 1986 (*source:* Fig. 6)

mainly of investment by the LAPFs, and only secondarily of discretionary saving by households. There is also other saving by other parts of the personal sector, notably UIBs and PNBs.

Figure 7 shows the relative size of these flows. Investment income is over one-third of the LAPFs' income. Employers' contributions and life-assurance premiums are each over one-quarter. Employees' contributions are one-tenth, and just over a third as much as employers' contributions; the propor-

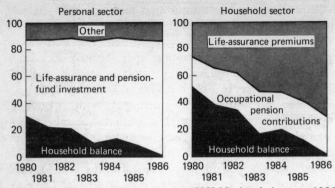

8. Changing shares in saving (*source: UK National Accounts* 1986, tables 4.1, 4.4, 4.5)

tion is higher for contributory schemes. Pensions account for nearly half the outgo, investment just over two-fifths, and administration costs one-tenth. Details of the flows of funds into and out of the LAPFs are published by the Bank of England in a quarterly Press notice on institutional investment, about fifteen weeks after the end of each quarter.

Two main definitions of saving are analysed in Figure 8, showing changes in their composition since 1980. Discretionary saving by households has fallen from 31 per cent of total personal sector saving to below zero, while investment by LAPFs has risen from 56 to 86 per cent, and the saving of the rest of the personal sector other than households has stayed roughly in the 12 to 15 per cent range. On the right-hand graph of the figure, two of the main elements of con-tractual saving by households have been added to show the bulk of discretionary plus contracted saving by households as opposed to the personal sector as a whole. The share of discretionary saving in this total has fallen from 52 per cent to below zero since 1980. That of life-assurance premiums has risen from 26 to 73 per cent, while that of occupational pension contributions has risen only from 22 to 29 per cent. This suggests that the dominance of the pension funds over discretionary personal saving may have been exaggerated. Individuals are putting far more into life-insurance contracts than into pension contributions; it is their employers who are making by far the largest payments into pension funds.

Since personal sector saving is by definition that part of PDI not spent on consumption, it is sensitive to what is included in consumption, and what in capital expenditure. For example, in 1984 the Central Statistical Office decided to reclassify the rapidly growing expenditure on home improvements out of consumption and into capital expenditure. This increased the saving ratio for 1983 by $1\frac{1}{2}$ percentage points, a substantial change. The saving ratio is also revised each year for up to ten years after the year to which it relates, as better information becomes available. The average revision after one year is an increase of $\frac{1}{2}$ per cent, but it is likely to be downwards by smaller amounts in later years. For example, the 1974 saving ratio began life in 1975 at 12.7 per cent, then rose each year to 14.4 per cent in 1978, then fell each year to 11.8 per cent in 1984 – but this would have been 12.5 per cent using the financial-asset method of estimation (see Table 8). In the 1987 Blue Book, the personal sector saving ratio was revised downwards by an average of 0.9 per cent a year for each of the previous seven years.

It is thus no surprise that, among the personal sector statistics, saving gets the lowest grading (D) for reliability, which means that it can be over 20 per cent out either way (see Table 10). Wages and salaries, by contrast, get an A grading, since they can be fairly accurately assessed from PAYE returns. Other forms of personal income, which have to be inferred from inadequate information, get only a C; so PDI, combining the two forms of income, comes in between with a B. The government naturally has A-grade information about its own payments and receipts, social-security grants and contributions, and income tax.

Consumers' expenditure

Consumers' expenditure can be measured more easily and quickly than other items in the personal income, expenditure and saving account, which is published in fairly detailed form in a CSO Press notice twelve weeks after the end of

Table 10. Reliability of personal-sector statistics

A. + or − less than 3 per cent:	Wages and salaries
	Current grants from central government
	Taxes on income
	National-insurance contributions
	Consumers' expenditure
B. + or − 3–10 per cent:	Personal disposable income
C. + or − 10–20 per cent:	Self-employment income
	Rent, dividends and interest
D. + or − more than 20 per cent:	Transfers abroad
	Personal saving

Source: U K National Accounts: Sources and Methods, p. 62.

each quarter. A simple one-page preliminary estimate of quarterly consumers' expenditure at constant (1980) prices is therefore published only four weeks after the end of each quarter. It is partly forecast, since it is based on incomplete data. It is therefore subject to revision by half a per cent either way when the fuller accounts are published about eight weeks later.

Consumers' expenditure, as defined in the national accounts, is not confined to the expenditure of consumers in the usual sense, just as personal income is not merely the income of persons. It is defined as the current expenditure of the whole personal sector. As the consumption line in Table 9 shows, consumers' expenditure of the personal sector is considerably greater than the spending of households on current goods and services. In 1986 it was £234 billion, compared with £210 billion for the household sector, about 11 per cent more. The difference is accounted for by imputed rent deemed to be paid by owner-occupiers to themselves (£14 billion), final expenditure by PNBs (£5 billion) and administrative costs of L A P F s (£5 billion).

It is still true that nearly nine-tenths of 'consumers' expenditure' comprises households' spending on goods and services. The Press notice highlights the percentage change between the latest quarter and the previous quarter, and between the latest quarter and the same quarter a year ago. The figures are seasonally adjusted, so as to avoid mis-interpretation of the big leap in purchases which occurs in the fourth quarter of each year as Christmas approaches.

Table 11 illustrates the importance of distinguishing be-tween these two types of comparison in analysing the trend. The year 1986 had a strong 4.7 per cent real increase in consumer spending compared with the previous year. In each quarter of the year spending was about this much higher than in the same quarter of the previous year. Yet the level of consumers' expenditure was actually flat between the third and fourth quarters of 1986, and continued to be so in the first quarter of 1987, giving a nine-month plateau following a steep rise in the quarterly trend.

The spotting of such trends is the key to forecasting. Let us see the result of extrapolating the plateau for consumers' expenditure through 1987. The first quarter still shows re-assuringly high growth over the same quarter of 1986, be-cause the rise was so steep between the first and third quarters of 1986. By the third and fourth quarters of 1987, the projection shows no rise at all over the previous year, any more than over the previous quarter. It was an analysis along these lines which led some – wrongly as it happens – to question the government's March budget forecast of 4 per cent private consumption growth in 1987.

Retail sales

An even earlier indication of the trend of consumers' expendi-ture is given by the provisional monthly estimate of retail sales published by the Department of Trade and Industry (DTI) only two weeks after the end of each month. A final estimate is published three weeks later, five weeks after the end of the month. These figures are published in index form, since they are based on percentage changes from the refer-ence year (1980 at the time of writing) when sales values in pounds were calculated. One index gives the current value of sales, not seasonally adjusted. The more useful index, par-ticularly for comparison with the consumers' expenditure

Table 11. Short-term changes in consumption and retail sales, 1986–7: quarterly, at 1980 prices, seasonally adjusted (percentage changes)

	Quarters	Consumers' expenditure			Retail sales		
		£ billion	On previous quarter	Year ago	Index	On previous quarter	Year ago
1986	1	39.0	1.0	4.3	119.3	1.2	4.2
	2	39.6	1.5	5.3	121.3	1.7	4.7
	3	40.3	1.8	5.2	123.7	2.0	5.5
	4	40.3	0.0	4.4	126.5	2.3	7.3
1986	Year	159.2	1.1	4.7	122.6	1.8	5.3
1987	1	40.3	0.0	3.3	125.4	− 0.9	5.1
Projection[1]							
	2	40.3	0	1.8	127.4	1.6	5.0
	3	40.3	0	0	125.7	− 1.3	1.6
	4	40.3	0	0	125.7	0	− 0.6
1987	Year	161.2	0	1.3	126.0	− 0.2	2.8

1. Assumptions: consumers' expenditure unchanged from Q1 1987, retail sales from May 1987. The projection illustrates a statistical point, and is not to be interpreted as a forecast.
Source: Press notice CSO (87)39, 30 April 1987; DTI Press notice 313, 8 June 1987; *British Business*, 24 April 1987.

figures, is that which gives the volume of retail sales, seasonally adjusted.

The data on retail sales are obtained by the DTI by means of a voluntary inquiry to a panel of 3,200 retailers, including a sample of the smaller independent retailers, who account for one-third of retail sales, and nearly all the very large retailers. The information used in the early provisional estimate covers over three-quarters of all retailers by turnover, and in the most recent year has differed by an average of 0.3 per cent either way from the final figure. The data go back to 1955. There are sub-indices for food retailers, mixed food and non-food, and non-food, including as separate categories clothing and footwear, household goods and other goods.

Every two years the retail sales index is re-based to reflect the changes in the pattern of expenditure. The most recent re-basing was carried out in April 1987, using 1984 as the new base year, so as to incorporate the results of the fuller inquiry into retailing carried out in that year. (The index continued to be referenced on 1980, because of the convenience of keeping it at 100 in 1980.) The result of the re-basing was to increase the volume of retail sales by 0.26 per cent a year for each of the five years to 1986, so that the level of the index in that year suddenly jumped by 1.3 per cent. This result was due to such factors as the greater weight (proportion) of electrical and electronic goods in retail sales in 1984 than in 1980. These goods went up less in price than other goods – their prices actually fell in 1986 – so an increase in their weight lowered the average price deflator (rate of inflation) applied to the value index of retail sales, leading to a rise in the volume index.

Table 11 shows that the volume of retail sales tends to rise by more than the volume of consumers' expenditure. This does not necessarily mean that purchases in shops are increasing faster than those made through non-retail outlets, for example purchases of services. The difference may be partly due to different statistical methods of measurement. For example, consumers' expenditure on food is estimated from the National Food Survey as well as from shop sales.

The trend of retail sales can diverge sharply from that of consumers' expenditure in the short run. For example, in the first quarter of 1987, retail sales fell by nearly 1 per cent, while consumers' expenditure remained static. This led the CSO to conclude that expenditure through non-retail outlets had increased. Over longer periods, the retail sales index tends to rise about 0.6 per cent a year faster than consumers' expenditure (see Table 12). Nearly 0.3 per cent of this is due to the re-basing on 1984, which took place in 1987. The extra 0.3 per cent may disappear again when consumers' expenditure is re-based using 1985 constant prices, as it is expected to be in 1988.

The composition of retail sales differs markedly from that of consumers' expenditure. Retail sales cover 41 per cent of consumers' expenditure, or 46 per cent of household purchases of goods and services. Food accounts for 14 per cent of consumers' expenditure, but 38 per cent of retail sales

Table 12. Consumption and saving trends, 1980–86: annual percentage changes

Year	Real personal disposable income	Consumers' expenditure, 1980 prices	Retail sales volume	Percentage of disposable income	
				Personal sector saving	Household sector balance
1980	1.4	0.0	−0.6	14.2	4.8
1981	−1.4	−0.1	0.2	13.1	3.2
1982	−0.2	0.8	1.9	12.2	2.8
1983	2.3	4.0	5.2	10.7	1.2
1984	2.7	2.1	3.6	11.2	1.6
1985	2.7	3.7	4.6	10.4	0.9
1986	4.2	5.7	5.3	9.1	−0.1
Average:	1.7	2.3	2.9	−0.6[1]	−0.5[1]

1. Average cumulative change in percentage points, from 13.0 and 4.0 in 1979.
Source: Blue Book 1987, tables 4.1, 4.6, 4.9; D T I Press notice 313, 8 June 1987.

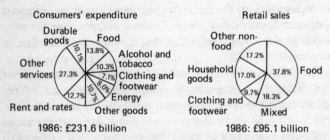

1986: £231.6 billion   1986: £95.1 billion

9. Shares of consumers' expenditure and retail sales, 1986 (*source: consumers' expenditure: Monthly Digest of Statistics,* April 1987, table 1.5; *retail sales:* D T I Press notice 313, 8 June 1987)

(see Figure 9). The main categories of consumers' expenditure not principally sold through retail shops are energy, rent and rates, and other services. The other categories exceed the estimated value of retail sales by only about 9 per cent, so clearly they are sold mainly in shops.

Distributive trades survey

In July 1983 the CBI began publication of a monthly distributive trades survey, based on a weighted sample of nearly 600 respondents. It uses a similar technique to the CBI industrial-trends survey, which has been conducted since 1963 (see page 77). The survey comprises four variables: sales volume; volume of orders placed with suppliers; volume of sales, for the time of year (a form of seasonal adjustment); and volume of stocks in relation to expected sales. Respondents are asked to give the present position in the current month, and the expected position next month. Each question allows for three possible answers; the same, up, or down, compared with the same month a year before; so here too there is an implicit form of seasonal adjustment. The survey gives the percentage of respondents, giving each answer for the month in which it is published and the next month. It then expresses these percentages in balance form, showing the difference between the 'ups' and the 'downs', and ignoring the 'sames'. The percentage balances are shown for each month in the previous year, and attempts are made to discern trends from them. The present position for each month is also compared with what it was expected to be in the previous month.

The distributive trades survey has too short a history for its usefulness to be properly assessed. The changes in the percentage balances from month to month do not appear to bear much relation to changes in the index of the volume of retail sales published by the DTI compared with its level a year ago. They are, if anything, somewhat less erratic. One weakness of surveys of this kind is that the same percentage balance figure can be obtained with widely different percentages of 'same' answers.

The CBI provides useful commentaries, interpreting the figures, and breaks the results down when appropriate to show divergent trends for retailers, wholesalers and different kinds of product.

The economic theory of consumption and saving

Consumption and saving are one of the most important branches of modern economic theory. Keynes and Friedman are among those who have made major contributions. So central is the part played by consumption that a theory about the whole economy is required to explain it. Employment, labour income, investment, the rate of interest, economic growth, inflation, fiscal policy, and personal wealth are all linked with consumption and saving. Consumption and saving are two sides of the same coin. They can be seen as simultaneously determined in the allocation of personal disposable income. Some theories emphasize one, some the other, but any explanation of one implicitly explains the other. Saving is what is left of P D I after consumers' expenditure, and consumers' expenditure is what is left of P D I after saving – by definition.

We can isolate a section of the whole economy, and begin with personal income as given, since it is the starting-point of the indicators under discussion in this chapter. The main variable which then determines personal disposable income is income tax and employee national-insurance contributions. The government controls these variables in the annual Budget. As we have seen in Table 7, the total effect of income-tax and national-insurance changes has been to reduce the growth of P D I below that of total personal income since 1979. Let us now take P D I as given by personal income and tax policy. What can we now say about the propensity to consume (or save), as Keynes termed the proportion of P D I spent on consumption? It is obvious from Table 12 that when real consumers' expenditure rises faster than real P D I, the saving ratio must – by definition – be lower, because the consumption ratio is higher – a higher proportion of income is consumed. This has been true of every year from 1980 to 1986, with the exception of 1984, when the saving ratio rose from 10.7 to 11.2 per cent. Thus, as shown in Table 7, consumption rose faster than P D I as the saving ratio fell, and indeed faster than total personal income. So consumers responded to a higher tax burden by saving less. They restored to the economy the purchasing power which the government had removed.

The average propensity to consume is the proportion of personal disposable income spent on consumption (or one minus the saving ratio). The income elasticity of consumption is the ratio of the percentage increase in consumption to a one per cent increase in income. The marginal propensity to consume is the income elasticity of consumption times the average propensity to consume. For example, the average propensity to consume in the U K was 85.8 per cent in 1980. The personal sector consumed this proportion of its disposable income after tax, and saved 14.2 per cent. Between 1980 and 1986, disposable income rose by 60 per cent, and consumption by 70 per cent, in rounded numbers. The income elasticity of consumption was therefore 70/60, or 1.16. The marginal propensity to consume, the proportion of additional income consumed, should therefore have been 0.858×1.16, which is roughly equal to one. On looking at table 4.1 of the 1987 Blue Book, we find that this is confirmed by the figures. Disposable income rose by £97 billion, from £160 billion to £257 billion, and consumption went up by £97 billion, from £137 billion to £234 billion. Saving was thus unchanged at £23 billion. The marginal propensity to consume was 97/97, or 100 per cent. All the increase in income was consumed and none of it saved. The saving ratio fell from 14.2 to 9.1 per cent. The average propensity to consume must rise if the marginal propensity is higher. It did rise, to 90.9 per cent. This does not mean that total saving was falling, but that the increase was matched by extra personal borrowing, which allowed consumption, physical investment and financial investment all to rise faster than disposable income.

We have an arithmetical tautology here which can be expressed by the simple formula $dC/dY = C/Y \times (dC/dY \times Y/C)$. This tells us nothing to explain consumption behaviour in the U K, however striking the simple facts may be; they are more so since the sharp upwards revision of consumption and downwards revision of saving that were revealed in the 1987 Blue Book.

The explanation can start with time trends, even though they may be difficult to discern among stronger short-term influences. It can be argued that, as real income rises, so does the saving ratio. People save more to buy houses and build financial assets. These are both 'superior goods', for which the demand rises with income, or so it is maintained. The argument can also be applied to those in higher income groups, to explain why they save more than those in lower income groups. If income is redistributed to higher income groups – as Mrs Thatcher has done – this will raise the saving ratio. If it is redistributed to lower income groups – as Keynes wished to do – this will raise the consumption ratio.

The opposite argument was put in a famous paper on saving by Ramsey. He argued that as people became more prosperous, they would approach a state of satiety called 'bliss'. They would feel less need to save for new investment in a still higher standard of living in future. This theory is plausible, but premature in its application to most economies. One possible exception is the United States, where the personal saving ratio has fallen as national income has risen.

During the 1970s, the saving ratio rose with inflation rates in most countries. It had previously been thought that inflation would stimulate consumption, as people forsook money for goods. This may sometimes be true of economies in a state of hyperinflation. But it is now well established that moderate inflation in single or low double figures is associated with higher saving. The reasons for this are disputed. The fear of recession and unemployment following government action to control inflation could have led to saving from precautionary motives. It is more widely agreed that people react to the depletion by inflation of the real value of existing stocks of savings by saving more so as to restore the loss. On the other hand, if inflation increases the value of personal equity holdings, there is a 'wealth effect' tending to increase consumption. So inflation does not necessarily reduce the value of all types of saving; only those with fixed capital repayment. Conversely, the rise in the price of consumer goods may make them appear expensive compared with investments, such as houses or financial assets. This would lead to less consumption, and more saving.

At this point the rate of interest enters the argument. It is linked with the inflation rate, since the two tend to move together. It may thus be difficult to tell the effects of one apart from the effects of the other. If the interest rate is higher than the inflation rate, the real rate of interest is positive. It could be said that this more than protects the stock of savings against inflation, so it is not necessary to save more. If the nominal rate of interest is less than the inflation rate, then the previous line of reasoning applies, and people save more because of the inflation. On the other hand, a positive real rate of interest may encourage people to switch out of consumer goods and into financial assets. This is one of many cases in economics where the 'income effect' of real interest rates in increasing the return on savings is in conflict with the 'substitution effect', when a higher price for savings encourages people to put money into them.

Our own research suggests that interest rates have a positive effect on saving. The substitution effect is stronger than the income effect. A 1 per cent rise in bank seven-day deposit rates was found to lead to a 0.6 per cent rise in the personal saving ratio, but with a constant element of 7 per cent in the ratio, owing to contractual saving through life assurance and pension funds. The practice by banks and building societies of crediting interest to savings accounts would in itself explain part of the tendency of saving to rise with interest rates.

This view may seem intuitively obvious, but it has been widely questioned, and there is evidence on the other side. The case for the 'income effect' has never been better put than by the Italian economist Vilfredo Pareto: 'Saving . . . is the effect of people acting according to animal instinct. This is why people would not stop saving, even if the rate of interest on savings became zero; it may even happen that certain individuals save more . . . when the interest on savings goes down.'

3

Industry and Commerce

'After the latest batch of brokers' circulars sniffing out the end of the great bull run, Lloyds Bank has chipped in with its own bearish review of the prospects for company profits. Mr Christopher Johnson, the Bank's chief economic adviser, argues that the market has been taking an over-sanguine view of profit progression because it looks at company results – boosted by the stock profits generated by historic accounting – rather than the aggregated official figures.'

Lex, *Financial Times*, 3 August 1987

Industrial and commercial companies (ICCs) are a major influence on the whole economy. The performance of the other sectors depends on whether industry and commerce are in advance or in retreat. These companies account directly for nearly a fifth of GDP, because of their profits and other income. They provide about three-fifths of all employment incomes through the wages and salaries they pay their employees. They undertake nearly two-fifths of all fixed capital investment. They are responsible for most British exports of goods and services. They are major users and sources of finance for the banks and the capital markets. On their 'animal spirits' or the lack of them the good health of the economy depends.

Official statistics about the ICCs are notoriously difficult to compile, often late or incomplete, subject to interminable later revisions, and extremely tricky even for financial experts fully to understand. The financial Press and the stock market are influenced more by the results of individual companies than by the aggregated official figures, which come out later and use different accounting concepts. The value of the CSO and DTI statistics is that they give a broader and more balanced picture than any results of individual companies, however large, and are a better guide to the performance of the economy as a whole.

Macro-economic commentators in the UK devote surprisingly little attention to company profits compared with their counterparts in the USA. This is due partly to the low degree of accuracy of the statistics, partly to the relatively low priority attached to profits in the UK academic culture.

There are about 4,500 public limited companies (PLCs), which are the main constituent of the company sector, plus a million or so smaller private companies. They are defined as resident in the UK, rather than British-owned. UK affiliates of foreign companies are thus included, while foreign affiliates of UK companies are excluded. Public corporations are excluded, until they are privatized; their inclusion then swells the ICCs' ranks in a way that distorts the statistics. UIBs and PNBs are also excluded, being in the personal sector. The main distinction within the company sector is between ICCs and financial companies. These can be divided into the monetary sector (mainly banks, see page 171) and the other financial institutions (OFIs). The OFIs include insurance companies, building societies, investment and unit trusts, and life-assurance and pension funds, whose ownership lies in the personal sector, while their financial transactions take place in the company sector. Leasing companies were transferred from the ICCs to the OFIs a few years ago. Property companies remain among the ICCs.

The ICCs and financial companies have different functions in the economy, which can be summed up as providing goods and services, and providing finance, respectively. The two subsectors cannot be simply added together, because much of the income of financial companies is interest paid by ICCs – and, to a lesser extent, vice versa. Such items have to be consolidated out, because by convention the accounts for a sector must exclude transactions that take place inside it.

North Sea oil companies are a major subsector within ICCs. It is important to treat their profits separately from those of other ICCs, because they fluctuate even more, as the price of oil rises or falls. For much of the time profit trends among North Sea and non-North Sea companies are not only of different magnitudes, but of different signs (one is minus when the other is plus). North Sea oil profits are highly accurate, to within 3 per cent, because they are based on direct returns by oil and gas companies to the Department of Energy. The profits of other ICCs have in recent years deteriorated from being 3–10 per cent to being only 10–20 per cent reliable. Estimates are based mainly on Inland Revenue assessments for corporation tax, which are made in arrears and sometimes reassessed for many years, leading to revision of the official statistics. More up-to-date, but not very reliable, estimates are made by means of a quarterly profits inquiry to 750 large companies, and by checking against published results from individual companies. The profits of financial companies are only 10–20 per cent reliable, although some of their other figures are within 3 per cent, being based on direct returns to the Bank of England or the DTI.

Industrial and commercial companies

The CSO published two separate quarterly Press notices on ICCs until mid-1985. These have been combined into one, which appears with a time-lag of one quarter. It contains three detailed tables, covering appropriations, capital expenditure, and financial transactions. (See page 29 for indicators of output of the production industries, which we cover as part of GDP, and page 74 for broader indicators of capital expenditure.)

Gross trading profits (GTPs) are the most important single indicator in the ICCs' Press notice (see Table 13). They are seasonally adjusted, quarterly and annually, and divided between North Sea oil and other companies. They are given net of stock appreciation, which is the same basis as that on which they are given as part of GDP (see Figure 4).

Table 13. Industrial and commercial company profit trends: percentage changes, 1980–86 (A includes, B excludes British Telecom)

	Total income		North Sea oil		Gross trading profits							
					Other				Total			
	Nominal	Real	Nominal	Real	Nominal		Real		Nominal		Real	
					A	B	A	B	A	B	A	B
1980	0.2	−15.1	53.3	29.8	−3.6		−18.4		8.8		−7.8	
1981	7.7	−3.8	34.9	20.5	−2.4		−12.8		9.2		−2.4	
1982	8.1	−0.5	17.1	7.8	18.1		8.6		17.7		8.2	
1983	19.4	14.1	23.2	17.8	18.1		12.9		20.1		14.8	
1984	19.3	13.7	21.2	15.4	17.2		11.6		18.8		13.1	
1985	13.8	7.3	−3.4	−9.0	34.7	23.6	27.0	16.5	19.6	12.9	12.7	6.4
1986	−4.0	−7.2	−54.3	−55.8	21.6	22.4	17.6	18.4	−2.8	−3.7	−6.0	−6.8
1980–86 average	8.9	0.7	6.9	−1.1	14.1	12.8	5.6	4.4	12.8	11.7	4.3	3.3

Note: The RPI has been used to deflate nominal to real. Gross trading profits do not include stock appreciation.
Source: Blue Book 1987, table 5.4. (Version A)

This means that the amount required to compensate for the extra cost of replacing stocks due to inflation has to be subtracted from profits. When profits were lower, and inflation higher, in the mid-1970s and again in the early 1980s, stock appreciation was a more substantial charge on profits than in the mid-1980s. GTPs were just under four-fifths of ICCs' total income in 1986. The rest was rent, mainly to property companies; non-trading income, notably interest on bank deposits; and income from foreign affiliates, net of tax, which does not count as part of UK profits or GDP.

The significance of the GTP and income figures can be grasped only if they are expressed in the form of percentage changes, and deflated to real terms. Table 1 provides this supplement to the ICCs' appropriation account in the CSO Press notice. It can be seen that ICCs' total income rose hardly at all in real terms in 1980–86. Total GTP fared rather better, rising at 4 per cent a year in real terms, and thus increasing the share of profits relative to wages in the national income. However, the volatility of GTPs is shown by the fact that they fell in real terms in 1980 and 1981, because of the recession, and in 1986, because of the fall in oil prices and profits. In between, there was a strong profit recovery, by an average of 12 per cent a year in real terms, for the four years 1982–5. North Sea oil companies were the most volatile. Their profits multiplied by $2\frac{1}{4}$ times in the five years to 1984, helped by the rise in prices and output, then by the depreciation of the pound against the dollar. They then fell by 60 per cent in real terms in the next two years, as the pound rose and the oil price fell. North Sea profits fell from 39 per cent of all ICCs' GTP in 1983 to 15 per cent in 1986 (see Figure 10).

The GTPs of other ICCs were relatively steady in their growth, after falling 28 per cent in real terms in the 1980–81 recession. Over the five years to 1986, profits growth was 15 per cent a year in real terms, and their real level doubled. However, the effect of including the recession is to bring the real growth rate of profits down to $5\frac{1}{2}$ per cent for the whole of 1980–86. The pre-tax real return on capital of non-North Sea ICCs, as calculated by the Bank of England, rose from 3 per cent in 1981 to 9 per cent in 1986.

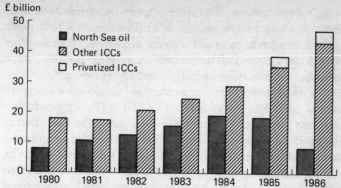

10. Gross trading profits, 1980–86, industrial and commercial companies (net of stock appreciation) (*source:* Blue Book 1987, table 5.4)

The CSO explained the effect that the inclusion of British Telecom (BT) had had on the 1985 figures in its March 1986 Press notice, but this is not sufficient. Since then, BT and other privatized corporations have been added to the ICCs' account without any further estimates of the effects. There is a strong case for publishing two separate profit series, at least from 1985 onwards until 1990, one without, and one with privatized corporations. Otherwise a serious exaggeration of profit growth of the ICCs will result. This has been done in the 'B' columns in Table 13.

BT's GTP in 1985 is estimated at £3.2 billion, including interest and depreciation, which are not deducted at this stage in the national accounts, as they are in company accounts. This rose to about £3.6 billion in 1986. BT was privatized in November 1984. The privatization of British Gas in November 1986, and of British Airways in February 1987, could add another £1.5 billion and £0.5 billion respectively to GTP. If it is assumed that BT's GTP is £4 billion in 1987, GTP in that year could be swelled by £6 billion by privatization profits, without mentioning a host of lesser privatized companies.

The real increase in non-North Sea GTP without BT was 16 per cent in 1985, not 24 per cent as shown in the

CSO Press notice. The 1986 change is unaffected, since both 1985 and 1986 include BT. The result is that profit growth is seen to be much steadier in 1983–6, staying within 14–16 per cent in real terms each year, while the real rate of profit growth in 1980–86 falls from $5\frac{1}{2}$ to $4\frac{1}{2}$ per cent.

Table 14 shows the other sources of ICC income described above for 1986, in addition to GTP. The appropriation account published by the CSO then shows the allocation of income. Dividends are shown net of advance corporation tax, which is included in UK taxes. These taxes comprise mainly corporation tax, and, for oil companies, petroleum-revenue tax; we have added oil royalties, which are grouped with interest payments in the CSO figures, as a form of rent. Profits due abroad are those remitted to parent companies overseas by their UK affiliates. These and income from abroad include unremitted profits too. What remains is undistributed income, or the saving of the ICCs.

Table 14 also shows how these figures would appear in a conventional accounting presentation, if the ICCs were one big company. Depreciation would be deducted from income; we show replacement-cost capital consumption on a national accounts basis, because the lower figure for historic-cost depreciation charged by most companies is not available. We also deduct interest payments, and income from abroad, so as to isolate the accounts of UK resident companies. Taxable profit is then seen to be well under half the CSO total income figure. UK taxes appear to be 44 per cent of taxable profit, but this would be lower if taxable profit were raised by deducting only historic-cost and not replacement-cost depreciation from total income. On any estimate retentions in the conventional sense are only a fraction of CSO undistributed income, but if depreciation is added back, the two figures are much closer.

Table 14 shows for comparison how different the financial company accounts are from those of the ICCs. (They are not published in a Press notice, only in the GDP figures in *Economic Trends*.) Financial companies such as banks have negative GTP, because their costs, which are a deduction from GTP, are greater than their service charges. Most of

Table 14. Company appropriation account 1986

	Industrial and commercial		Financial	
	£ billion	%	£ billion	%
Sources of income				
Gross trading profits	55.6	76.6	−6.7	−16.8
North Sea oil	8.4	11.6		
Other	47.2	65.0		
Stock appreciation	1.9	2.6	0	
Rent and non-trading	7.3	10.1	38.7	97.2
Income from abroad [1]	7.8	10.7	7.8	19.6
Total income	72.6	100	39.8	100
Allocation of income				
Dividends	8.7	12.0	2.2 [2]	5.5
Interest [3]	11.4	15.7	23.8	59.8
Profits due abroad [1]	4.8	6.6	0.7	1.8
UK taxes [4]	13.5	18.6	1.6	4.0
Undistributed (saving)	34.2	47.1	11.5	28.9
Total	72.6	100	39.8	100
Conventional accounting presentation				
Total income	72.6		39.8	
Less: Depreciation [5]	20.8		3.3	
Interest	11.4		24.8 [6]	
Income from abroad [1]	7.8		7.8	
Taxable profit	32.6		3.9	
Less UK taxes	13.5 (41%)		1.6 (41%)	
Profit after tax	19.1		2.3	
Dividends	8.7		1.2	
Retentions	10.4		1.1	

1. Net of taxes.
2. Including interest on loan stock.
3. Including dividends on preference shares.
4. Including North Sea oil royalties.
5. Capital consumption at current replacement cost, which differs from historic-cost depreciation in company accounts.
6. Including £1 billion interest on loan stock.
Source: Blue Book 1987, tables 5.4, 5.7.

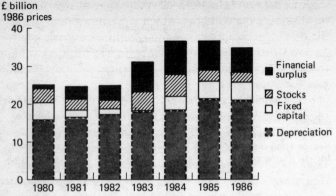

11. Industrial and commercial companies' use of savings, 1980–86
(*source:* Blue Book 1987, tables 5.4, 5.6)

their profits come from rent and non-trading income, which exceeded interest payments by £16 billion in 1986, nearly double their negative GTP. (Because interest counts as a transfer payment in the UK national accounts, it is not part of GDP, and is therefore excluded from gross trading profits.) Financial companies' income has risen to one-third that of all companies as the role of the financial sector has increased. This falls to about one-fifth on consolidation, because of the netting out of interest payments between financial companies and ICCs.

Capital account and financial surplus

The function of ICCs' saving, or undistributed income, is to finance their capital expenditure, which can be divided into stocks and gross domestic fixed capital formation (GDFCF). The difference between the two is the financial surplus or deficit. The way in which saving is split among the different claims on it is shown in Figure 11. Stocks accounted for between 8 and 17 per cent of ICCs' saving in different years in the 1980s. However, this was very differently split between the physical increase in stocks and stock appreciation (the rise in the cost of financing stocks) in different years. In 1980–82, there were sharp run-downs in physical stockbuilding, which were more than offset by the cost of stock appreciation in conditions of high inflation. In 1983–6 there was little change in the physical value of stocks, and inflation moderated, so that stock appreciation rose more slowly.

Fixed capital expenditure including depreciation costs, the main claim on saving, fell from 84 per cent of saving in 1980 to 62 per cent in 1984, because saving rose considerably faster than GDFCF. The opposite happened in 1985 and 1986, when GDFCF rose again to 76 per cent of saving. The extent of new net investment as opposed to replacement of old investment can be judged by the difference between depreciation and gross capital expenditure. This had sunk almost to vanishing point by 1983, but rose again by 1986.

The financial balance of the ICCs rose as a result of these transactions from virtually nothing in 1980 – following a deficit in some years in the 1970s – to a surplus of 20 per cent in 1983, and a few points on each side of that figure in more recent years. There is no particular merit about ICCs being in surplus. It may be a sign that they are lacking in investment opportunities, just as a deficit may show that they are gearing up to expand by means of ambitious capital programmes. On the other hand, the accumulated surplus of ICCs denotes greater financial strength after the weakness of the 1980–81 recession years.

In most years, the ICCs have a net borrowing requirement (NBR), in spite of being in financial surplus (see Figure 12). The third table in the CSO Press notice on ICCs analyses the NBR by giving the financial transactions of the ICCs, showing how they dispose of their surplus. The NBR can be explained in two ways. It can be seen as the excess of security purchases and overseas investment over and above the financial surplus. These transactions are mostly similar in function to capital expenditure; they include the purchase of other companies' shares for take-overs or trade investments, investment in foreign subsidiaries, including unremitted profits, and some trade credit. Or the NBR can be seen as the excess of borrowing through

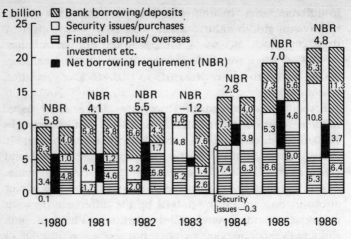

12. Industrial and commercial companies' flow of funds, 1980–86 (*note:* liabilities are on the left, assets on the right of each pair of bars) (*source:* Press notice CSO (87)59, 29 June 1987)

banks or security issues over the acquisition of liquid bank and other deposits.

The doubling of total financial transactions in nominal terms during the 1980s is a sign of the increasing involvement of ICCs in financial as opposed to industrial and commercial sources of profit. Each type of transaction can be followed through the bar chart. Direct investment abroad has increased, but not as rapidly as purchases of company securities, which rose from £1 billion in 1980 to a peak of £4.6 billion in 1985. Most of this sum was the cash, as opposed to the share, element in take-overs and mergers, but in real terms these were still below the peak of 1972, and the even higher peak of 1968. In many years, such as 1986, the main use of ICCs' funds was to build liquid assets, mainly bank deposits, which became an important source of interest income to supplement trading profits for many companies. The ICCs added slightly more to their liquid deposits in 1980–86 than they borrowed in bank loans; twice as much in 1986 alone. Their fund-raising from the securities markets, after an eclipse in 1984, rose rapidly to nearly £11 billion in 1986, over twice as much as their bank borrowing. This marked the 'securitization' of credit. Banks found it more convenient to lend, or arrange loans, and companies to borrow, in the form of tradable securities than to use traditional bank loans. The main types of issue have been rights issues in the equity market, and Eurobond issues. The equity market for new issues, and the traditional listed UK bond market, have been less important sources of finance. The Bank of England publishes a monthly Press notice on capital issues and redemptions in the UK, about six days after the end of the month.

ICCs' financial transactions include many items which are difficult to measure accurately. The result is a residual error, or 'balancing item', which gives the statisticians a lot of trouble, and casts doubt on the reliability of this whole section of the official statistics. For example, preliminary estimates for 1984 indicated an unidentified acquisition of assets of nearly £10 billion by ICCs. This has since been reduced to £2 billion by subsequent revision of other figures. There is still an average £1.8 billion balancing item, which can be positive or negative, for each of the years 1980–86. It has been included with overseas investment and other items on the bottom right-hand section of the bars in Figure 12.

Fixed-capital expenditure

The Department of Trade and Industry (DTI) publishes a provisional quarterly Press notice on fixed capital expenditure seven weeks after the end of each quarter, and a revised estimate eleven weeks after. Capital expenditure includes improvements to existing equipment, but excludes repairs – sometimes a difficult distinction to draw in practice. It is limited to spending on physical goods, and excludes additions to productive capacity by buying other companies, since they do not add to the total stock of fixed capital.

The capital expenditure figures are collected mainly by means of quarterly inquiries by the Business Statistics Office to companies purchasing capital equipment, which are backed up by the Annual Censuses of Production, and other

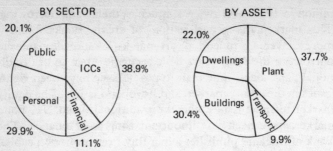

13. Shares of capital expenditure by sector and by asset, 1986 (*source: by sector: Financial Statistics,* May 1987, table 1.2; *by asset: Monthly Digest of Statistics,* April 1987, table 1.7)

annual inquiries to the services sector. Another possible method is by reference to the producers of capital goods; these can result in better classified data by type of product, but exports have to be subtracted, and imports added, in order to reconcile the findings with the other method. In the UK, this method is used only for private dwellings and agriculture. The figures extend back to 1955. The estimates in total are 3–10 per cent reliable, though some are within 3 per cent, and others up to 20 per cent, depending on the industrial sector.

As Figure 13 shows, 39 per cent of total GDFCF was by ICCs in 1986. Another 11 per cent was by financial companies. About another 16 per cent was by UIBs in the personal sector, and by public corporations in the public sector. Thus about two-thirds was business investment, and the other one-third new dwellings and central and local government investment on health, education, roads and other public services. New dwellings were 22 per cent, and other buildings and works 30 per cent. Transport equipment, such as cars, lorries, aircraft and ships, was 10 per cent. So 38 per cent was plant, machinery and other productive equipment.

The analysis of capital expenditure (capex) by industrial sector in Figure 14 may be compared with that of GDP in Figure 2. Manufacturing, sectors 2–4, accounts for 13 per cent of capex, and 26 per cent of GDP. Energy and water,

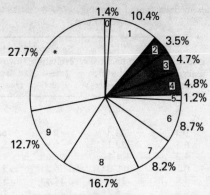

KEY 0 Agriculture, forestry and fishing
    1 Energy and water-supply industries
    2 Extraction of minerals and ores other than fuels; manufacture of
      metals, mineral products and chemicals
    3 Metal goods, engineering and vehicles industries
    4 Other manufacturing industries
    5 Construction
    6 Distribution, hotels and catering; repairs
    7 Transport and communication
    8 Banking, finance, insurance, business services and leasing
    9 Other services
    * Ownership of dwellings
NOTE: The shaded area comprises manufacturing industry.
14. Shares of capital expenditure by industry, 1986 (*source: Monthly Digest of Statistics*, April 1987, tables 1.7–1.9; *British Business*, 26 June 1987)

including North Sea oil, accounts for over 10 per cent of capex, and just under 10 per cent of GDP. Services, sectors 6–9, account for 46 per cent of capex, and 49 per cent of output, a somewhat closer match. The main mismatch is in ownership of dwellings, which accounts for 6 per cent of GDP, but 27 per cent of capex. The DTI Press notice covers only divisions 1–8 of the standard industrial classification. It omits division 9, comprising mainly public services such as health and education, and it omits housing investment. There is a special calculation in which leased assets, normally shown under division 8, financial services, are partly reallocated to the manufacturing divisions 2–4.

Table 15. Trends in fixed capital spending, 1980–86 (at 1980 prices, percentage changes)

	Agriculture, energy, water	Manufacturing (including leased assets)	Services (excluding leased assets)	Dwellings (including land transfer)	Total
1979 weight	15.2	18.7	40.9	25.2	100.0
1980	0.1	−11.1	−2.9	−6.6	−5.0
1981	6.5	−22.1	−5.9	−13.4	−9.4
1982	4.2	−1.7	3.6	4.1	4.1
1983	0.1	−0.8	6.2	13.9	5.9
1984	−4.8	18.6	14.8	5.3	9.0
1985	−9.9	5.7	10.2	−4.2	1.8
1986	−5.9	−4.7	0.3	8.8	0.6
1980–86[1] average	−1.5 (−0.2)	−3.0 (−0.6)	3.5 (1.4)	0.7 (0.2)	0.8 (0.8)
1982–6[1] average	−3.4 (−0.5)	3.1 (0.6)	6.9 (2.8)	5.4 (1.4)	4.2 (4.2)

1. The figures in brackets give the contribution of each column to the total.
Source: DTI Press notice, 18 June 1987; *Monthly Digest of Statistics*, April 1987, table 1.7.

Leasing was used to finance £1.2 billion of manufacturing investment in 1986, raising the total by about 2 percentage points to 15 per cent.

Trends in fixed-capital spending, given in constant 1980 prices in the DTI Press notice and in the *Monthly Digest of Statistics*, show little real increase, less than 1 per cent a year, in 1980–86 (see Table 15). The capex cycle is more pronounced than that of GDP as a whole. Capex fell by 14 per cent in real terms in 1980–81, then rose by 23 per cent, over 4 per cent a year, in 1982–86. There was a 9 per cent real increase in 1984, because of the incentive to bring forward investment owing to the phased withdrawal of capital allowances against tax in that year's Budget. Capex rose in real terms in the energy sector even in the recession year 1981, because of the effect of rising North Sea oil prices and profits in stimulating new offshore developments. It then fell in 1984–6 because oil prices were falling, even when it was buoyant in other sectors. North Sea investment thus offset to some extent the cyclical trend of investment in manufacturing.

Manufacturing investment fell by 30 per cent in real terms in the 1980–81 recession, stagnated for the next two years, then rose 25 per cent in the two years 1984–5, only to fall again in 1986 as the incentives from the 1984 Budget ran out. Investment in services, which was already more than double manufacturing investment in 1979, followed a similar cycle in less extreme form, keeping up a real rise of $3\frac{1}{2}$ per cent a year in 1980–86 as a whole. Investment in housing showed a rather different cyclical pattern; private housing tends to react to the interest-rate cycle, while council housing has suffered from public-expenditure cuts.

Stockbuilding

The DTI publishes quarterly Press notices on stockbuilding about a week after those on fixed capital expenditure. They are also at constant 1980 prices, with quarterly and annual data. Manufacturing is more important in stockbuilding than in GDFCF, accounting for nearly half all stocks in the economy. The Press notice therefore subdivides manufacturing stocks into material and fuel, work in progress, and finished goods, each accounting for about one-third of the total. Nearly a quarter of total stocks are accounted for by wholesale and retail distribution, which are each given separately.

Stockbuilding figures are highly volatile, and difficult to interpret and compile because of the problems of stock valuation. The CSO Press notice would benefit from more information about stock levels, so that changes in stocks could be compared with them. This has been supplied in Table 16. It can be seen that stocks have been falling from 32 per cent of GDP in 1979 to 26 per cent in 1986, a decline of 19 per cent in the stock–output ratio. Similar stock–output ratio figures are given in *Economic Trends* every month. Stocks have either been declining faster than GDP, as in 1980–81, or, when they have been rising, they have risen less rapidly,

Table 16. Stockbuilding trends, 1979–86: changes in physical stocks (at 1980 prices)

	Previous year-end level (£ billion)	Percentage of GDP (at market prices)	Change in stocks			
			£ billion	Percentage of level	Percentage of GDP	Impact on GDP
1979	69.6	29.5	2.5	3.6	1.1	—
1980	72.1	31.3	−2.9	−4.0	−1.2	−2.3
1981	69.2	30.4	−2.4	−3.5	−1.1	+0.1
1982	66.8	29.1	−1.1	−1.6	−0.5	+0.6
1983	65.7	27.6	0.7	1.1	0.3	+0.8
1984	66.4	27.3	0.0	0.0	0.0	−0.3
1985	66.4	26.3	0.5	0.8	0.2	+0.2
1986	66.9	25.9	0.6	0.9	0.2	0.0

Source: D T I Press notice 87/348, 23 June 1987.

as in 1983, 1985 and 1986. The change in stocks is often expressed as a percentage of GDP. It is rarely over 1 per cent, and usually less. To gauge the impact of stock changes on GDP changes, we have to take the difference in stockbuilding as a percentage of GDP between one year and the next – a figure still surprisingly absent from most official statistics. It is remarkable that the whole of the 1980 recession was accounted for by the change from a positive to a negative stockbuild of 1.1 per cent of GDP from 1979 to 1980. The other components of demand were in sum unchanged in real terms. Stockbuilding made an important positive contribution to recovery in 1982–3. In 1984, the negative contribution of the coal strike to GDP(O) was reflected in a draw-down of coal stocks which took one-third of a per cent off GDP(E).

There are three main reasons for the falling stock–output ratio. First, high interest rates have made it expensive to carry stocks. Second, firms have become more efficient in controlling stock levels. Third, stock relief for price increases against tax was removed in the 1984 Budget, on the rather spurious grounds that inflation was no longer a problem.

CBI industrial trends survey

Once a quarter the CBI sends a questionnaire to manufacturing firms, and publishes the results from a weighted sample of about 1,500. A simpler questionnaire is sent out in the intervening months. Thus, about three weeks after the end of each month, the CBI issues to the Press either a monthly or a quarterly industrial trends survey. It covers both the situation during the previous month when the questionnaire is filled in, and the expectation for the following month, which is the month when the survey is published. Although the replies are qualitative rather than quantitative, they do make it possible to assess developments in manufacturing industry before the official statistics are available. Some fairly complex interpretation is required, however, in order to relate the CBI series to the official series of monthly and quarterly statistics. The CBI surveys are also published as part of its quarterly *Economic Situation Report*, and as a monthly addition to it, together with a commentary by the confederation's economics staff.

The CBI monthly inquiry covers total order books, export order books, stocks of finished goods, the volume of output, and average prices. The quarterly inquiry also covers optimism about the business situation and exports, capital expenditure, numbers employed, new orders, deliveries, stocks of raw material and work in progress, length of order books, factors limiting output and exports, adequacy of capacity, reasons for expanding it and factors limiting capital expenditure. Full results are available for nine subsectors within manufacturing industry. The CBI's questions take the form of a three-way option between up, same or down (see page 55). The results over a period are put in terms of positive or negative balances between ups and downs, ignoring the sames. The survey was introduced in 1958. It was fully described and discussed on its twenty-fifth anniversary in October 1983 in a CBI publication appropriately entitled *Twenty-five Years of 'Ups' and 'Downs'*.

CBI research suggests that the level of the balances is better correlated with changes in the level of the corresponding official statistics than with the levels themselves. In other words, if 20 per cent more businessmen think output will go up rather than down month after month, the implication is that output is rising by the same amount each month, rather than that it is staying at the same level each month without rising. This conclusion is not clear-cut, however. The CBI is continuing research into how the survey results might be used either to estimate official statistics in advance of publication, or to forecast the future course of key variables such as employment, output, exports and capital expenditure.

There is particular interest in the context of this chapter in the CBI forecasts of capital expenditure, based on the survey question about authorizations during the next twelve months. These can be compared in *Economic Trends* with the DTI investment intentions survey, which is published as a Press notice in June and December each year. The survey covers capex in manufacturing, with leasing shown separately, and in services. As an example, intentions for 1988 are first given in qualitative terms in December 1986 and in June 1987, and then in precise volume percentages in December 1987 and in June 1988. The average error of the second pair of the forecasts is about 5 per cent, with little gain in accuracy between the second December and the second June forecast. The survey can thus hardly be considered a reliable forecasting tool.

The theory of profits and investment

One economic theory maintains that profits are a reward to the entrepreneur for taking risks. This is not particularly helpful to the forecaster who is trying to explain and predict what gross trading profits will be in a particular year. For this purpose, profit is better understood in an accounting sense, as the difference between the proceeds of the company sector's outputs and the costs of its inputs. In each case, proceeds and costs can be broken down into a volume component and a price component.

The volume of companies' output depends on the various kinds of demand, for consumer goods, investment goods, and exports. The price depends on costs and on margins, which are governed by the extent of competition in the market, and on the degree of capacity utilization; the higher it is, the greater the incentive to firms to respond to additional demand by raising prices rather than output. In export markets, the exchange rate is an additional influence on profits; the higher the pound, the lower are foreign prices converted into sterling, but if sterling prices are raised, demand for UK exports falls. If the pound falls, the reverse applies.

The volume of companies' inputs depends on productivity, on the quantities of labour, capital and materials required to produce a given output of goods and services. The price of labour, which includes national-insurance contributions as well as wages, is dominant, but can be offset by productivity increases reducing unit costs (see Table 24). The price of materials is far more variable, since it depends on the commodity cycle and on the exchange rate. The rapid growth of profits in UK industrial companies in recent years has been partly due to the fall in world commodity prices, which were in 1987 starting to rise again.

Profits are themselves one of the determinants of capital investment. Retained profits provide equity finance for investment, and profits are a measure of the rate of return that is required to justify the risk of expanding capacity. Expectations of the demand for future output also determine investment plans, but these tend to be based on experience of demand in the recent past. According to the 'accelerator' theory of investment, capital expenditure changes by a multiple of demand for firms' output. Since it takes at least two units of capital to produce a unit of output, an increase in demand of one unit will require an increase in investment of at least two units. The theory works in reverse. During the 1980–81 recession, capital investment fell by about twice as much as output. Investment is also determined by the price of capital, which is the rate of interest on loans and the earnings yield on equity investment. When the earnings yield is high, it is expensive to issue your own equity, but cheap to buy other people's. Firms will therefore tend to expand by take-overs rather than by investing in physical capital. The ratio of share prices to the price of capital goods is called the valuation ratio. When it rises with an increase in share prices, take-overs become expensive, and physical capital comparatively cheap.

It is not the price of capital in isolation, but its price relative to the price of labour, which influences investment decisions. The high pay increases in British industry in recent years have provoked manufacturing industry into lay-offs, accompanied by labour-saving capital investment. The productivity of labour has thus increased, but only because profits have been sufficient to remunerate the additional capital equipment which makes labour more productive.

4

Labour Statistics

'A week after winning a third term in power, Mrs Thatcher's government was given a flying start yesterday with the news that unemployment has fallen below the three million mark for the first time in three years.'
George Jones, *Daily Telegraph*, 19 June 1987

The most conspicuous labour statistic is unemployment. Together with employment, earnings and productivity, it appears in one compendious monthly Press notice from the Department of Employment, which forms the basis of this chapter. Unemployment is often cited by voters as the most important political issue facing the country. The change in unemployment appears to have become more important than its high level, in both the economic and the political spheres. Pay bargaining is influenced more by the change than the level, so that earnings can be rising faster if unemployment is falling, even while its level is still about three million. Mrs Thatcher's government was also able to turn unemployment from an electoral liability into an asset, because it fell, if only by one percentage point, in the year before the June 1987 election.

The employment figures have been almost as important as those for unemployment. Even when unemployment is not falling, it may be possible to point to a rise in employment. The earnings and productivity figures are causally linked with those for employment and unemployment. High rises in earnings can cause unemployment, because they discourage the demand for labour. They can also lead to productivity increases, since these are required to validate and meet the cost of the pay increases. The steady $7\frac{1}{2}$ per cent rate of increase of underlying earnings has for the four years to 1987 become a sort of Planck's Constant of the British economy, impervious to changes in the rate of inflation, union power or anything else. The Chancellor of the Exchequer has spoken out against excessive pay increases, but in a free labour market at a time of economic recovery, and with incomes policy banished to the wilderness of Keynesian heresies, it is hard to see how they can be avoided. The Confederation of British Industry, powerless to prevent high pay increases, has justified them as the price for a high-productivity economy. Labour productivity has indeed expanded rapidly during the recovery, as the government has frequently pointed out. However, the rise has been more impressive in manufacturing than in services, has been achieved only by massive lay-offs and closures, and has followed a very up-and-down pattern.

The definition of unemployment

Unemployment is not only an important statistic but, perhaps as a result, a highly disputed one. There are many different ways of defining it, and the official definition in use in the UK has been so frequently changed that it is difficult to grasp the underlying trends as they occur. The definition of unemployment is a question more of semantics than of economics. Politicians, like Humpty-Dumpty, can make the word 'unemployment' mean what they choose (see page 164). It is not sufficient to say that anyone not working is unemployed. There are millions of pensioners who have retired from work, and housewives who prefer to work in the household rather than in the labour market. We would not normally think of them as unemployed. More precise criteria are required (see Table 17). These are: claiming benefit as unemployed; seeking work; wanting a job; being available for work; and not working. Different definitions of unemployment can be categorized with reference to these criteria. They are independent of each other, although there is a high correlation between them.

Table 17. Criteria for being unemployed and alternative definitions of unemployment

		Criteria for being unemployed						
		Sought work in last		Wants a job	Available for work	Worked in last		Number (000s)[1]
	Claiming benefit	Week	Four weeks			Week	Four weeks	
1.	Yes	Yes	—	—	Yes	No	—	2,002
2.	No	Yes	—	—	—	No	—	826
3.	Yes	—	Yes	—	Yes	—	No	101
4.	No	—	Yes	—	Yes	—	No	47
5.	Yes	—	No	—	Yes	—	No	859
6.	Yes	—	No	—	Yes	—	Yes	206

Note: A dash indicates that the criterion at the head of the column does not form part of the definition summarized by the row.
1. As of spring 1986.

Alternative definitions of unemployment

		(000s)	(%)[2]
Labour Force Survey estimate	1 + 2 =	2,828	10.6
Alternative (ILO/OECD) estimate	1 + 2 + 3 + 4 =	2,976	11.2
UK national definition: claimants	1 + 3 + 5 + 6 =	3,168	11.7
Widest definition	1 + 2 + 3 + 4 + 5 + 6 =	4,041	14.3

2. Percentage of employed labour force plus unemployed.

Source: 1986 Labour Force Survey.

The most restrictive definition in the UK is that used in the Labour Force Survey. This is that a person should have sought work within the last week, and not have done any paid work in the last week – not even one hour. By this criterion 2.8 million people were unemployed in Great Britain in spring 1986, or 10.6 per cent of the work-force. This can be broadened in the way recommended by the OECD, following the ILO, to include all those who have sought work and not done any work in the last *four* weeks, and are available for work. This gives 3 million, or 11.2 per cent.

Those who wish to minimize the unemployment problem have experimented with more restrictive definitions. For example (see Table 18), we could reduce the unemployed to

Table 18. Unemployment by age, sex and duration, April 1987

	Age			Sex		Duration in weeks		
	Under 25	25–54	55 and over	Male	Female	Up to 26	26–52	Over 52
(000s)	1,026	1,708	373	2,158	949	1,180	632	1,295
Percentage	33	55	12	69	31	38	20	42

Source: Employment Gazette, July 1987, table 2.5.

only 55 per cent of their present numbers by cutting out all those under twenty-five, on the grounds that they could be in education and training, and all those over fifty-five, as candidates for early retirement. We could cut out the 30 per cent of the unemployed who are women, on the grounds that many of them are married and could be supported by their husbands. We could eliminate the 38 per cent who have been unemployed for less than six months, because they are in between jobs, or taking their time to search for a good job, rather than just any job. If we did all three at once, as recommended many years ago by an Institute of Economic Affairs pamphlet, we could reduce unemployment as of April 1987 to 828,000, or only 27 per cent of its official level.

It is also possible to play down unemployment figures by suggesting that many of the unemployed are doing paid work in the black economy. An investigation of limited scope by Sir Derek Rayner published in 1981 found that 8 per cent or more were unlawfully working while claiming benefits, but the Department of Employment was doubtful about the accuracy of his findings. In 1987 it was claimed by the department that about £50 million a year was being saved by fraud investigators prosecuting or warning people about taking jobs while still drawing benefit, but that this was only a small proportion of the total numbers suspected of fraud. This can hardly amount to more than about 10,000 claimants, compared with the 250,000 or so implied by the Rayner figure of 8 per cent of the unemployed. It is estimated that £750–£1,000 million is being saved, by contrast, through people entitled to benefit failing to claim it. Thus on balance the state gains far more than it loses by the failure of the benefit system to apply exactly to those for whom it was intended. The political right will always play up the fraudsters, while the political left emphasizes the poor who fail to get their entitlements.

There are undoubtedly some cases of people doing full-time jobs yet claiming unemployment benefit. In 1986, 3,650 people were prosecuted. There were far more frequent instances of unemployed people doing odd jobs to supplement the 'dole', and straying above the 'disregard' limits. Those on unemployment benefit can have up to £2 a day earnings disregarded, and still receive benefits; if they earn over £2, they lose the whole of the benefit, which is currently £4.50 a day. For those unemployed over one year, who are on supplementary benefit, only up to £4 a week is 'disregarded', and anything above that is docked one-for-one from the benefit. In the former case the implied marginal tax rate starts at infinity; in the latter it is 100 per cent. In the circumstances, few unemployed odd-jobbers can be expected to declare earnings above the disregard limit. Even if a good deal of this kind of petty fraud occurs, it does not remove the need for such people to be found proper jobs. If the disregard limits are increased, as was intended in the context of the social-security reform, many odd-jobbers now claiming benefit fraudulently will cease to be guilty of fraud.

The UK official definition of unemployment was until October 1982 based on the numbers of unemployed registered at jobcentres, which tried to find them jobs. Jobcentres and social-security benefit offices were physically separated in 1974, but only in 1982 was registration at jobcentres made voluntary, which ruled it out as a criterion for unemployment. It was therefore decided to take claiming – and receiving – benefit as unemployed as being the criterion. This gives 3.2 million, or 11.7 per cent, rather more than either Labour Force Survey definition. Since being 'available for work' is a necessary condition of receiving benefit, this criterion also applies to the UK official definition, but not to the UK Labour Force Survey definition of unemployment.

The benefit criterion is easy to measure on a monthly basis, but it is conceptually unsatisfactory. It gives only about a two-thirds overlap with the Labour Force Survey definition. It excludes about 800,000 work-seekers who do not claim benefit because they are not entitled to, like many married women for example, or fail to claim their entitlement for one reason or another. It includes 860,000 who have not looked for work in the last four weeks, but are entitled to benefit because they are available for work. There are also about 200,000 who have had work of some kind within the last month, whom there is a good case for counting as unemployed, but who fall outside the UK Labour Force Survey definition. The benefit criterion is also flawed in its application. It includes a small number of fraudulent claimants, although many of them are odd-jobbers, and are thus unemployed for most of the time. It also excludes possibly larger numbers of unemployed people who would be entitled to benefit but fail to claim it. Since both the benefit-claimant definition and the Labour Force Survey definition cover people who might be regarded as unemployed for different reasons, it would seem logical to merge them. We then find that there were 4 million unemployed, or 14.3 per cent of the working population, in spring 1986.

The unemployment numbers are difficult to understand properly if they are not expressed as a percentage. Until 1986, they were expressed as a percentage of the unemployed plus employees in employment. A change was then made, to include the self-employed and HM forces as part of the denominator (the bottom half) of the fraction, on the grounds that unemployment can be ended by self-employment as well as by employment. This resulted in a reduction of 1.4 percentage points in the unemployment rate, as shown in Table 19. The table also shows the difference between the unadjusted 'headline' unemployment total, including school-leavers, and the seasonally adjusted total excluding school-leavers, which gives a better idea of the trend. The exclusion of school-leavers, who currently average 90,000

Table 19. The UK unemployment percentage, December 1986

| | Numbers (000s) | |
	Actual	Seasonally adjusted
1. Employees in employment	21,763	21,682
2. Self-employed	2,678	2,678
3. HM forces	320	320
4. Employed labour force (1 + 2 + 3)	24,761	24,680
5. Unemployed (excluding school-leavers)	3,140	3,119
6. School-leavers unemployed	89	93
7. Working population (4 + 5 + 6)	27,990	27,892
'Old' unemployment percentage	12.9	12.6
	$(5 + 6)/(1 + 5 + 6)$	$5/(1 + 5)$
'New' unemployment percentage	11.5	11.2
	$(5 + 6)/7$	$5/7$

Source: Employment Gazette, July 1987, tables 1.1, 2.1.

unemployed a month, takes 0.3 per cent off the unemployment percentage in the average month; more in the autumn, when many of them are still searching for jobs, and less as the year goes on. School-leavers have been disqualified from getting benefit between the end of the summer term when they leave and the beginning of September. This reduces the headline total by about 100,000 in June, July and August.

How the unemployment statistics were reduced

Unemployment seldom went into double-figure percentages before the 1980s. It exceeded 10 per cent in 1879, 1886 and 1921. Only in 1930–35 was it consistently high, peaking at 15.6 per cent in 1932; this was 3.4 million. During the Second World War, and for thirty-five years after it, unemployment was in low single-figure percentages. Looking back, it is hard to see it as having been a problem; yet at the time, rises even in that low level of unemployment were viewed with concern. It was always a policy goal to reduce unemployment at such times, without lapsing into inflation or balance-of-payments crises.

In 1950, when the present series of data begins, there were only about a quarter of a million unemployed. The numbers rose to a peak of just under half a million in 1959 and again in 1963. By 1966, unemployment had fallen back to 350,000 or 1.3 per cent. It doubled to 2.6 per cent by 1970, and at the 1972 peak there were three-quarters of a million unemployed. The rapid 1973 expansion cut this by a quarter of a million in one year, but by 1980 unemployment had trebled to $1\frac{1}{2}$ million, and reached about 6 per cent. It then doubled again to 3 million and around 12 per cent in the four years to 1984. The rate of increase slowed down, but only in 1986 did unemployment begin to fall. The story since 1971 is shown in Figure 15.

The history of unemployment since 1981 has become difficult to follow because of frequent changes in the way in which the statistics are compiled (see Table 20). Each change has been defensible on grounds of greater accuracy or practicality. Yet because all the changes but one minor one have operated in the direction of reducing published unemployment totals by a cumulative 424,000, as well as 1.4 points in percentage terms, the suspicion lingers that one motive behind them was to reduce the damaging political effect of high unemployment. After all, accuracy would also have been improved by adding to the count some of those not claiming benefit who are defined as unemployed in the UK's own Labour Force Survey (see Table 17).

By changing the definition of unemployment so frequently, the government made it difficult to follow the trend. Figures have been published by the Department of Employment for earlier periods on the new basis, but not for later periods on the old basis. The Unemployment Unit has made an estimate which shows that unemployment would have risen to 3.6 million, or 14.3 per cent, by September 1986

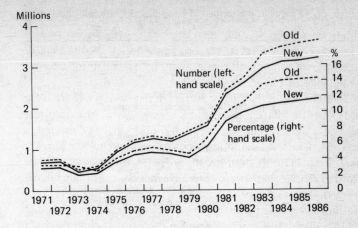

15. Unemployment in the UK, 1971–86 (September) (*source: Economic Trends*, Annual Supplement, tables 102, 103; *Employment Gazette*, July 1985, p. 275; *Unemployment Unit briefing*, October 1986)

if the statistics had not been changed (see Figure 15). On the new basis, they were 3.2 million, and 11.6 per cent. The size of the unemployment problem was thus cut by one-fifth.

The most important change was from the clerical count of those registering at jobcentres to the computer count of those claiming benefits at social-security offices (see page 85). This reduced the unemployment figure by 190,000, about one-third of it because of greater accuracy in counting, but about two-thirds of it by removing job-seekers not entitled to benefit (23,000 severely disabled were added to the count, who might well have been left out by any criterion other than the claiming of benefit). Another 200,000 over-sixties were removed from the count in two stages by being given higher long-term benefits, which resulted in their leaving the definition, but not the condition, of unemployment. The long-term unemployed without jobs for over a year, some of them over sixty, are now over two-fifths of the total. The longer they remain without a job, the less likely it is that

Table 20. Changes in the method of compiling the unemployment statistics, 1979–86

Date	Change	Effect
October 1979	Fortnightly payment of benefits	+ 20,000
November 1981	Men over sixty offered higher supplementary benefit to leave working population	− 37,000
October 1982	Registration at jobcentres made voluntary Computer count of benefit claimants substituted for clerical count of registrants	− 190,000
March 1983	Men sixty and over given national-insurance credits or higher supplementary benefit without claiming unemployment benefit	− 162,000
July 1985	Correction of Northern Ireland discrepancies	− 5,000
March 1986	Two-week delay in compilation of figures to reduce over-recording	− 50,000
		424,000
Total effect of changes to seasonally adjusted figure without school-leavers in April 1987		458,000
July 1986	Inclusion of self-employed and H M forces in denominator of unemployment percentage	− 1.4%

Source: Employment Gazette, October 1986, p. 422; *Unemployment Bulletin*, no. 20, summer 1986, pp. 14–15, and statistical supplement, May 1986, p. 6.

they will get one. Some, like the Employment Institute, have argued that this is a reason for giving them priority in the labour market, not for removing them from the unemployment count.

The other main change is not in the number of unemployed, but in the percentage (see Table 19). The percentage is a fraction, with the unemployed as the numerator. What should the denominator be? Unemployed as a percentage of what? Between the wars it was as a percentage of contributors to national insurance, which artificially boosted the percentage, but not the numbers. For most of the post-war period, it was a percentage of the unemployed themselves, plus employees in employment. Then, in 1986, the self-employed and HM forces were added to the denominator. Unemployment was expressed as a percentage of the unemployed plus the employed labour force (including self-employed), which is by definition equal to the 'working population' of whom over 10 per cent are currently *not* working. This immediately caused a 1.4 per cent drop in unemployment, which was that much greater because of the rapid increase in self-employment. All previous data were similarly adjusted by the addition of the self-employed and HM forces to the denominator, causing about a 10 per cent drop in unemployment percentages. Not only did the change involve a somewhat Orwellian rewriting of history, it brought a new source of revision into recent figures as well. Self-employment is notoriously difficult to measure. It has to be estimated on the basis of the 1981 census, and annual labour-force surveys. Thus when self-employment numbers are revised, unemployment percentages must be as well. While the change was in itself logical, because the unemployed can become just as much self-employed as employees, it raises as many problems as it solves. Again, political motives may have tipped the balance.

Both employment and unemployment can be put in perspective, by expressing them as a percentage of the total population (see Figure 16). The unemployed are just over 5 per cent of the total population, and another 5 per cent are self-employed. Less than two-fifths have a job, of whom one-fifth (8 per cent) are part-time women workers. Thirty per cent are over-sixteens classed as 'economically inactive'. Of these, about half are of working age and could be regarded as employable, while the other half are over working age; some of these do work, and others would, if 'ageism' were given its head. While only 5 per cent of the total population are officially unemployed, 45 per cent of the population over sixteen are either officially unemployed or 'economically inactive'.

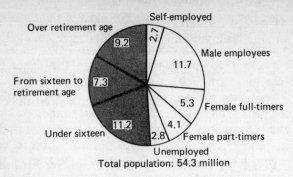

16. Economic status of the UK population (activity rate (active as percentage of sixteen and over) = 61.7 per cent; unemployment rate (unemployment as percentage of active) = 10.5 per cent) (*source*: Labour Force Survey)

Table 21. The effect of special employment measures: numbers off the unemployment count, March 1987 (000s)

1. Job-creation programmes	Community Programme	220
	New workers' scheme	6
	Enterprise allowance scheme	15
2. Administrative/statistical measures	Job-release scheme	23
	Availability-for-work test	6
	Restart scheme	104
	Benefit changes	15
3. Training schemes	Job-training scheme	0[1]
	Youth Training Scheme	0[1]
		389

1. Numbers are difficult to estimate, and thought to be negligible.
Source: Charter for Jobs Economic Report, May 1987, table 1.

The other way in which the government has reduced unemployment is by means of 'special measures' (see Table 21). These are estimated to have reduced the unemployment count by nearly 400,000. So if there had been neither statistical redefinition nor special measures, unemployment – even on the rather restrictive official definition – would have reached 4 million by 1986. The numbers removed from the count by special measures are less than those taking part in them, since many of them would not have counted as unemployed.

The most important special measure is the Community Programme, which gives work on special projects for six months. It was estimated to have taken 220,000 off the unemployment count in March 1987. Large numbers are also involved in the Youth Training Scheme, but few of them would have counted as unemployed had they not been involved. The YTS should be seen as improving job prospects by raising qualifications, rather than as contributing statistically to the reduction of unemployment, which excludes school-leavers in the definition generally taken as most indicative of the trend.

Another 150,000 have been removed from the count by statistical measures. These consist not of changing definitions so much as applying existing definitions more rigorously. The most notable case is the Restart scheme, introduced in July 1986, which interviewed 1.5 million people over the following year. About 10 per cent of them are estimated to have come off the unemployment count. There is evidence that only $\frac{1}{2}$ per cent of them got jobs directly as a result, but some of the others may indirectly have been helped to find jobs quicker than they would otherwise have done. About 1 per cent have been disqualified from benefit, but others may have left the count for fear that this would happen if it was found out that they were doing some paid work. There is also some evidence that the criteria for receiving benefit are being more strictly applied, quite apart from the Restart interviews. Thus an unemployed person who is looking after a sick relative and cannot make alternative arrangements quickly enough could fail to qualify for benefit, and thus not count as unemployed.

Unemployment and employment

The position from March 1979 to March 1987 is shown in Figure 17 and Table 22, which analyse changes in Great Britain both over the period and in the two subperiods

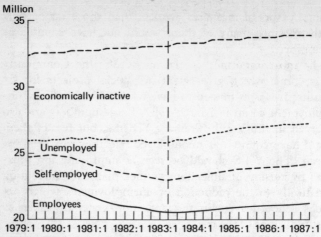

17. Population of working age, Great Britain, March 1979 to March 1987 (*source: Employment Gazette*)

before and after 1983. Employment in manufacturing industry fell by about 2 million to 5 million between 1979 and 1983, but the fall was much slower after 1983, because manufacturing output was rising instead of falling; the rise was slower than the increase in productivity, so employment continued to fall. Employment in other industries and services fell slightly before 1983, but grew by 1.1 million afterwards – still only a 1.8 per cent annual increase on a base of 15 million. The number of all employees fell by 2 million in 1979–83, then rose by 700,000 in 1983–7, giving a net loss of 1.3 million.

The number of jobs lost before 1983 was slightly offset by the rise in self-employment, and the number created after 1983 considerably augmented by it. The self-employed increased by 800,000 during the whole period, reducing the net loss of jobs from 1.3 million to 500,000. However, the figures for self-employment are unreliable, and have recently had to be revised downwards. In any case, many of the self-employed are part-time, and may be no more than odd-jobbers who are looking for permanent employment. Similarly, it is estimated that 545,000 of the 728,000 jobs created

Table 22. Changes in employment and unemployment in Great Britain, 1979–87 (seasonally adjusted)

| | March 1979 level (000s) | March 1983 | | | | March 1987 | | | | | | |
| | | Level (000s) | Change from March 1979 | | | Level (000s) | Change from March 1983 | | | Change from March 1979 | | |
			000s	%	% p.a.		000s	%	% p.a.	000s	%	% p.a.
1. Manufacturing employees	7,129	5,485	−1,644	−23	−6.3	5,075	−410	−7.5	−1.9	−2,054	−29	−4.2
2. Other employees	15,413	15,044	−369	−2.4	−0.6	16,182	+1,138	+7.6	+1.8	+769	+5.0	+0.6
3.[1] All employees	22,542	20,529	−2,013	−8.9	−2.3	21,257	+728	+3.5	+0.9	−1,285	−5.7	−0.7
4. Self-employed	1,843	2,147	+304	+16	+3.9	2,644	+497	+23	+5.3	+801	+43	+4.6
5. H M forces	314	322	+8	+2.5	+0.6	320	−2	−0.6	−0.2	+6	+1.9	+0.2
6.[2] Employed labour force	24,699	22,998	−1,701	−6.9	−1.8	24,221	+1,223	+5.3	+1.3	−478	−1.9	−0.2
7. Unemployed	1,199	2,828	+1,629	+136	+24	3,116	+288	+10	+2.5	+1,917	+160	+13
8.[3] Working population	25,898	25,826	−72	−0.3	−0.1	27,337	+1,511	5.9	+1.4	+1,439	+5.6	+0.7
9. Inactive population	6,672	7,474	+802	+12	+2.9	6,730	−744	−10	−2.6	+58	+0.9	+0.1
10.[4] Working-age population	32,570	33,300	+730	+2.2	+0.6	34,067	+767	+2.3	+0.6	+1,497	+4.6	+0.6
Activity rate[5]	79.5%	77.6%				80.2%						

1. 1 + 2 = 3.
2. 3 + 4 + 5 = 6.
3. 6 + 7 = 8.
4. 8 + 9 = 10.
5. Activity rate = 8 ÷ 10.

Source: Employment Gazette, Historical Supplement no. 1, and 'Labour force outlook for Great Britain', May 1987; Department of Employment Press notice 156/87, 16 July 1987.

between 1983 and 1987 were for part-timers, mainly women. While this may in many cases have satisfied personal preferences, it has been argued that only the equivalent of 270,000 full-time jobs were thereby created, reducing the number of new full-time jobs created to less than half a million during 1983–7. It is also estimated that another 270,000 of the new jobs created are 'double jobs', done by someone who already has a job, perhaps part-time. This would, on one interpretation, reduce the number of full-time equivalent jobs created in the four years to 1987 to only 200,000.

A major distortion of the true employment position occurred when 800,000 people of working age dropped out of the 'working population' in 1979–83 because they were discouraged by rising unemployment from looking for jobs, and did not qualify for benefit, and then (nearly all) returned to it in 1983–7 as the economic climate improved. They are shown in line 9 of Table 22 as 'inactive population'.

The population of working age was rising by about half a per cent a year during this period as the 'bulge' passed out of the schools and universities. It rose by 1.5 million during 1979–87. Before 1983, the increase of about 750,000 was more than offset by the numbers giving up work or unemployment. The economic-activity rate dropped by two percentage points to 77.6 per cent. Unemployment therefore rose only by the numbers put out of work. It was not augmented by the increase in the population of working age, which would have added about $2\frac{1}{2}$ percentage points to the unemployment rate. After 1983, the rise in the economic-activity ratio back to over 80 per cent made unemployment worse than it would otherwise have been. The number of jobs created – including part-time and double jobs – was roughly equal to the numbers joining the population of working age. On top of this, there was an increase in self-employment of about half a million, so the unemployed should have fallen by this much. Instead, the extra 750,000 or so who shifted back across the frontier between 'inactivity' and 'activity' absorbed all the increase in self-employment and added a net 250,000 to the unemployment count.

The whole episode illustrates how sensitive perceptions of

reality are to statistical definition. Had unemployment been defined on the basis of a constant activity rate, the problem would have looked far worse in 1979–83, far better in 1983–6, but not so good in 1986–7, as the following analysis of the figures for the year to June 1987 shows.

For most of the 1979–83 period, employment was falling and unemployment was rising. Between March 1983 and mid-1986, unemployment was still rising, but so was employment. Over the year to mid-1987, employment and self-employment continued to rise, but unemployment fell by about the same amount: 285,000. Yet the Labour Force Survey had predicted a rise in the working population of about 195,000; 150,000 of it for demographic reasons, 45,000 because of a rise in the activity rate. Instead of rising, the activity rate fell, and about 145,000 workers were defined as 'inactive', accounting for two-thirds of the reduction in unemployment. This fall in the activity rate was due to Restart interviews, and other measures which discouraged people from claiming benefit, even though they would previously have counted as unemployed by other criteria. Of the 195,000 extra working population, 50,000 were absorbed by the Youth Training Scheme, so 145,000 became neither employed nor unemployed, but economically inactive.

Half of the fall in unemployment during the year was thus due to a change in the activity rate brought about by official policy. To put it in another way, half of the jobs created merely sufficed to prevent the extra population of working age from becoming unemployed, rather than reducing unemployment in any real sense. On the widest definition of unemployment (see Table 17), there would probably still be 3.9 million unemployed in mid-1987, a reduction of only 100,000 from mid-1986. The re-merger of jobcentres and benefit offices, which were separated in 1974, will reduce unemployment further by making it easier for the authorities to put pressure on the unemployed to either take up job offers or lose benefit.

As a footnote to the unemployment figures, it must be noted that most refer to the United Kingdom, but some only to Great Britain. This can be a source of confusion.

There are about 125,000 unemployed in Northern Ireland – 18 per cent of the working population – who account for the difference between the U K and the G B figures. The reason for using G B figures from time to time is that they can be related to figures for employment and for the Labour Force Survey that do not include Northern Ireland. The novice can imagine that he or she is looking at a big change in unemployment when he or she has merely inadvertently switched from a U K to a G B set of figures.

The Department of Employment Press notice gives details of job vacancies notified at jobcentres. These are estimated to be only one-third of all vacancies in the economy, because many employers use private channels. The changes rather than the levels of vacancies may still be taken as indicating a trend. They tend to move in the opposite direction to changes in unemployment, as an indicator of labour-market conditions. For example, vacancies rose by about 50,000 to 233,000 over the year to June 1987, as unemployment was falling.

It is a naïve mistake to think that the number of un-employed could be reduced if only vacancies could be filled from their ranks. The average vacancy lasts only a month, so that the figures indicate more the trend of labour-market turnover than the number of posts that cannot be filled.

Earnings, productivity and labour costs

Statistics for earnings, productivity and labour costs used to be the subject of a separate Press notice, but they are now part of the monthly Department of Employment release of unemployment and employment figures. The earnings index in its present form goes back only to 1980. It is based on a monthly inquiry to a sample of employers, and covers a much wider range of industries, particularly in the services sector, than the old index which it replaced. It can be analysed on the basis of the 1980 standard industrial classi-fication. Sub-indices are quoted in the Press notice for production, manufacturing and service industries.

Because the earnings index is based on payments actually

made, as opposed to those which accrue on paper, its behaviour is uneven from month to month; during 1986, its year-on-year increase jumped around randomly between 6.1 and 8.6 per cent, averaging 7.9 per cent. The Department of Employment therefore calculates an underlying increase by smoothing the fluctuations. It makes seasonal adjustments, and allows for arrears or advances in payment of wages resulting from pay negotiations, and for the effect of industrial disputes. The result is almost too stable to be true; for the four years 1984–7, the underlying increase of earnings was $7\frac{1}{2}$ per cent almost every month, except for a few months in which it was $7\frac{3}{4}$ per cent.

Earnings should be distinguished from pay settlements. They include overtime and various forms of wage drift, such as 'grading drift', which occurs when the proportion of higher-graded posts rises. These are not included in settlement figures, which have recently been $1\frac{1}{2}$–2 per cent less than earnings increases. Earnings are averages per head, and therefore need to be multiplied by changes in the number of employees in employment to calculate changes in the total wage bill. Table 23 shows that earnings increased faster than prices from 1981 onwards, giving a real increase of just over 2 per cent a year. The figures were artificially depressed in 1984, and boosted in 1985, because of the coal strike. The underlying rate gives a less bumpy pattern of real increases, but still shows a big jump to 4 per cent in real terms in 1986, because inflation fell to only 3.4 per cent.

Figures are also given in the Press notice for output per head, in manufacturing and in the whole economy, in other words labour productivity; and earnings per unit of output, or unit labour costs. Both are given in index form, with the index starting at 100 in 1980, as for earnings. The increase in earnings divided by the increase in labour productivity is equal to the rise in unit labour costs. Productivity growth can thus reduce the increase in unit labour costs below the rise in earnings.

The government has made much of the growth in manufacturing productivity of over 5 per cent a year in 1982–6, which reduced the average earnings increase of 9 per cent to

Table 23. Average earnings in Great Britain, 1981–6: percentage increase on a year earlier

	Nominal earnings		Prices (RPI)	Real earnings	
	Actual	Underlyings		Actual	Underlying
1981	12.9	13.0	11.9	0.9	1.0
1982	9.4	9.6	8.6	0.6	0.8
1983	8.4	7.7	4.6	3.6	3.0
1984	6.1	7.6	5.0	1.0	2.5
1985	8.5	7.5	6.1	2.3	1.3
1986	7.9	7.5	3.4	4.3	4.0
1981–6 Average	8.8	8.8	6.6	2.1	2.1

Source: Economic Trends, April 1987, tables 40, 42; *Employment Gazette*, July 1987, table 5.1.

a unit-labour-cost increase of just under 4 per cent. The figures were less good in 1980 and 1981, so their inclusion brings productivity growth in manufacturing over the seven years 1980–86 down to $3\frac{1}{2}$ per cent, and raises the average annual unit-labour-cost increase to 7 per cent. It should also be noted that manufacturing productivity reached a peak increase of 8.5 per cent in 1983, then fell year by year to 2.6 per cent in 1986. It leapt to over 7 percent in the first half of 1987, reducing unit-labour-cost increases to virtually zero for the first time since 1983. It remains to be seen whether manufacturing industry can manage such spurts for long; they are due more to sudden surges in output in response to demand rather than to revolutions in shop-floor practices.

The productivity picture is not as good for the whole economy as for manufacturing. Just as manufacturing outperforms the whole-economy average, services underperform it. The productivity increases in Table 24 are, as whole-period averages, close to the GDP growth figures (see page 19). That for 1980–86, of 1.9 per cent, is slightly higher than GDP growth of 1.7 per cent, because there was a reduction of 500,000 in the employed labour force over the period.

Table 24. Earnings, productivity and labour costs, 1980–87: percentage changes

	Manufacturing			Whole economy		
	Average earnings	Output per head	Earnings per unit of output	Average earnings	Output per head	Earnings per unit of output
1980	17.6	−3.9	22.4	19.8	−2.1	22.4
1981	13.1	3.5	9.3	11.9	2.0	9.7
1982	11.2	6.6	4.3	9.7	3.7	5.8
1983	8.9	8.5	0.4	8.6	3.9	4.5
1984	8.7	5.4	3.1	5.7	1.5	4.1
1985	9.1	3.2	5.7	7.4	2.1	5.2
1986	7.7	2.6	5.0	7.8	2.4	5.3
1987[1]	8.0	6.9	1.1	7.8	4.1	3.6
1980–86 average	10.8	3.6	7.0	10.0	1.9	8.0
1982–6 average	9.1	5.2	3.7	7.8	2.7	5.0

Note: $\dfrac{(1 + \text{average earnings change})}{(1 + \text{output per head change})} = (1 + \text{earnings per unit of output change})$.

Average earnings are calculated from output per head and earnings per unit of output, and differ slightly from the earnings figures in Table 23.

Source: Economic Trends, April 1987, tables 34, 40; Department of Employment Press notice 156/87, 16 July 1987.

1. Partly estimated.

That for 1982–6, of 2.7 per cent, is the same as the GDP growth figure, and benefits equally by the omission of the recession years 1980–81. Productivity in the services sector of the economy rose by only $1\frac{1}{4}$ per cent in 1980–86, compared with 3 per cent in 1965–73, the period which Mrs Thatcher and her supporters criticize for its bad economic management. The growth of manufacturing productivity in these two periods was almost identical at $3\frac{1}{2}$–$3\frac{3}{4}$ per cent. (See the *Financial Statement and Budget Report 1987–88*, table 3.11.)

The economics of unemployment, pay and productivity

We can only hope to summarize briefly here some of the complex linkages between unemployment, pay and productivity, variables which are at the heart of modern macroeconomic theory. We list some of the current ways of explaining unemployment, together with the policy remedies derived from them.

1. *Unemployment is due to a deficiency of demand in the economy*. It can therefore be reduced by fiscal expansion, by increasing the budget deficit, either raising public expenditure or cutting taxes. Against this it is argued that there has in fact been a brisk increase in nominal monetary demand, but too much has gone into higher prices, and not enough into higher demand for real output. Any further increase in monetary demand might fuel inflation rather than increasing real demand and thus reducing unemployment. There may nevertheless be a trade-off, where some extra inflation is accepted as the price of reducing unemployment. Such a difficult choice could be avoided if a workable incomes policy could be devised so as to forestall the inflationary element in demand expansion.

2. *Unemployment is due to too high a real exchange rate*, in other words one that raises UK exporters' costs and prices relative to those of their competitors, particularly those in the newly industrializing countries such as Hong Kong or Taiwan. It can therefore be remedied by a real devaluation, bringing export-led growth. Here the objection is that devaluation brings inflation, and contains a greater nominal than real element; the competitiveness that comes with lower export prices is taken away by higher import costs, leading to domestic price and pay inflation. As well as causing inflation through the exchange rate, devaluation can cause inflation through capacity constraints as the demand for output increases. It makes little difference whether the extra demand is self-generated, as in paragraph 1 above, or comes from outside. While the UK's high real exchange rate during much of the 1980s helped to keep inflation down, it was the real devaluations, particularly that of 1986 following the oil-price fall, which helped to check unemployment.

3. *Unemployment is due to the price of labour being too high* compared with that of other factors of production. Real wages, or at least their rate of increase, should be cut, there-fore, in order to stimulate employers' demand for labour, and its substitution for capital. Although this is a classical economics argument, it is similar to the Keynesian argument for incomes policy put forward in paragraph 1. The objec-tion is that trade unions, for all the reduction in their powers, would not agree to real wage cuts; it is also difficult to achieve a real wage cut of a given size, since cuts in the rate of nominal wage increases lead to lower price increases, which put real wages up again. A cut in real pre-tax wages, if it can be achieved, also cuts demand, and thus employment, unless it is offset by an income-tax cut. The high pay increases of the 1980s, far from being discouraged by high unemploy-ment, were one of its causes. In order to validate higher pay, employers had to get higher productivity, which meant laying off workers rather than raising output.

4. *Unemployment is an inevitable result of technological pro-gress.* We should therefore adopt 'small is beautiful' labour-intensive methods of alternative-society production and industrial organization. There is a grain of truth in this argu-ment, to the extent that manufacturing industry is becoming more capital-intensive, and is likely to need fewer workers, whatever the price of their labour. However, the converse is that the relatively labour-intensive services sector accounts for a growing proportion of the economy. It should therefore be possible to shift employees from manufacturing into ser-vices to combat 'technological' unemployment. This is what has in fact happened in the UK (see Table 22). Even in manu-facturing, higher productivity means greater competitive-ness, more sales, and thus even possibly more employees. If economic growth is fast enough, manufacturing employment may decline relative to that in services, but not absolutely.

5. *North Sea oil has caused unemployment by raising the ex-change rate.* This has led to a deficit in manufacturing trade, offsetting the surplus in oil trade. Oil exports use hardly any

labour, while manufacturing imports destroy British jobs. As in paragraph 2, the remedy would have been to lower the exchange rate, with the same objections. It was Sir Michael Edwardes, then Chairman of BL, who put forward to the CBI conference the more drastic nostrum: 'It would have been better to leave the bloody stuff in the ground.' However, a lower exchange rate would actually have increased the UK's already large balance-of-payments surplus from oil by improving the balance of manufacturing trade. If it had been accompanied by fiscal expansion as in paragraph 1, the surplus would have been absorbed by higher imports. Instead of investing a surplus abroad, the UK could have increased its investment in industrial capacity and jobs at home. Like other forms of expansion, this would have had its cost in terms of higher inflation.

5

Inflation

'City analysts floored as inflation edges up to 4.2 per cent.'
Christopher Huhne, *Guardian*, 11 July 1987

There are many ways of measuring the rate of change of prices. This is usually called the rate of inflation. Some economists seek to distinguish once-for-all price increases from inflation, which they define as 'a process of steadily rising prices' (*Penguin Dictionary of Economics*). The two cannot easily be separated, and inflation has come to be equated with any kind of price increase. On the rare occasions when prices fall, it is termed negative inflation, or deflation. The Retail Prices Index (RPI) is the best-known way of measuring price changes. It is also the most widely publicized of all the UK economic indicators. Other measures of inflation covered in Press notices are the Tax and Price Index (TPI), and the Producer Prices Index, formerly known as the Wholesale Prices Index. In this chapter we also give a version of the RPI excluding owner-occupation costs, and the gross domestic product and consumers' expenditure deflators (CEDs). The latter are often used by economists, but attract little public attention.

The Retail Prices Index

The RPI measures the rate of change of consumer prices. It is an index number, such as 107.4, which has no meaning on its own, but only when it is compared with the same index at a different point in time. It shows how the price level has changed since the index was restarted at 100 in January 1987. It is the change in the index over a period, not its level, which shows how much prices have gone up (or, very occasionally, down).

The control of inflation is a top policy priority for every government. The RPI is the 'judge and jury' on whether they are succeeding, according to Mr Nigel Lawson, Chancellor of the Exchequer, speaking in 1986. The financial markets watch the RPI as a pointer to the government's interest-rate policy, operating through the effect of interest rates on the exchange rate. If the RPI is higher than expected, interest rates may be raised to bring it down. If it is lower than expected, interest rates may be allowed to fall. (As we shall see, the way in which the RPI measures housing costs may give a perverse result to such policy actions in the short run.) The Thatcher government originally appeared to give the conquest of inflation an overriding priority, even over such objectives as full employment and economic growth. More recently, the government has sought to use the reduction of inflation more as a means to stable expansion than as an end in itself. The target of zero inflation has been glimpsed only intermittently. It has little real attraction, because of its cost in rising unemployment, and the diminishing political returns to be expected from further reductions once inflation is in low single figures.

The RPI has many uses in the economy. The government uses the RPI increase over the year to each December to 'index' tax allowances for the next financial year in the Budget the following March. This means that they are normally raised in line with inflation so as to keep their value to the taxpayer constant. (In some years they are raised by less, in others by more than the inflation rate.) This applies to the main personal allowances, and, more approximately, to the higher-rate bands, the capital-gains-tax exemptions and indexation reliefs, the inheritance-tax scales, and the VAT exemption limits. The government uses the RPI increase over the year to each September to uprate pensions and some other social-security benefits from the following April. It also uses the RPI to increase the principal value of index-linked gilt-edged securities and National Savings certificates. To say that they are 'index-linked' means that their value changes with the RPI.

The RPI is used as the starting-point for pay claims. Employee representatives generally bargain for an increase in line with the movement of the RPI, plus some real increase to allow for other factors such as productivity. They are likely to choose whichever is the higher of the last year's RPI increase, or the next year's forecast RPI increase. The RPI varies considerably from month to month, so the date of an annual pay negotiation may influence the amount of the claim.

The RPI has many uses in statistics. It is often used to deflate amounts in money terms so as to express them in real terms, taking out that part due purely to rising prices rather than rising quantities. This makes it possible to assess changes in, for example, the standard of living over a period. The RPI can be used to turn conventional company accounts into constant purchasing power (CPP) accounts. This is one of a number of possible forms of inflation accounting. It has not been used by UK companies in practice.

The history of the RPI

There are records of price changes of staple commodities going back to the Middle Ages, which can be used to provide a rough-and-ready idea of inflation trends. The immediate precursor of the RPI was the national cost-of-living index set up in 1914, which lasted until 1947. This was followed by an interim index until 1956, when a new index of retail prices was instituted. It took on its present form only in 1962, when the components began to be given new weights each year in line with changes in family expenditure. The index itself is restarted at 100 from time to time, most recently in January 1987, and before that in January 1974. It is as if the price of the 'basket' of goods and services used for the RPI were set at 100 units in those months, and then increased by the percentage increase shown by the whole basket.

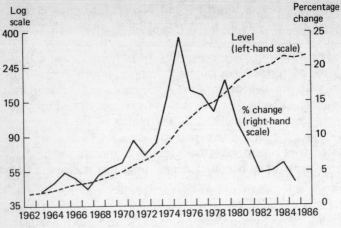

18. The Retail Prices Index, 1962–86

Figure 18 shows that the level of the RPI has been rising since 1962. Its most rapid rate of increase, given by the steepness of the curve, was in the mid-1970s. By the mid-1980s it had returned to the more gentle rate of increase of the early 1960s. The jagged line shows more clearly how the annual rate of change of the RPI has fluctuated, from 1.9 per cent in 1963 to 24.2 per cent in 1975, and back to 3.4 per cent in 1986. In the century 1850–1950, prices fell in thirty-five years and rose in sixty-five, of which ten were war years. The price level was about the same in 1900 as it had been in 1850, with some fluctuations in between. It multiplied three and a half times between 1900 and 1950, but the annual average inflation rate for the period was still only $2\frac{1}{2}$ per cent. The price level then multiplied ten times in the thirty-five years 1951–86, with an average inflation rate of 6.8 per cent a year. By 1986, prices had multiplied about five times in the fifteen years since 1971, and doubled in the eight years since 1978.

The Retail Prices Index Advisory Committee (RPIAC) was set up as the Cost of Living Advisory Committee in 1946 to advise the government on the construction of the

RPI. It did not meet between 1977 and 1984, but was then called upon to advise on possible changes. Its report was published in July 1986, and partly carried into effect from January 1987, leaving other recommendations to be implemented later. The RPIAC's report made a number of minor technical recommendations. Its main recommendation of substance was that the coverage of the RPI should be extended to items then excluded, which had come to represent about 5 per cent of expenditure in the Family Expenditure Survey (FES). The most important is holiday spending, of which three-quarters is abroad and one-quarter in the UK, accounting together for about $2\frac{1}{2}$ per cent of the average family budget. The committee recommended including only payments made in the UK for foreign holidays, and not payments made abroad. Another 1 per cent of budgets goes on fees and subscriptions for education, health, trade unions and professional bodies, and this too is to be included. Perhaps the same amount is spent on financial services, such as bank charges and certain types of insurance. These items pose measurement problems, so could not all be included at the same time as other charges in the indices introduced in January 1987.

The RPIAC's proposals for restructuring the components of the RPI into more meaningful categories were carried out from January 1987. The changes, together with the proposed additional items, are shown in Table 25. The former catch-all categories of 'miscellaneous goods' and 'services' have been replaced by more precise subdivisions. There is now 'household services', including domestic and cleaning services, and postal and telephone charges. On the other hand there is 'personal goods and services', comprising such items as chemists' goods, watches and hairdressing. 'Transport and vehicles' has been split into 'motoring expenditure' and 'fares and other travel' costs. The new 'leisure goods' category includes audio-visual, photographic and sports equipment, and 'leisure services' now takes in entertainment and recreation, and is to take in holidays. The new categories will give a more meaningful basis on which to analyse the relative price

Table 25. Changes in RPI weights between 1986 and 1987

1986		1987	
Category	Weight	Category	Weight
Food	185	Food (excl. pet food)	167
Meals out	44	Catering	46
Alcoholic drink	82	Alcoholic drink	76
Tobacco	40	Tobacco	38
Housing	153	Housing	157
Fuel and light	62	Fuel and light	61
Durable household goods	63	Household goods	73
		Household services	44
Clothing and footwear	75	Clothing and footwear	74
		Personal goods and services	38
Transport and vehicles	157	Motoring expenditure	127
		Fares and other travel	22
Miscellaneous goods	81	Leisure goods	47
Services	58	Leisure services	30
	1,000		1,000

Source: Employment Gazette, April 1987.

changes of different types of consumer activity and their changing weights in total expenditure.

The RPIAC made some important changes in the housing category. It was asked to re-examine the treatment of housing costs. These include mortgage-interest payments, which have been included in the RPI since 1975 to represent the costs of owner-occupied housing. The committee decided to keep mortgage costs in, but with a number of changes which reduced their weight in the index from 54 per 1,000 in 1986 to 44 per 1,000 in 1987. At the same time it increased the weight of rents and domestic rates by recommending that rent and rate rebates should no longer be 'netted off' rents and rates. Rents and rates are now given gross, on the grounds that the RPI's job is to record prices, not costs. The committee took the view that discriminatory subsidies to selected groups should not be deducted, as opposed to discounts built into prices which are taken into account in compiling the RPI.

Method of compilation of the RPI

The RPI is based on the prices at which 600 different items are sold in 180 areas in different regions of varying characteristics, and in different kinds of shops. On one day in the middle of each month 130,000 prices are recorded. National average prices are published only for products which are standard in different kinds of shop, mainly food. For example, on 14 April 1987, 181 different prices were logged for vacuum-packed back bacon. The average used for the RPI was £1.64 a lb, but prices ranged from under £1.04 to over £2.10, with 20 per cent of them falling outside even these limits.

Each item is given a weight, which is the percentage of consumer expenditure that it represented in a base period, according to the Family Expenditure Survey (FES) conducted by the Department of Employment. Total expenditure is set equal to 1,000 units, and each item is given a weight equal to so much per mille out of 1,000. The index is then recalculated each month. The proportionate change in the price of each item is multiplied by its weight in the total index to give the average change for all items. This procedure can be followed in Table 26. Column 2 shows the percentage change in the price of each category of expenditure during 1986. Column 3 shows the percentage weight of each category, set in January 1986 on the basis of the FES for the year to mid-1985. Column 5 gives the result of multiplying each percentage increase by the appropriate weight, to give the contribution of each category to the total rise in prices of 3.9 per cent. For example, food prices increased by 3.8 per cent in the year to January 1987. The weight of food in the index was 185 per mille, or 18.5 per cent. Its contribution to the total RPI increase of 3.9 per cent was therefore 0.7 (3.8 × 0.185).

Once the 'all items' index has been calculated, it can then be used to work out the rate of inflation, or the change in the RPI, over different time periods. As Table 27 shows, this is found by dividing the latest index figure by a previous index figure, then subtracting 1 and multiplying it by 100, to get the percen-

Table 26. Analysing RPI increases over time

	Percentage change to January 1987 over		Percentage weight in family expenditure		Contribution to change over latest year	Average annual percentage change, January 1974–87
	Latest month (1)	Latest year (2)	1986 (3)	1973 (4)	(= 2 × 3) (5)	(6)
Food	1.2	3.8	18.5	24.8	0.7	10.2
Alcoholic drink	1.4	4.0	8.2	7.3	0.3	12.1
Tobacco	0.0	10.5	4.0	4.9	0.4	14.8
Housing	0.3	8.3	15.3	12.6	1.3	13.2
Fuel and light	0.2	−0.2	6.2	5.8	0.0	13.3
Durables	−0.8	0.2	6.3	5.8	0.0	7.8
Clothing and footwear	−1.5	2.5	7.5	8.9	0.2	6.6
Transport and vehicles	0.9	1.7	15.7	13.5	0.3	11.2
Miscellaneous	−0.2	2.5	8.1	6.5	0.2	11.5
Services	0.5	4.0	5.8	5.3	0.2	11.4
Meals out	0.4	6.6	4.4	4.6	0.3	12.4
All items	0.4	3.9	100.0	100.0	3.9	11.1

Sources by columns:

1, 6: Department of Employment Press notice 40/87.

2, 3, 5: *Employment Gazette*, March 1987, p. 119, table 1.

4: *Monthly Digest of Statistics*, January 1987, table 18.1.

tage change. The RPI change is generally given in the Press as that over the last twelve months. The Press notice also gives the figure over the last month and over the last six months, which is sometimes regarded as the best indication of a trend.

The Press notice gives an index for all items except seasonal foods – fresh fruit and vegetables, eggs, home-killed lamb and fish – and another index for all items except housing. Although they represent only 2½ per cent of total expenditure, seasonal foods have a marked effect on the trend of the index, because their prices tend to rise in the first half and fall in the second half of the year. The fluctuations in housing costs are caused mainly by the ups and downs of mortgage-interest rates. The two derivatives of the index ex-

Table 27. Calculating the RPI

	Time intervals			
	Latest, January 1987	One month, December 1986	Six months, July 1986	One year, January 1986
A. Level of index	394.5[1]	393.0	384.7	379.7
B. Level of index divided into January 1987 level	—	$\dfrac{394.5}{393.0}$	$\dfrac{394.5}{384.7}$	$\dfrac{394.5}{379.7}$
C = B minus 1		0.0038	0.0255	0.0390
D = C × 100 rounded to one place		0.4	2.5	3.9
E = D at annual compound rate		4.7	5.2	3.9

1. The index was re-based at 100 for January 1987, the figure shown in later Press releases. The earlier index numbers in the table can be converted to the new base by multiplying them by the ratio of the new and the old January 1987 numbers, i.e. 100/394.5 = 0.2535. The January 1986 index number would thus be 96.2. The new index numbers can also be converted to the old basis by multiplying them by the reciprocal of this ratio, i.e. 3.945.

Source: Department of Employment Press notice 40/87.

cluding seasonal foods and excluding housing costs therefore show more stable trends.

In the USA, more emphasis is given to the monthly change in consumer prices, which is sometimes expressed as an annual rate. When the monthly RPI change is as volatile as it is in the UK, this can be highly misleading. In 1986, the UK's monthly inflation figure, expressed at an annual rate, varied between $12\frac{1}{4}$ per cent in April and minus $3\frac{1}{2}$ per cent in July. However, the USA does better than the UK in publishing a seasonally adjusted version of its consumer price index.

Confusion often arises over different ways of expressing annual inflation rates. One common practice is to take the

Table 28. Averaging the RPI, 1986

	Percentage increase year-on-year (1)	Quarterly average of column 1 (2)	Annual average of column 1 (3)
January	5.5 ⎫		
February	5.1 ⎬ 1	4.9 ⎫	
March	4.2 ⎭		
April	3.0 ⎫		
May	2.8 ⎬ 2	2.8	
June	2.5 ⎭		
July	2.4 ⎫		3.4
August	2.5 ⎬ 3	2.6	
September	3.0 ⎭		
October	3.0 ⎫		
November	3.5 ⎬ 4	3.4 ⎭	
December	3.7 ⎭		

Source: Economic Trends, January 1987, table 4.2.

average of the twelve monthly figures showing the increases year-on-year in the RPI for each month (see Table 28). For some purposes, it may be more appropriate to take the rate of inflation through the year, as represented by the December-on-December RPI increase. In 1986 the two figures were not very different: 3.4 and 3.7 per cent. When the rate of inflation is changing rapidly, the two figures can differ markedly. For example in Brazil in 1986 the average inflation rate was 50 per cent, but the rate through the year to December was 66 per cent. The rate of inflation can also be expressed in quarterly averages, and the annual average will then be the average of the four quarterly figures.

Strengths and weaknesses of the RPI

The RPI does not attempt to measure the cost of living of the top 4 per cent in the income scale, nor of the 14 per cent of households which rely for at least 75 per cent of their income on state pensions and benefits. It gives a higher weight to those on higher incomes who are included, because it is based on total expenditure and not on a 'democratic' head count which would give as much weight to price increases incurred by those spending half the average as to those spending double the average. On the basis of the 1985 data, for example, the weight given in the RPI to the wealthiest 5 per cent of the population was not 5 per cent, but about 12 per cent, because this was their share of total consumer expenditure. This matters because in the eight years to January 1982 the RPI overstated the rate of inflation by about 0.3 per cent a year for the top decile (one-tenth) covered, and understated it by about 0.4 per cent a year for the bottom decile. This occurred because those on higher incomes tended to spend more on goods and services whose prices went up less than the average while those on lower incomes did the opposite.

There is a separate index for pensioners, who tend to spend more on food and less on housing than the rest of the population, but it has not recently diverged significantly from the main RPI. There are not separate RPIs for each income group, although the Institute for Fiscal Studies has done a sample calculation of them from FES data, from which we have taken our figures. The effect of providing such indices regularly would probably be to tilt the balance of pay bargaining and tax changes more in favour of those on lower incomes.

The RPI does not fully take account of changes in the quality of goods, and may thus systematically overstate the inflation rate, since quality improves over the years in the majority of cases. Extra quality, like extra quantity, is a real increase in consumption, and we should therefore exclude it from any measurement of the rate of inflation. Some part of price rises corresponds to improvements in quality, but these are hard to define, since they may go with changes in product or model. Indeed, the quality of some goods, such as electronic wares, has been rising while their price has been falling.

The RPI is always out of date, because it is based on the expenditure recorded in the FES eighteen months previously (on average). By the current year, people are likely to have switched their expenditure, buying more of the goods and services that have risen relatively little in price and less of those whose prices have risen relatively a lot, because relative price changes encourage switching from more expensive to cheaper goods. This defect matters more in years when there are big relative price changes, such as the fall in petrol prices during 1986. However, the re-weighting of the index, which has been done each year from 1962, does enable it more or less to keep pace with long-run changes in consumption patterns.

Owner-occupation and the RPI

Dwelling prices have been rising in the last decade by 2.7 per cent a year more than the RPI, which is the same as the long-term trend (see Table 29). Their upwards movement is uneven, with increases below that of the RPI in three out of the last ten years, but above it in seven. In 1986 and again 1987, dwelling prices rose by over 10 per cent more than the RPI. Mortgage-interest costs, which are used to measure owner-occupation in the RPI, have risen even faster, by an average of 4.3 per cent a year more than the RPI. They are even more erratic, with annual changes ranging from − 10 to + 50. They reflect house-price increases, which are used to estimate the increase in debt on 'standard' mortgages. However, interest-rate changes are the overriding short-term influence on mortgage costs, making them even more volatile as well as raising them in recent years owing to the rise in interest rates.

Far from worrying about house-price inflation, some countries, such as France, Italy and Switzerland, exclude owner-occupation from the consumer-price index altogether. There is a good case for including rent, as the purchase of a service, and a more dubious one for including local-authority rates, on the grounds that VAT, another indirect tax, is

Table 29. The price of owner-occupation, 1977–87: percentage changes (annual averages)

	Dwelling prices	Mortgage interest (MI)	RPI	RPI ex MI	Weight of MI in RPI [1]
1977	7.6	12.1	15.8	16.0	2.7
1978	15.8	−4.8	8.3	8.6	2.3
1979	29.3	49.9	13.4	12.2	3.1
1980	21.2	9.0	18.0	18.3	3.8
1981	5.5	45.3	11.9	10.2	4.2
1982	2.5	9.5	8.6	8.7	4.1
1983	11.6	−10.8	4.6	5.1	3.4
1984	9.7	19.8	5.0	4.4	3.9
1985	8.6	26.9	6.1	5.1	4.6
1986	14.1	−0.2	3.4	3.6	5.4
1987 [2]	15.0	8.3	4.3	4.1	4.4
1977–86	12.3	14.1	9.4	9.1	

1. Each year's weight is based on expenditure during the previous period.
2. Forecast based on first three–five months of the year.
Source: Building Societies Fact Book; *Monthly Digest of Statistics*; *Employment Gazette.*

included. The case for excluding owner-occupation is that it is a form of investment – for many households by far the most important – and thus should not be included in a measure of consumer-price movements any more than the purchase of stocks and shares. Because of the fluctuations in many measures of housing costs, their inclusion tends to make the RPI erratic. This has recently raised such problems of macro-economic management that the Chancellor of the Exchequer, Mr Nigel Lawson, made no secret of his wish to see mortgage interest taken out of the RPI. Figure 19 shows why. In the two years 1985 and 1986, the monthly figure for year-on-year changes in the RPI fluctuated between 2.4 and 7.0 per cent. Without the 5 per cent or so weight of volatile mortgage costs, the RPI would have moved only between 3.2 and 5.6 per cent during this period. Its inclusion thus widened the range of variation from 2.4 to 4.6 percentage points. The higher inflation numbers damaged the cause of pay moderation more than the low

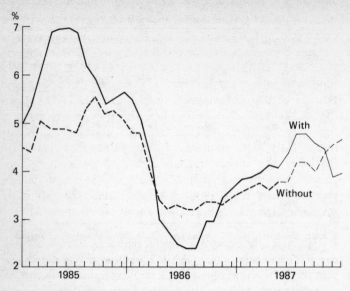

19. The RPI with and without mortgage costs, 1985–7

numbers benefited it. Over the last decade, the variance from trend (twelve-month moving average) of the RPI has been 2.5 percentage points, which falls to 2.3 if mortgage interest is removed. The inclusion of mortgage interest has added 0.3 percentage points to the annual inflation rate over the last ten years.

Governments can, on the other hand, derive short-term advantage from the inclusion of housing in the RPI when interest rates are falling. The figure shows that in the last quarter of 1985 the RPI was on a falling trend, coming down to the Treasury's forecast of 4 per cent. If mortgage interest had been excluded, the trend would have risen towards 5 per cent.

One argument for including owner-occupation costs is that most consumers, rightly or wrongly, regard them as part of the cost of living, and would feel that the figures were being fiddled if they were removed. The RPIAC's reasons for not wishing to exclude owner-occupiers' housing costs from the index did not rest primarily on this point but on a recognition that, by living in their houses, owner-occupiers are involved in consumption of a service, and that this service has a price attached to it even though no money changes hands. The price therefore has to be measured by means of a proxy. The RPIAC recommended some changes to the Department of Employment in their July 1986 report, but they left mortgage payments in the RPI, with some technical modifications, partly on the basis of a survey indicating that 80 per cent of consumers thought they should be included. The trade unions also expressed their opposition to the removal of housing costs from the RPI, although this was not mentioned in the report.

The possibilities set out here draw upon, but go beyond, the RPIAC report (see Table 30). Our three criteria are: that the RPI should measure actual expenditure on owner-occupation; that it should separate changes in the price from changes in the volume of owner-occupation; and that it should prevent the whole RPI from being affected by volatility in the chosen measure of owner-occupation costs. The chosen measure should be used to determine the annual weight of owner-occupation costs in the RPI, as well as month-to-month changes.

Imputed rent. This was the measurement used before 1975, when the switch was made to mortgage interest on the recommendation of the RPIAC. It still appears as a form of consumers' expenditure in the national accounts and in the Family Expenditure Survey (FES). It is an attempt to measure the consumption of housing services by estimating how much rent owner-occupiers would be paying if their property was rented. It measures notional, not actual, spending, and is subject to the vagaries of housing rents, which are used as a basis for imputation. Because rents have been rising faster than inflation in recent years, imputed rent had reached a notional 6 per cent of consumers' expenditure in

Table 30. Weight of owner-occupation expenditure, 1985

Criterion	£ billion	Percentage of CE[1]
Imputed rent	12.8	6.0
Dwelling purchases:		
All dwellings	53.7	21.1
First-time buyers	17.5	8.0
New dwellings[2]	10.7	5.1
User cost[3]	8.7	4.2
Mortgage payments:		
Actual	8.7	4.2
FES[4]	11.3	5.4
New RPI[5]	9.8	4.7

1. Consumers' expenditure (CE) in the national accounts, deducting imputed rent and adding back amounts in first column.
2. Including dwellings purchased from public sector.
3. Mortgage interest, plus opportunity cost of unmortgaged housing stock measured by long gilt yield, plus 2½ per cent depreciation, minus rise in capital value of housing stock.
4. Family Expenditure Survey data used for 'old' RPI weight, and scaled up.
5. Cost of standardized mortgage used for 'new' RPI weight, and scaled up.

Source: UK National Accounts, 1986, table 4.8; *BSA Bulletin*, April 1987, tables 12, 13; *Methodological Issues Affecting the Retail Prices Index*, Cmnd 9848, July 1986; Vanessa Fry and Panos Pashardes, *The RPI and the Cost of Living*, Institute for Fiscal Studies, May 1986.

1985. Imputed rent is less volatile than mortgage payments, but fails to correspond to any expenditure in the real world.

Dwelling purchases. The amount spent by owner-occupiers moving house was estimated at £54 billion in 1985, or 21 per cent of adjusted consumer expenditure. It is tempting to attach this weight to house purchase in the RPI, and apply the increase in house prices to it, treating houses like cars or furniture or any other consumer good. This would increase the RPI inflation rate, because house prices tend to increase in real terms. It would also ignore the fact that about half of all home-buyers obtain funds from selling their previous homes. Their only costs are transaction costs of a few per cent, unless they 'trade up' into a more expensive house. There is therefore a case for including only house purchases by first-time buyers, on the grounds that they cannot raise funds by selling. Since first-time buyers, though half the total, buy cheaper houses, this would reduce the weight of house purchase in consumer spending to 8 per cent.

First-time buyers may, however, obtain funds directly or indirectly from last-time sellers, notably by inheriting property from dead relatives. There is a case for netting out all house sales and purchases within the personal sector, even if some householders withdraw equity by spending the proceeds of house sales, and others then have to borrow more. This would lead us to include only newly built houses and those bought from the local authority and other public sector sources, giving a weight of 5.1 per cent, not much different from that actually used in 1985. Since second-hand house prices change more or less in line with new prices, this measure would act as a proxy for all house-price changes. It would, however, be made volatile by fluctuations in the new-housing construction cycle, and in the numbers of dwellings purchased from the public sector.

User cost. Whatever the cost of housing, it is sometimes argued that the tax-free capital gains accruing to owner-occupiers should be deducted from it. The Institute for Fiscal Studies has published a measure of 'user cost' which does this (see Table 30). It takes the cost of owner-occupation as the interest on mortgage debt, plus the opportunity cost of the investment in the unmortgaged part of the housing stock (a long gilt yield is one way to measure it), plus a depreciation allowance. The capital gain on housing is then deducted. This is an economically admirable concept. Yet nothing in it except mortgage interest and the small number of capital gains realized on sale reflects any actual transaction. User cost is highly variable, containing as it does three volatile elements: mortgage interest, financial yields and house prices. In 1985, user cost happened to give exactly the same expenditure figure as mortgage payments, but in years of big house-price increases it may be negative, with the weird result that housing inflation, far from adding to normal inflation, would make a negative contribution to the RPI, supposedly offsetting the price increases for all other goods.

Mortgage costs. We come therefore to mortgage costs, as the closest reflection of what households regularly spend. There are at least three ways of measuring them. The obvious way would be to apply the mortgage-interest rate, net of tax, to outstanding mortgage debt, giving a weight of 4.2 per cent of consumers' expenditure in 1985. This underestimates housing expenditure, because it excludes repayments of principal, which many householders do not clearly distinguish from interest. It overestimates it, because it includes mortgages for home improvement and 'equity withdrawal', in other words consumption. It is also volatile, because it records fluctuations in the mortgage as a percentage of the purchase price, which are independent of the change in owner-occupation itself. Finally, it gives a figure for all consumers, and does not exclude the top 4 per cent of the income scale. The RPI does not purport to measure their expenditure, and they may be heavy mortgage borrowers.

The RPI between 1975 and 1986 adopted the simple alternative of using the FES to make annual estimates of the weight of mortgage interest, because it covers the same households as the RPI. This overestimates mortgage payments, because many households include repayments of principal, and others are judged by the statisticians to have artificially high interest payments because of switching from repayment to endowment mortgages. Like the previous measure, it also includes home-improvement loans and equity withdrawal. The RPIAC therefore changed the definition and the method of weighting mortgage interest so as to overcome these defects. The new method would have reduced the 1986 weight from 5.4 to 4.7 per cent, and gave a weight of 4.4 per cent for 1987.

The new method, set out in Annex Two to the RPIAC report, is complex, but similar to the method previously used to calculate changes from month to month in the level of mortgage payments. This is now used instead of the FES to fix the weight of mortgage interest in consumers' expenditure each year. It standardizes mortgages by assuming that 60 per cent of owner-occupiers take out a mortgage, and borrow 65 per cent of the purchase price. These figures are based on the averages of the last decade, and underestimate current increases in mortgage debt, on the grounds that it is owner-occupation, rather than the extent to which it is financed by mortgages, that is being measured. The old method held the percentage of the purchase price fixed, but allowed the number of mortgages to reflect those actually taken out, rather than setting it at a fixed proportion of owner-occupiers. The new method does, however, reflect the growth in the total number of owner-occupiers, irrespective of the extent to which they change their use of mortgage finance.

The new method, which came into use from January 1987, will thus reduce variations arising from changes in the extent of mortgage finance. It will still be plagued by volatility in house prices and in interest rates, since these are still its two main variables. There are strong arguments against including mortgage interest in the RPI. A mortgage is a financial transaction, and interest does not count as value added in the national accounts. Interest on other loans is excluded, so why include it on mortgages? Owner-occupation is as much the investment of savings as it is the consumption of services. Only one-quarter of the value of the housing stock is mortgaged, and thus mortgage interest is acting only as a proxy for three-quarters of what it purports to measure. Both interest on bank and building-society deposits and capital gains on housing can and should be offset against mortgage interest. Worst of all, when the government raises interest rates to curb inflation, mortgage rates go up, and so does the RPI. When it cuts income tax to boost the economy, mortgage interest rises, because the tax relief is less, and the rise in the RPI acts as a brake on expansion. Some of these arguments were forcefully put by the Building Societies Association in the commentary of its October 1984 *Bulletin*. The RPIAC were not convinced by these arguments, and concluded that the case should prevail for continuing to include mortgage interest in the RPI as the best proxy for the costs of owner-occupation services. If, on the other hand, we accept the case for excluding mortgage interest from the RPI, what follows?

There are two ways out. The first is to return to the FES to see what households actually spend on mortgage interest plus repayments; and supplement it by further survey evidence, which would show that mortgage payments fluctuate far less than interest rates, because of variable repayment terms. The other, which we would prefer, is to exclude owner-occupation from the RPI altogether, on the grounds that it is investment, not consumption. Some of the alternatives are too clever by half, and suffer from the difficulty that even the most sophisticated householders would have in understanding them.

What is in the RPI basket?

The components of the RPI can be thought of as items in a huge shopping basket which holds the average household's purchases, even though no single household conforms to the average pattern. For example, hardly any household pays both rent and mortgage interest, but both have to be in the basket, because some households pay rent, and others are buying their home on a mortgage. Columns 3 and 4 of Table 26 give an indication of how the shares of the different categories in total family expenditure have changed since 1973. Column 6 shows the differing annual rates of inflation of each category over the same period. There is no clear correlation between changes in share and changes in relative price. The share of food has fallen from 25 to 18½ per cent, although it has risen in price 1 per cent less a year than the whole RPI. On the other hand, the share of housing has risen three percentage points to 15½ per cent, even though

		Relative price	
		Down	Up
Relative volume	Up	Clothing Footwear	Transport Communication
	Down	Food Household goods	Alcohol Tobacco Fuel and light Housing

20. Consumption changes, 1975–85 (*source: U K National Accounts*, 1986, tables 4.8, 4.9)

its price has risen 2 per cent a year faster than the general index.

Nor is there any clear correlation between changes in the relative prices of consumer goods and the relative volume of expenditure on them. Figure 20 shows that the main categories of consumer spending which figure in the RPI occur in every possible combination. In the top left-hand box are clothing and footwear, whose relative prices have fallen – in other words they have risen less than the RPI for all items. The relative volume of expenditure on them has risen, i.e. it has increased faster than total consumption.

This exhibits the usual negative price elasticity of demand. Lower relative prices stimulate more spending. Food and household goods have also fallen in relative price, yet the relative volume of expenditure on them has fallen, see the bottom left-hand box. Even though more has been spent on them than if their prices had risen faster, the negative price elasticity of demand has been overridden by the negative income elasticity of demand; as incomes rise, people spend a smaller share of them on food and household goods. For some goods and services, the income elasticity of demand is positive. In the top right-hand box are transport, including cars, and communications, including telephones. The demand for them rises with income. Even though their prices have risen relative to the RPI, the resulting setback to expenditure has been swamped by the positive income effect.

In the bottom right-hand box are the items whose relative price has risen, and on which the relative volume of expenditure has fallen. This again shows the negative price elasticity of demand, with higher prices discouraging consumption, in some cases assisted by negative income elasticity. People would have spent a smaller proportion of their income on these goods and services even if their prices had not risen so fast. They are alcohol and tobacco; their prices include heavy excise duties, and consumption has slowed for health reasons. Fuel has become more expensive because of the energy crisis, which has encouraged conservation. Housing, as we have seen, has risen in price. Owner-occupation has risen with income, but housing as a whole has not, because of the fall in the share of the rented sector.

Short-term behaviour and the RPI

Some short-term movements in the RPI can be seen as once-for-all changes rather than as indicators of inflation, which can be defined as a continuous upward trend. Such movements can be explained partly by regular seasonal factors, and partly by random changes in the more volatile components of expenditure. The Budget, which has in recent years been in mid-March, nearly always includes annual increases in excise duties more or less in line with the previous year's inflation rate. Dutiable items make up about 18 per cent of the RPI, and the duties themselves 9 per cent since they account for about half the price. An increase of, say, 4 per cent in the duties therefore puts up the RPI by 0.36 per cent, most of it in April (strictly, mid-March to mid-April). Local-authority rents and rates also go up every year in April, in recent years by considerably more than the general inflation rate. Since they have together a 7 per cent RPI weight, a 10 per cent increase causes a 0.7 rise in the RPI. Thus in April alone the RPI can go up by 1 per cent or more.

Seasonal foods make up only $2\frac{1}{2}$ per cent of expenditure, but they have a noticeable influence on the RPI, generally rising in the first half of the year – by 15 per cent in the first half of 1986, for example – and falling in the second half. Thus in 1986, seasonal foods added about 0.1 per cent to the RPI in three of the first six months, causing the inflation rate to be 0.6 percentage points a year higher at an annual rate, and subtracted about the same amount in three months out of the last six. Another seasonal factor is the 'sales' in January, and to a lesser extent in July, which cause cuts in the price of clothing, footwear and consumer durables, followed by equivalent rises in the next month. This takes 0.1 per cent or more off the January RPI, and adds it back in February. Such variations clearly show up more when the inflation rate is down in the 2–4 per cent range, as it was in 1986.

The two main random shocks to the RPI are changes in the price of petrol (weight 4.7 per cent in 1986), due to oil-price movements, and in mortgage interest (weight 5.4 per cent in 1986), because of monetary-policy changes. In March 1986 a drop of $4\frac{1}{2}$ per cent in petrol prices took 0.2 per cent off the RPI; there was a similar movement the other way in September when petrol prices rose again. An $8\frac{1}{2}$ per cent cut in the mortgage rate in May 1986 – from 12 to 11 per cent – took 0.45 per cent off the RPI for June, but a 12 per cent increase in October added 0.65 per cent to the November RPI.

The Tax and Price Index (TPI)

The TPI has a wider scope than the RPI. The RPI includes indirect taxes, such as VAT, excise duties and local-authority rates, but not direct taxes, such as income tax. As well as the rise in prices, including indirect taxes, the TPI also seeks to measure the change in direct taxes, comprising income tax and employee national-insurance contributions. The change in the TPI combines the rise in prices and the change in direct taxes into a composite figure. Prices are given a weight equal to post-tax income as a proportion of gross taxable income, and direct taxes a weight equal to their share of gross taxable income. The TPI shows the change in gross taxable income which would be required to maintain constant purchasing power in the face of changes in prices and direct taxes. If taxes always changed in line with prices, the TPI would be the same as the RPI, and would become redundant. Direct taxes hardly ever change at the same rate as prices, so the TPI provides additional information.

For example, the average RPI in 1983 was 4.6 per cent. The average increase in personal direct tax payments was 2 per cent, less than the RPI, because income-tax allowances and thresholds were increased by more than the inflation rate. The average tax rate for taxpayers was 25 per cent, we estimate from the Inland Revenue's *Survey of Personal Income 1983–84*, so after-tax income was 75 per cent of gross income. The combined rate of increase of taxes and prices was therefore $(0.25 \times 2) + (0.75 \times 4.6) = 4$. Because taxes went up less than prices, the TPI went up less than the RPI. An increase of only 4 per cent in gross taxable income was needed to keep pace with price inflation of 4.6 per cent.

The TPI was invented by Mrs Thatcher's first administration as a way of presenting its first, controversial Budget of June 1979 in a better light. The Budget cut the basic rate of income tax from 33 to 30 per cent, but raised value-added tax from 8 to 15 per cent, thus making a big switch from direct to indirect taxation while leaving the total personal tax burden little changed. Because VAT but not income tax is included in the RPI as part of the prices of goods on which it falls, the effect was to raise the RPI by 4 percentage points between June and July 1979, to $15\frac{1}{2}$ per cent. The message of the TPI, introduced in August 1979, was that there was no increase in a broader inflation index which brought the income-tax cuts into the reckoning. The TPI came too late to undo the damage to pay bargaining caused by a 4 per cent increase in the RPI. Then, for the two and a half years from the middle of 1980, the TPI began to show bigger year-on-year increases than the RPI, because the government was increasing the burden of personal taxation in order to reduce the Budget deficit. The TPI was subsequently consigned to obscurity, because its message had become that pay needed to rise by even more than inflation in order to maintain purchasing power. Although a monthly Press notice on the TPI is still published, it receives little coverage. It is surprising that the government has not again put more emphasis on it, because during the five years starting in 1983 it has been rising more slowly than the RPI, thanks to income-tax cuts.

Table 31 shows for the first time a calculation which is not published by the government. That is the annual average of the year-on-year TPI increases published each month, and calculated back to 1975, covering the four years before the TPI was initiated. In years when personal taxation was increased, the TPI increase was higher than that of the RPI. These were 1975, 1976, 1981 and 1982. In all the other years since 1977 personal taxes rose by less than inflation, and the TPI went up less than the RPI. The average difference between the two indices is 2 per cent a year, but this tends to cancel out in the long run. Over the whole period 1975–86, the TPI rose on average by 0.1 per cent a year less than the RPI, but over the decade 1977–86 it rose by 0.85 per cent less. This shows that income-tax cuts during this period, including both Labour and Conservative governments, had a significant effect on purchasing power.

The TPI has been criticized for covering only taxpayers. Like the RPI, it excludes roughly the top 4 per cent of the income distribution, specifically all those with incomes over £22,415 a year in January 1987, which includes most higher-rate taxpayers. It also excludes about a quarter of all households because they are non-taxpayers. It is thus relevant only to basic-rate taxpayers, rather than averaging out the effect of income-tax changes on all RPI households. It has the disadvantage for pay-bargaining purposes that the lower-paid, who pay little or no tax, are entitled to dismiss it as irrelevant when it shows a lower increase than the RPI. As they do not benefit from income-tax cuts, they require the full RPI increase to compensate them for inflation.

The TPI shows what increase in gross income the average

Table 31. The RPI and other inflation indices, 1975–86

| | RPI | Deflators | | Producer prices | | | RPI Excluding mortgage costs |
		CE	GDP[1]	Output	Input	TPI	
1975	24.2	23.7	27.3	23.0	11.6	29.3	—
1976	16.5	15.7	14.5	16.2	24.8	18.8	16.9
1977	15.8	14.9	12.3	18.2	15.2	14.8	16.0
1978	8.3	9.2	12.3	9.9	3.5	3.0	8.6
1979	13.4	13.6	12.7	10.9	13.0	12.0	12.2
1980	18.0	16.1	18.8	14.0	8.5	17.4	18.3
1981	11.9	11.4	10.3	9.6	9.2	14.8	10.4
1982	8.6	8.7	7.0	7.7	7.3	9.9	8.6
1983	4.6	5.0	5.7	5.4	6.9	4.0	5.1
1984	5.0	4.7	4.7	6.2	8.1	3.9	4.4
1985	6.1	5.3	5.7	5.5	1.6	5.2	5.1
1986	3.4	3.7	3.0	4.5	−8.1	1.9	3.6
1975–86	11.2	10.9	11.0	10.8	8.2	11.0	—
Average absolute difference from RPI							
	0.0	0.6	1.8	1.6	5.1	2.0	—

1. At factor cost.
Source: Press notices; *UK National Accounts*, 1986, table 1.16; *Economic Trends*, table 42.

basic-rate taxpayer needs to maintain his or her purchasing power with a given rate of inflation and a given income-tax change. The Institute for Fiscal Studies published an alternative index, at about the same time in 1979, called the Gross Earnings Deflator. This averages out the effects of income-tax changes over non-taxpayers as well as taxpayers. It also shows, as the TPI does not, what increase in gross income is required to keep pace with a given rise in the RPI if there is no change in tax rates. It illustrates the point that, when income rises, tax rises by more, because the marginal rate on the additional income is higher than the average rate of tax on existing income. In other words, the income elasticity of income tax is higher than 1. To return to our 1983 example, assume that income is 100 units, of which 25 is paid in tax. RPI inflation is 4.6 per cent. The marginal tax rate, including national insurance, was 38 per cent. If there is a rise in pay of 4.6 units, 1.75 are paid in tax, and there is an after-tax increase of 2.85, which is a rise of only 3.8 per cent on net pay of 75. The Gross Earnings Deflator is calculated by multiplying the RPI increase by

$$\frac{1 - \text{average tax rate} = 0.75}{1 - \text{marginal tax rate} = 0.62} = 1.21\%.$$

This gives a GED of 5.6 per cent (4.6 × 1.21). If the pay increase is 5.6, 2.1 goes in tax, and the remaining 3.5 is a 4.6 per cent increase in the net pay of 75.

The TPI shows the lowest increase just after any Budget which reduces the burden of personal tax. For example, in April 1986, the month-to-month increase in the RPI was 1 per cent, the year's highest, because of the annual increases in excise duties and local-authority rates. Yet the TPI fell by 1.8 per cent in the same month, because of the cut in income tax from 30 to 29p in the pound. In subsequent months, the TPI tends to rise by more than the RPI, because price increases continue through the year, but there are no further cuts in tax rates after the Budget, and tax payments, as we have seen, rise faster than income.

Producer prices

Two producer price indices are published each month by the Department of Trade and Industry. One covers output prices of home sales of manufactured products, the other input prices of materials and fuel purchased by manufacturing industry. Although manufacturing industry currently accounts for only about one-quarter of the UK's GDP, it gives a good indication of inflationary trends in the economy. Materials and fuel make up about one-third of manufacturing industry's costs, labour about two-thirds. Their prices are more volatile, because they are partly imported, and thus vary with the exchange rate and world commodity prices. Fuel, in the form of petroleum products, which has a weight of 10 per cent in the index of materials and fuel inputs, has been particularly volatile because of the ups and down of crude oil prices. The input-costs index also shows big monthly fluctuations because of seasonal variations in electricity and food prices. It is therefore also published in a seasonally adjusted version.

The producer price indices are the successors to the old wholesale-price indices, which have been published since the early 1950s. Because changing relative prices of different sectors of output and input lead to changes in their relative weights within each index, these indices have been re-weighted about every five years, and re-based at 100. As we have seen, the RPI is re-weighted every year, and was last re-based in January 1987. The wholesale-price indices were last re-based in 1983, but using 1979 weights and setting 1980 at 100. They were also rechristened 'producer-price' indices, because they give prices at the factory gate rather than at the stage of wholesale distribution. They were also based on the new standard industrial classification of 1980, and the energy industries were taken out of manufacturing; this resulted in petroleum products from refineries becoming part of the input rather than the output index, and crude oil no longer being part of the input index, since it became an input within the energy-industry sector.

The output price index is given separately for food, drink and tobacco manufacturing – about 11 per cent of total manufacturing – because it has a high raw-material content, and for other manufacturing industry. It is built up from separate indices for eighteen broad sectors of manufacturing industry, whose indices are also published. The input price index is similarly divided according to the sectors purchasing the inputs. In both cases the indices cover only transactions with other sectors, and not transactions within the sector. On the input side, separate indices are given for fuel and for materials, and monthly and annual prices movements are shown for petroleum products, electricity, food-manufacturing materials and other materials, the two latter each showing home-produced and imported materials separately.

The differences in the movements of input and output prices can be seen as an indicator of manufacturing industry's 'terms of trade'. For example in 1986 producer prices rose by $4\frac{1}{2}$ per cent, but input prices, excluding the food, drink and tobacco industries, fell by $10\frac{1}{2}$ per cent, so the terms of trade rose by 17 per cent. A rise of 5 per cent in unit labour costs was exactly offset by the fall in fuel and materials costs to give a total cost change of zero for the year. Producer output prices still went up by $4\frac{1}{2}$ per cent, and the result was a steep rise in profits. These indices enable us to trace how the sharp fall in oil prices in 1986 went mainly into higher non-oil profits rather than into lower wages or consumer prices (see page 33).

Other inflation indices

Press releases are published on only three inflation indices, the RPI, the TPI and producer prices. Of almost equal importance are the implied index numbers of costs and prices published in the *UK National Accounts* Blue Book on an annual basis, which can also be calculated on a quarterly basis from the *Monthly Digest of Statistics*. These are not published in Press releases, because they are quarterly, published only with some delay, and subject to subsequent revision (the GDP deflator does appear in the Press release on GDP). These indices are sometimes confusingly known as 'deflators' because they show by how much current price figures have to be deflated in order to arrive at constant price, or volume, figures. The deflators are derived from indices showing the costs and prices of GDP and its various expenditure components, such as consumers' expenditure, capital expenditure and exports net of imports.

The GDP deflator is an index of home costs, which shows the contribution of pay and profits per unit of output to the increase in prices in the economy. As its name implies, it excludes import costs and prices; these also make a major contribution to prices in the UK, since imports of goods and services were 31 per cent of GDP in 1986. The consumers' expenditure deflator (CED) is more comparable with the Retail Prices Index. It is in fact a slightly more accurate measure of inflation, for several reasons:

1. It covers the whole of consumers' expenditure as it is

defined in the national accounts, instead of excluding the 4 per cent top-income households and the 14 per cent pensioners dependent on the state pension for 75 per cent of their income.

2. It uses the expenditure weights of the current year, rather than those of the base year, which is on average eighteen months before the current year, owing to the timing of the FES. In other words it shows the price increases of goods and services purchased in the current year, rather than those purchased in the previous year. It can thus take account of changes in weights due to switching from more expensive to cheaper goods and services.

3. Like consumers' expenditure in the national accounts, it takes imputed rent as a measure of owner-occupation, rather than mortgage costs as does the RPI. This makes it slightly lower in the long run, and a bit less volatile in the short run.

There is little difference between the twelve-year rate of inflation as measured by the different indices (see Table 31), with the exception of the producer input-prices index. This shows an inflation rate nearly 3 per cent lower than the RPI, and varies from it by an average of 5 per cent either way each year. This index is sensitive to the time-period chosen. The effect of including 1974, when oil prices rose sharply, and excluding 1986, when they fell sharply, would be to give an annual rate of input-price inflation much closer to that of output-price inflation. Producer output prices have risen by 0.3 percentage points a year less than the RPI, which suggests a rise in the price of services and other industries relative to manufacturing. In the average year manufacturers' producer prices diverge by 1.6 per cent from the RPI increase.

The GDP deflator hardly differs from the RPI in the long run, but diverges by 1.9 per cent one way or another in an average year, mainly because of the differing contributions of home and import costs to consumer prices. The GDP deflator was particularly low at 3 per cent in 1986 because of the halving of North Sea oil prices and profits. The CED is the closest to the RPI from among the alternative indices, but is still 0.2 per cent a year less, and the absolute divergence averages 0.7 per cent a year. The differences between the indices are greatest when the rate of inflation is at either a high or a low turning-point, as in 1975, 1978, 1980 and 1986. The CED has an important disadvantage. It is revised every few years as the relative volume of different kinds of consumers' expenditure is changed in line with its re-basing on the prices of a later year. The RPI has the supreme merit among indicators that, whatever its defects, its definition is such that it never needs to be subsequently revised. This was so until it was discovered that, owing to a computer programming error, the RPI had been underestimated by 0.1 per cent in most months between February 1986 and October 1987.

Economic influences

The two main medium-term influences on the RPI are the costs of home-produced goods and services, and import prices. Home costs, measured by the GDP deflator (see page 133), are about 40 per cent profits and rent, and about 60 per cent wages. Producer prices reflect changes in costs per unit of output rather than total costs. Increases in productivity, which reduce costs per unit of output, can thus wholly or partly offset increases in wages and profits. Import prices depend partly on the prices charged by other countries which export to the UK, in terms of dollars, D-marks or other currencies, and partly on the exchange rate of the pound against these currencies. A falling pound can worsen an already rising trend in import prices, as in 1974, when the oil price rose, or it can be offset by falls in the price of oil and other imported commodities, as in 1986.

While changes in profits and labour costs per unit of output are the main influence on UK inflation, they are less volatile than import prices, including exchange-rate changes, which can have a bigger short-term effect, since 31 per cent of domestic demand for goods and services is satisfied by imports. The RPI includes imported goods and services, and those with imported components and materials, so it is subject to changes in import prices in a way that the GDP deflator is not. However, importers have a choice whether to pass on import-price changes into retail-price changes, or allow them to have their impact on profit margins rather than prices.

According to the monetarist school of thought, inflation is caused by excessive increases in the supply of money (see page 162). This linkage has appeared to operate at certain times in recent UK history, but not at others. In the last five years, the rate of inflation has been low or even falling, while the broad monetary indicator, sterling M3, has been rising rapidly. Monetary expansion may be associated with rising pay and profits, or with a falling exchange rate leading to higher import prices, but this is not always the case. The RPI itself, rather than the money supply, has come to be regarded as the main indicator of inflation, and thus of possible government measures to deal with it.

6

The Balance of Payments

'Anything unexpected could affright the pound.'
Peter Day, *Business News*, the *Today* programme,
22 July 1987, on the trade figures to be issued that day

There are three main sets of indicators about the UK's accounts with the rest of the world which appear in Press-notice form. Towards the end of each month, the Department of Trade and Industry publishes the current account of the UK balance of payments for the previous month. This is popularly known as the trade figures, because its coverage is almost entirely restricted to visible trade, in some detail. Each quarter, about two months after the end of the quarter, the Central Statistical Office publishes preliminary figures for the UK balance of payments on a wider basis. It gives few details of visible trade, but more on invisibles: services; interest, profits and dividends; and transfers. It also gives the capital account, which consists of changes in UK overseas assets and liabilities. Finally, the Treasury publishes a short monthly notice on the official reserves of gold and foreign exchange, only two days after the end of the month covered.

The balance of payments on current account is the difference between exports of goods and services plus inflows of other 'invisible' income, and imports of goods and services plus outflows of other 'invisible' income. Only by coincidence is it likely to be in balance, with the two amounts equal. It is generally in surplus or deficit. This surplus or deficit is by accounting convention offset by a corresponding deficit or surplus on the capital account, which consists of flows of direct and portfolio investment, and bank loans and deposits. A current-account surplus necessarily gets invested abroad, and a deficit has to be financed by foreign borrowing. If the UK sells more to foreigners than it buys, it has to lend them the money, and if it buys more than it sells it has to borrow the money. This leads to an increase in UK assets or liabilities vis-à-vis foreigners.

One special kind of UK foreign asset is the official reserves. These comprise gold, convertible currencies and special drawing rights held in the Exchange Equalization Account together with the United Kingdom reserve position in the IMF; convertible currencies may be held in the form of financial instruments. It was once the UK's practice to enter movements in the reserves and certain other transactions in official borrowing in a special category of the balance of payments known as 'official financing'. The total of official financing with the sign reversed equalled the 'balance for official financing' (i.e. the sum of the current-account balance, the capital-account balance and the balancing item). The role of government was thus presented as being to invest or finance the residual surplus or deficit of the whole of the rest of the balance of payments by buying or selling reserve assets. Now changes in the reserves and other transactions in official borrowing are included among other types of transactions in the UK external assets and liabilities so that the sum of the current and capital accounts (including these official transactions) equals the balancing item (p. 154) with the signs reversed. Transactions in official debt not only include those in the debt of central government, but also those under the public sector exchange cover scheme, so it is misleading to take changes in the reserves as the only significant form of official transaction.

The trade figures

The monthly trade figures have been perhaps the most important of all the indicators for most of the post-war period.

During the Bretton Woods period of fixed exchange rates up to 1972, a deficit or a series of deficits in the trade figures was regarded as the signal for a rise in bank rate, which would both bring in capital to finance it and slow down the growth of the economy, so as to switch resources into exports and reduce the demand for imports. If this treatment did not work, bad trade figures could trigger off speculation about a devaluation of the pound against the dollar, which only actually happened twice, in 1949 and in 1968. (The pound was revalued upwards against the dollar in late 1971, six months before the final collapse of the fixed-exchange-rate system.) When the UK and other countries moved to floating exchange rates in 1972, the trade figures became a signal of changes in the exchange rate, which led only at one remove to changes in interest rates, particularly if a persistent fall in the pound was developing. It was only when the UK moved into substantial current-account surplus in the first half of the 1980s that the trade figures took a back seat. Certainly the surpluses went with a rise in the pound's exchange rate. But interest rates, far from falling as a result, might be rising because of the need to control the money supply, which became the more important indicator (see page 162).

With the return to deficit on current account from 1986 onwards, the trade figures again became important. For example, in May 1987, there was a deficit of £561 million, according to the Press notice issued in late July (delayed by a Customs strike). Coming as it did after four successive months of surpluses, this deficit had a big impact on financial markets. Although it did no more than bring the first four months' figures back on track for the government's March forecast of a current account deficit of £2½ billion for the whole year, it upset the markets' expectations, based on the forecasts of City economists that there would be a small surplus.

According to the Royal Economic Society's figures, the UK's largest ever current-account surplus was in 1913. The surplus, which had been only 1 per cent of GDP in 1901, rose to 10 per cent by 1913. By 1918, the surplus had changed into a deficit. However, by 1920 there was a surplus of 6 per cent of GDP. By 1931, the account had moved back into deficit, and stayed there through the 1930s. In 1940, the deficit ballooned to 12 per cent of GDP, and remained high until 1947.

The UK current account has been in surplus more often than in deficit, in twenty-four years out of the forty-one from 1946 – when the present run of figures begins – to 1986. The surpluses have been larger than the deficits. Yet the balance on visible trade in goods was in surplus for only six of these years. In every year, however, except 1946 and 1947, the invisibles account was in surplus. In eighteen years out of forty-one, there was a visible trade deficit which was outweighed by an invisibles surplus, giving a current-account surplus. The UK was thus able to use current surpluses to fund capital outflows. Its traditional role as a capital exporter was reversed for most of the 1970s, when US capital was imported to develop North Sea oil.

The changing composition of the current-account balance is shown in Figure 21. The visible-trade balance can easily be analysed from the Press notice into manufactures, food and raw materials, and fuels. Before 1974, the UK's traditional stance was a surplus in manufactures and in invisibles, more often than not exceeding a deficit in food, raw materials and fuels. In 1974, because of the rise in the price of oil, the fuels deficit rose so as to put the current account into deficit by nearly 3 per cent of GDP. By 1981, the development of the North Sea had switched the fuels account into surplus. With surpluses continuing in manufactures (because of the recession) and in invisibles, the UK had a current-account surplus as large in relation to GDP as the deficit of seven years earlier.

By 1985, the positions had changed again, with manufactures crossing over into deficit; but by this time the fuels surplus had grown so that it covered the manufactures deficit twice over. The loss of competitiveness due to the effect of North Sea oil on the exchange rate, together with the recovery in the economy, had changed the traditional pattern, but the current-account surplus survived, though on a

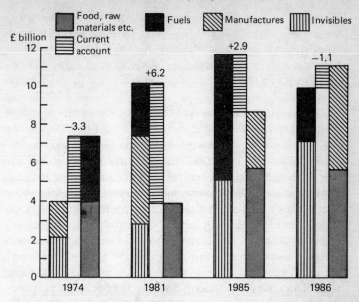

NOTE: For each year, the bars on the left are surpluses, and the bars on the right are deficits. The differences between them are the total current-account surpluses or deficits, shown as the bars in the middle, with the amount written above.

21. The changing composition of the current account, 1974–86 (*source: Monthly Review of External Trade Statistics, Annual Supplement*, 1987, pp. 7, 17, 19)

smaller scale. It was the halving of the oil price in 1986 which pushed the UK back into current-account deficit. From 1986 onwards, a falling oil surplus and an unpredictable invisibles surplus may not be enough to outweigh the traditional deficit in food and raw materials and the disconcerting new deficit in manufactures. The UK may thus again become a capital importer, this time of modern capital goods to re-equip manufacturing industry rather than to exploit North Sea oil.

While the long-run trends are easily discernible, the short-term monthly position is not always so clear. The trade figures are difficult to compile and interpret, and subject to frequent revision. The balance of payments in any particular month or year may later turn out to be quite different from that originally published. By that time the damage may have been done, because the market reaction to the original figures is seldom reversible, unless they are revised fairly soon afterwards.

The visible-trade figures are based on Customs records of goods entering and leaving the country, and thus depend on the accuracy and speed with which the documents are processed. The export figures are compiled from records received in the Customs central statistical office up to three working days before the end of the month. They take about two weeks to arrive. So the export figures actually cover exports between about the middle of the preceding month and the middle of the current month. For imports, records received up to three working days after the end of the month are used, but two-thirds of them are computerized, so there is no delay in transmission. The coverage of imports is thus much closer to the current month than that of exports. Irregular events such as docks strikes can therefore have a different incidence on the export and on the import sides of the trade balance, producing a larger deficit or surplus than if the timing was the same on both sides.

The trade figures are seasonally adjusted, both to allow for regular annual fluctuations, as with any other statistical series, and to allow for the fact that there is a different number of working days in each calendar month. There remain a number of irregularities which cause some volatility in the figures. To remove some of these, one version of the figures is published without ships, North Sea installations, aircraft, precious stones and silver (SNAPS), 'excluding the more erratic items'.

The visible-trade figures are first compiled on an 'overseas trade statistics' (OTS) basis, as they are received in Customs. This is the basis of the compendious monthly *Overseas Trade Statistics of the UK*, published by the DTI, in which exports and imports are classified by country and by product, and of some of the tables in the monthly Press notice. For some purposes, they have to be converted to a 'balance-of-payments' (BOP) basis. The main effect is to reduce published import figures by deducting carriage, insurance and freight (c.i.f.). There are other differences in the range of goods covered among both imports and exports. While there is little disparity between OTS and BOP exports, the difference on the import side was about 6 per cent in 1986, for example. The headline figures are given on a BOP basis.

The visible-trade figures are subsequently revised as later information comes in, but most revisions are relatively small. The same cannot be said for invisibles, for which data are collected in a variety of ways, some of them rather unreliable. Most information on invisibles is collected on a quarterly basis, so the monthly invisibles balance has to be an estimate based on the latest available quarterly figures. Since these are available with a two-month rather than a one-month delay, it is five months before the monthly invisibles figures begin to reflect accurately the invisibles figures of even the previous quarter, and these themselves are subject to revision. Even the quarterly figures are only estimates based on partial data, and are liable to fluctuate as more information becomes available. A typical example of the subsequent revisions in the invisibles account – even after the preliminary monthly estimates have been superseded – is given in Table 32. During the fifteen months from May 1986 to July 1987, there were eight different estimates of what the current account of the balance of payments had been in 1985. They ranged between a surplus of £2,919 million and one of £3,763 million, a difference of £800 million or so. The May 1986 estimate was a surplus of £2,952 million. This leapt to a surplus of £3,763 million in June 1986, then fell by stages to a surplus of £2,946 million in March 1987. It rose again to £3,450 million in May and June. In July 1987, it fell again to £2,919 million, close to the original May 1986 figure. The reader can amuse herself by checking the estimate for 1985 that will be given in the latest available balance-of-payments figures at the time of reading.

The revisions of the 1985 figures were due mainly to the six revisions of the invisibles account which took place during the period. There were only two revisions of the

Table 32. The changing trade figures for 1985

Time of estimate	1985 balances		
	Visible	Invisible	Current
1986 May	−2,068	+5,020	+2,952
June	−2,068	+5,831	+3,763
July	−2,068	+5,831	+3,763
August	−2,111	+5,713	+3,602
September	−2,111	+5,713	+3,602
October	−2,111	+5,713	+3,602
November	−2,111	+5,713	+3,602
December	−2,111	+5,660	+3,549
1987 January	−2,111	+5,660	+3,549
February	−2,178	+5,660	+3,482
March	−2,178	+5,124	+2,946
April	−2,178	+5,124	+2,946
May	−2,178	+5,628	+3,450
June	−2,178	+5,628	+3,450
July	−2,178	+5,097	+2,919

Source: D T I/C S O Press notices.

visible trade figures. Such revisions, like those of the public-sector borrowing requirement, are magnified because they occur in a relatively small balance between two much larger amounts, as can be seen in Table 33. The revisions are to totals of visible and invisible credits or debits, and only in the second place to the balance between them. The amounts on each side of the main balances in the total balance of payments are shown in Table 33. They correspond to the bars for 1986 in Figure 21. The coverage figures show the relative size of the balances, by giving exports as a percentage of imports. The current account shows a deficit of £1 billion, which was revised upwards in August 1987 from a deficit of £120 million; however, this figure was a June revision of the previous estimate of £1.1 billion, which turned out nearer the mark. The deficit was made up of an 11 per cent surplus on invisibles, which outweighed a 10 per cent deficit on visible trade. This in its turn was the result of a surplus on fuels of 45 per cent, and deficits of 9 per cent on manufactures and 45 per cent on food and raw materials.

Table 33. The UK current account, 1986 (£ billion)

	Exports/ credits	Imports/ debits	Balance	Coverage[1] (%)
1. Food and raw materials	7.5	13.6	−6.1	55
2. Fuels	8.7	6.0	+2.7	145
3. Manufactures	54.4	60.0	−5.6	91
4. Miscellaneous	2.2	1.7	+0.5	129
5.[2] Visible trade	72.8	81.3	−8.5	90
6. Services	25.0	20.0	+5.0[3]	125
7. Interest, profits and dividends	47.4	42.7	+4.7[3]	111
8. Transfers	3.8	6.0	−2.2	63
9.[4] Invisibles	76.2	68.7	+7.5	111
10.[5] Total	149.0	150.0	−1.0	99
Percentage of GDP at factor cost: 5 + 6	30.6	31.7		
10	46.7	47.0		

1. Coverage is exports as a percentage of imports.
2. 1 + 2 + 3 + 4 = 5.
3. Of these sums £9.4 billion was estimated to be the overseas earnings of the City of London.
4. 6 + 7 + 8 = 9.
5. 5 + 9 = 10.
Source: UK Balance of Payments 1987 (Pink Book).

The invisible figures, from the quarterly balance-of-payments Press notice, show a surplus of 25 per cent on trade in services. However, the UK's share of world trade in services has fallen slightly faster than its share of trade in manufactures; from 11.9 per cent in 1968 to 7.3 per cent in 1983, according to a study by the Bank of England. This poor performance is due mainly to the decline of the shipping industry. Other services, such as civil aviation, travel and tourism, and financial services, are better performers.

The UK has an 11 per cent surplus of interest, profits and dividends inflows over outflows. This results from the £114 billion surplus of overseas assets over liabilities (at the end of 1986), due to the investment of the North Sea oil current-account surpluses abroad. This is again the difference between two much larger amounts: assets of £731 billion, and liabilities of £617 billion. Since there was an 18 per cent asset surplus over liabilities, the 11 per cent earnings surplus is somewhat below par. Interest, profits and dividends (IPD) represented a 7.1 per cent return on average assets, but a 7.5 per cent cost of funding average liabilities. The difference is partly accounted for by the relatively high return on US oil-company investment in the North Sea.

Each year in July, a Press notice appears giving the overseas earnings of the City of London, which are published a month later in the *UK Balance of Payments* Pink Book. These earnings by insurance, banking, broking and institutional investment include both services and IPD (see Table 33). They amounted to a surplus of £9.4 billion in 1986, a big rise from £6.6 billion in 1985. The City's services earned £5 billion in 1986, accounting for most of the total UK surplus on services, which was in deficit in the case of some other service industries. Since there were few debit items – UK residents using financial services overseas – City services also made up about one-fifth of total services credits of £25 billion. The other £4.4 billion of the City's earnings was a surplus of interest, profits and dividends. About half of this was overseas earnings by insurance and pension funds, and investment and unit trusts, and the other half by banks and securities dealers. The City, in this broad sense, made up nearly four-fifths of the UK's IPD credits of £47.4 billion in 1986. But its surplus cannot be compared with the UK surplus of £5.1 billion on IPD, since the earnings on portfolio investment in the UK by foreign investment institutions are not deducted from the City's accounts, as they are in the UK balance of payments.

The transfers section of the invisibles account is generally negative, because of debits in official transactions with the European Community, and the UK development-aid programme. These are defined as unrequited transfers. They give rise to changes in assets or liabilities in the capital account, for which a compensating entry is made in the current account even though there is no transaction affecting goods,

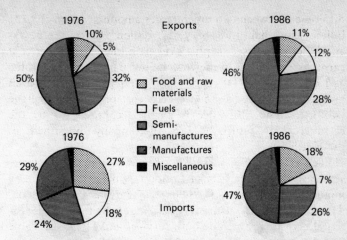

22. Commodity analysis of visible trade, overseas trade statistics basis, 1976 and 1986 (*source: Monthly Review of External Trade Statistics, Annual Supplement,* 1987, p. 72)

services or investment income. (The U K definition of transfers differs from the U S definition, in which 'transfers' cover interest, profits and dividends as well, but conforms with that of the I M F.)

The changing pattern of visible trade

The monthly trade figures give an analysis of exports and imports by commodity and by area. These can be traced back over longer periods in the *Monthly Review of Overseas Trade Statistics* and its *Annual Supplement*. Figure 22 shows how, between 1976 and 1986, the export share of fuels rose from 5 to 12 per cent (21 per cent in 1985, before the fall in the oil price), while their share of imports fell from 18 to 7 per cent. The share of manufactures fell from 82 to 74 per cent on the export side, and rose from 53 to 73 per cent on the import side, with most of the increase – ominously – in finished rather than semi-manufactures. The import share of food and raw materials fell, partly because of greater self-sufficiency in food due to the Common Agricultural Policy of the European Community.

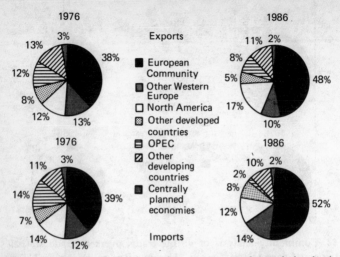

23. Area analysis of visible trade, overseas trade statistics basis, 1976 and 1986 (*source: Monthly Review of External Trade Statistics, Annual Supplement,* 1987, p. 73)

In the area analysis we see in Figure 23 how the share of the European Community, as a result of the UK joining in 1973, rose from 38 per cent in 1976 to 48 per cent in 1986 on the export side, but by rather more on the import side, from 39 to 52 per cent (but no more than 49 per cent in 1985). Between 1985 and 1986 the UK's deficit with the rest of the EC – on the rather overstated OTS basis – leapt from £3.2 billion to £9.5 billion, because of the fall in the value of North Sea oil exports to the Federal Republic of Germany, and the general rise in imports of manufactures. The fact that the current account as a whole was broadly in balance in 1986 nicely demolishes the facile alarmism caused by focusing on bilateral trade balances. The importance of North America as an export market rose with the vast US trade deficit, while that of OPEC fell with the oil price. The importance of oil imports from OPEC – equal to that of total imports from North America in 1976 – shrank as North Sea production expanded.

The changes in total exports and imports over time are

Table 34. Visible UK trade trends, 1977–87 (percentage changes)

	Exports				Imports				Terms of trade change
	Volume[1]		Unit value[2]	(Home prices (RPI)	Volume[1]		Unit value[2]	(Home prices (RPI)	
	Goods	(Goods and services)			Goods	(Goods and services)			
1977	7.8	(6.6)	18.4	(15.8)	1.9	(1.2)	15.8	(15.8)	2.3
1978	2.6	(1.9)	9.9	(8.3)	4.6	(3.9)	3.8	(8.3)	5.7
1979	4.9	(4.0)	10.7	(13.4)	10.7	(10.5)	6.7	(13.4)	4.0
1980	0.9	(–0.1)	14.2	(18.0)	–5.4	(–3.4)	10.0	(18.0)	3.7
1981	–0.7	(–0.6)	8.8	(11.9)	–4.7	(–2.5)	8.2	(11.9)	0.5
1982	2.6	(0.9)	6.8	(8.6)	5.4	(5.5)	7.9	(8.6)	–0.9
1983	1.9	(2.2)	8.2	(4.6)	8.1	(5.5)	9.2	(4.6)	–1.0
1984	8.4	(6.9)	8.2	(5.0)	11.0	(9.2)	9.6	(5.0)	–1.2
1985	5.5	(5.8)	5.5	(6.1)	3.4	(3.1)	3.9	(6.1)	1.4
1986	3.7	(3.0)	–4.8	(3.4)	6.3	(5.8)	–7.7	(3.4)	3.1
1977–86 average	3.7	(3.0)	8.4	(9.4)	4.1	(3.8)	6.6	(9.4)	1.7

1. Seasonally adjusted.
2. Not seasonally adjusted.
Source: Monthly Review of External Trade Statistics, Annual Supplement, 1987, p. 12; Economic Trends, April 1987, p. 79.

shown in Table 34. It is not particularly illuminating to analyse the movement of exports and imports in current pounds from year to year, since so much of the increases are due to price inflation. Exports cannot be deflated by the RPI, because their composition is so different from that of the basket of goods used for it. They can be scaled by relating them to GDP each year; for example exports of goods and services were about 30 per cent of GDP at factor cost in 1986, imports about 31 per cent. The usual method is to take the indices of the volume and unit value of exports and imports, which are given in the monthly trade figures Press notice. Both the volume and the unit-value indices are compiled from information about the prices and quantities of 9,000 different products collected by the Customs. They were re-based on 1980 rather than 1975 weights from September 1983, so the expectation is that in autumn 1988 they will again be re-based on 1985 weights. The weights are the proportions of each product in total exports and imports which are used to calculate the general changes in values and volumes over the whole range. As proportions change during each five-year period, the volume and value indices gradually become less accurate, because they implicitly assume no change since the base year.

The most obvious impact of the re-weighting on the 1980 base was that oil was given an increase in export weight from $3\frac{1}{2}$ to 13 per cent, and a decrease in import weight. This meant that the export unit-value index for all trade, including oil, rose by 47 per cent between 1978 and 1982 using the 1980 weights, compared with 43 per cent using the 1975 weights. Similarly, the volume increase in total exports during the same period was lifted from 6 to 8 per cent on account of the greater weight of rapidly rising oil exports.

Export volumes rose by an average of 3.7 per cent a year in 1977–86, import volumes by 4.1 per cent, while GDP was rising at 1.8 per cent. This reflects the general tendency of world trade to rise faster than world output, as national economies become more open to external trade and specialize in those products in which they have a comparative advantage. Exports of goods and services grew more slowly, at 3.0 per cent, because of the UK's relatively poor performance in shipping (as noted earlier). Imports of goods and services also increased less than those of goods alone, by 3.8 per cent a year. Exports of goods performed particularly well in years when the pound had fallen, such as 1977 and 1984–5, and badly when the pound rose, as in 1980 and 1981. Imports, instead of rising in volume as might have been expected in 1980 and 1981 because of the high exchange rate, fell because the recession reduced the demand for them.

Although import volumes were rising faster than export volumes in 1977–86, the visible deficit did not deteriorate in real terms, because export unit values were rising faster than import unit values, by 8.4 rather than 6.6 per cent a year. In other words, the terms of trade – the ratio of export to import prices – were moving in the UK's favour for most of the period. The average annual improvement was particularly marked in 1979–80, when the price of oil was rising. There was also an unexpected improvement of 3 per cent in the terms of trade in 1986; the price of oil fell, lowering export unit values by 4.8 per cent, but the price of other commodities also fell, bringing down import unit values by 7.7 per cent.

The price of exports over the period rose on average by almost as much as the price of home-produced goods, but the year-to-year movements tended to be less when the pound was rising, in 1979–81, and more when it was falling, in 1983–4. A high exchange rate reduces the sterling equivalent of foreign currency prices, while a low exchange rate increases it. The same effect is observable for import prices, but over the period they averaged a rise of only 6.6 per cent a year, compared with 9.4 per cent for home prices. Since imports are 31 per cent of GDP, a high-exchange-rate policy contributed in some years to keeping domestic inflation down by acting to lower import prices.

Capital account and reserves

Details of the capital account of the balance of payments are

Table 35. The capital account, 1986 (£ billion)

	Outwards	Inwards	Balance
1. Direct investment	11.4	5.4	− 6.0
2. Portfolio investment	22.9	8.2	− 14.7
3. Banking flows	54.5	67.7	+ 13.2
4. Official finance	3.4	0.2	− 3.2
5. Total capital account	92.2	81.5	− 10.7
6. Balancing item			+ 11.7
7. Current account			1.0

Source: Press notice CSO (87)50, 4 June 1987.

first given in the CSO quarterly Press notice, then in the annual Pink Book, the *UK Balance of Payments*. Further analyses by country are given with a time-lag of two years in Business Monitor MA4, *Overseas Transactions*. The UK has again become a major capital exporter in the 1980s. Even when the North Sea oil surplus was no longer giving the UK a surplus on current account, in 1986, identified outflows net of inflows of direct and portfolio investment came to £21 billion, or 6½ per cent of GDP (see Table 35).

Direct investment means investment by corporations, often multinationals, in production facilities in other countries. It is financed partly by unremitted profits, which count as an inflow in the current account of the UK balance of payments and as an outflow in the capital account, even though they do not move across any frontier, since they are notionally held to return to the country of the parent company before being reinvested overseas. Direct investment by US oil companies in the North Sea has been an important inflow, but it has recently been less than the outflows by major UK companies, in both oil and other industries. Portfolio investment increased strongly in the outwards direction after the removal of exchange controls in 1979. UK pension and insurance funds were able to increase the proportion of foreign shares in their portfolios from 5 per cent at the end of 1979 to 14 per cent by the end of 1984. There was a proposal in 1985 by Mr Roy Hattersley, the Shadow Chancellor of the Exchequer, that they should be persuaded by harsher tax treatment on overseas income to repatriate their

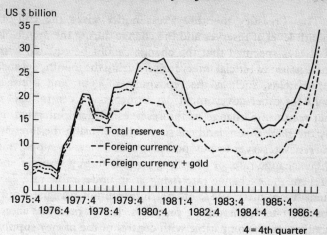

US $ billion

24. UK reserves: end-1975 to mid-1987 (*source: Financial Statistics*, table 10.3)

additional overseas investment so as to bring it back to 5 per cent. This was never implemented, since Labour lost the 1987 general election.

Much of the outwards portfolio investment – £7 billion in 1986 – has been by UK banks in overseas securities, mostly holdings of Eurobonds. The counterpart of these has been part of the large net inflows of short-term bank deposits, £13 billion in 1986, which are recorded in a separate section of the capital account. The majority of the banking flows, amounting to £68 billion on the inflow side in 1986, were of US dollars going in and out of the London Eurodollar market.

Movements in the official reserves of gold and foreign exchange constitute a further element in the capital account. (Changes in official debt, such as gilt-edged securities, held overseas count as inflows of portfolio investment.) The official reserves reached a low point of $4.1 billion at the end of 1976 (see Figure 24), rose to $27.5 billion by the end of 1980, fell again to $ 13.5 billion in the first quarter of 1985, then trebled to $34 billion in mid-1987. About $5.8 billion was gold, $3.4 billion claims on the IMF, and the rest foreign exchange, thought to be mainly US dollars, but with an increasing holding of D-marks.

The Treasury monthly Press notice gives the end-of-month level of reserves and the change during the month. It is always specified that the change cannot be equated with the amount of official intervention during the month, because other items, such as the repayment of debt, and transactions for other government departments and central banks, can result in a change in the reserves. Official intervention by the Bank of England consists either of using the foreign-currency reserves to buy pounds, with a view to supporting the exchange rate, or of selling pounds to buy reserves and prevent the exchange rate rising at an undesirable rate. For some years after 1977, official intervention was used only for short-term smoothing purposes. It was held that intervention was incompatible with control of the money supply, and that the exchange rate should be allowed to float freely. By 1987, intervention was being used as much as in the days of fixed exchange rates. The reserves rose by $22 billion during 1987, as the British government pursued the twin aims of capping the pound and supporting the dollar. Of this, $2.5 billion was due to the upward revaluation of non-dollar reserves which is carried out at the end of March each year.

In recent years the recorded deficit on capital account has been far greater than the recorded surplus on current account. The two accounts should cancel each other out, adding to zero. But in 1986, for example, there was a net outflow of £10.7 billion on capital account, and a deficit of £1.0 billion on current account. The sum of the two, the so-called 'balancing item', came to £11.7 billion. This is generally thought to consist of unrecorded capital inflows, mainly short-term, but it could be partly due to an underestimate of credits, probably invisibles, in the current account. In either case, the UK balance of payments is in better shape than the official statistics show. Either more capital is being invested in the UK, or the UK is doing better in its overseas earnings than is officially known. There could be a 'black economy' element in some of these financial flows, which may be concealed in order to escape the notice of the taxman. According to IMF figures, the world as a whole has a balance-of-payments deficit, which has been reduced from $107 billion in 1982 to $65 billion in 1986. This is in effect the extent to which recorded current deficits are overestimated or surpluses underestimated. If the UK's share of this statistical discrepancy is in proportion to its 6 per cent share of world trade, the current account could be an average of $4 billion (about £2½ billion) a year better off than is apparent. Indeed subsequent revisions of the latest figures may eventually prove the point, as more information about invisibles comes to light. The reasons for the discrepancy are believed to be mainly the under-recording of portfolio income, shipping earnings, and official transfers, as well as the absence of the Soviet Union and Taiwan in IMF statistics.

Exchange rates

Exchange rates are not the subject of a Press notice, since they are published daily by the Press. They are also published for the record in *Financial Statistics* and the *Bank of England Quarterly Bulletin*. In Table 36 we show annual average exchange rates of the pound against the dollar and the D-mark, and the effective rate index (ERI). The ERI is the best all-round exchange-rate indicator, because it is based on the pound's bilateral exchange rates against seventeen currencies, weighted according to their importance in UK trade. In financial markets, it is usually the dollar exchange rate which is quoted, since the dollar is the most widely used currency. In trade, the D-mark exchange rate is increasingly important, because it is at the centre of the European Monetary System, with whose members the UK does more trade than with any other area.

There are three main ways of quoting exchange rate statistics. They can be shown as rates at the end of a period, such as a month, a quarter or a year. This is the most useful statistic for balance-sheet purposes, in order to translate foreign-currency assets and liabilities into sterling on a particular day. They can be shown in terms of extreme points in a range of fluctuations; only a graph giving the range of

Table 36. Exchange rates, 1976–87 (averages)

	$/£		DM/£		Effective rate index	
	Level	Change (%)	Level	Change (%)	Level	Change (%)
1976	1.81		4.55		85.7	
1977	1.75	−3.3	4.05	−11.0	81.2	−5.3
1978	1.92	9.7	3.85	−4.9	81.5	0.4
1979	2.12	10.4	3.89	1.0	87.3	7.1
1980	2.33	9.9	4.23	8.7	96.1	10.1
1981	2.03	−12.9	4.56	7.8	95.3	−0.8
1982	1.75	−13.8	4.24	−7.0	90.7	−4.8
1983	1.52	−13.1	3.87	−8.7	83.3	−8.2
1984	1.34	−11.8	3.79	−2.1	78.7	−5.5
1985	1.30	−3.0	3.78	−0.3	78.7	0.0
1986	1.47	13.1	3.18	−15.9	72.9	−7.4
1977–86 average		−2.1		−3.5		−1.6

Source: Monthly Review of External Trade Statistics, Annual Supplement, 1987, p. 87.

rate for each day will pick up these turning-points. Finally, exchange rates can be shown as averages over a period. This is more helpful in judging their impact on trade over the same period, since extreme turning-points are generally short-lived. The yearly averages shown in Table 36 are the rates most relevant to an assessment of the impact of exchange rates on exports and imports.

The pound's effective rate often represents an average between the dollar rate, with a weight of 25 per cent in the basket, and the D-mark and the yen, with a weight of 14 per cent each. Thus from 1977 to 1980 the pound's average value rose by 33 per cent against the dollar, rose by 4½ per cent against the D-mark, and went up 18 per cent on the ERI. After UK interest rates and the price of oil had peaked in 1980–81, the pound fell most of the time over the five years to 1985. It fell by 44 per cent against the dollar, 11 per cent against the D-mark, and 18 per cent on the ERI. In 1986, the pound at last achieved what had been the government's preferred stance for some time. It rose 13 per cent against the dollar, which kept import prices down, and fell 16 per

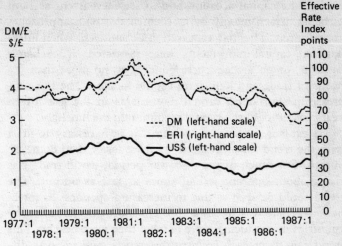

25. Exchange rates, monthly, 1977–87

cent against the D-mark, which put export profits up. In ERI terms, the fall was 7½ per cent. (See Figure 25.)

There is only a very rough correspondence between the direction of movement of the exchange rate and that of the terms of trade (see the right-hand columns of Tables 36 and 34). The terms of trade are the ratio of export prices to import prices. The immediate effect of an exchange-rate change, if both sets of prices are taken to be in sterling, is to change them all by the same proportion in foreign-currency terms, thus leaving the terms of trade unchanged. In practice, the terms of trade tend to rise when the pound goes up, because export prices in sterling fall by less than import prices, and to fall when the pound goes down, because export prices in sterling rise by less than import prices.

The economics of the balance of payments

The traditional approach to the balance of payments is to explain the current account – and regard the capital account as adjusting in the opposite direction to make the external account balance. More recently, economists have sought to explain the capital account, and to see the current account as being driven mainly by it. Elements of both approaches are required. The first appeared to be sufficient when international capital movements were restricted by exchange controls, or on a scale corresponding to no more than the needs of trade and long-term capital finance. The huge increase in short-term capital movements in the last fifteen years has brought the capital account into the limelight.

To explain the current account, it is necessary to start with the trend for all trade to increase faster than domestic output. For much of the post-war period, world trade was rising about one and a half times as fast as output. The trend could be seen as due to increasing openness as international trade was freed, and to enhanced specialization by countries in producing more of what they were best at. This trend can affect each country differently, and imports differently from exports. Thus in the UK there is some evidence that imports, in the absence of other influences, would tend to rise faster than exports.

In addition to, or instead of, the trend there is the relationship between the growth of demand and the growth of trade. This is the demand elasticity of imports in each country, often found to be in the region of 1.5. If domestic demand rises by 1 per cent, imports rise by about 1.5 per cent. In an ideal world, if this happened in each country, they would all benefit, because the faster rise in one country's imports than in domestic demand would translate into a faster rise in other countries' exports too. The demand elasticity of imports can be used to get the marginal propensity to import, by multiplying it by the average propensity to import. Thus if the UK's imports rise 1.5 times as fast as demand, and imports are on average 30 per cent of demand, the proportion of any additional demand satisfied by imports must be 45 per cent – the marginal propensity to import. (See p. 57 for a similar analysis of consumption.)

Exports depend partly on foreign demand. The growth of foreign markets for UK exports can be assessed by giving a weight to each country based on the existing pattern of exports. An increase in world demand will translate into a very different market-weighted rise for each country's exports. This depends also on the market elasticity of exports, in other words by how much they rise in response to a 1 per cent increase in market demand. In the absence of other factors, the rate at which any country can expand relative to the rest of the world may depend on the domestic demand elasticity of its imports, and on the foreign market elasticity of its exports. If the UK's imports grow 1.5 times as fast as its domestic demand, and its exports rise only just as fast as domestic demand abroad, then UK economic growth can be only two-thirds that of the rest of the world if exports and imports are to remain in balance with each other.

The other major trade variable is competitiveness, which can augment or offset the effect of movements in domestic and foreign demand. It is made up of three elements: labour costs; productivity, which reduces labour costs per unit of output (see Table 24); and the exchange rate, which changes domestic relative to foreign unit-labour costs. The use of import and export prices alone, while common in economic analysis, tends to disregard the fact that changes in costs may be greater than those in prices, especially where there is a 'law of one price' for similar goods competing in world markets. In such cases, the main impact of changes in competitiveness is not on prices, but on profits, which influence exporters' willingness to supply the product, rather than the demand for it.

The competitiveness elasticity of imports or exports is the percentage by which they change in response to a 1 per cent change in competitiveness. According to the famous Marshall-Lerner conditions, if a devaluation is to be effective, the price or competitiveness elasticities of imports and exports must add up to more than 1, if the terms of trade change to the full extent of the devaluation. Such conditions were found to hold for UK manufactures trade by a recent Bank of England study. The price elasticity of imports came out at 0.64, and that of exports at 0.37. According to the J-curve effect, however, a devaluation makes the trade balance in money terms get worse before it gets better. This happens because import prices rise before import volumes fall, causing domestic inflation, which worsens competitiveness before export prices in domestic currency have been cut enough to stimulate additional foreign sales. Favourable changes in the volumes of imports and exports may also be swamped by unfavourable changes in their relative prices – the terms of trade.

Different categories of traded product behave very differently. Much of the foregoing analysis has been applied to trade in manufactures, which were once a more important part of total UK trade than they are today. Oil and primary commodities do not react in the same way. The price of oil is established in a world market in terms of US dollars. Unit labour costs are negligible, and changes in the sterling exchange rate have no effect on the dollar price, but only on the profits of oil companies in the UK. Such changes are unlikely to have much effect even on the supply of oil, because in most cases they can be absorbed into relatively high profit margins.

The capital account is driven first by relative interest rates, and then by expectations about exchange-rate changes, which may enhance or nullify interest-rate differentials. Changes in other variables, such as relative inflation rates or money supplies, are studied for the impact they may have on interest and exchange rates. If interest rates on sterling assets are 5 per cent higher than on D-mark assets, capital flows out of D-marks and into sterling. If it is thought that sterling will fall by about 5 per cent against the D-mark over the next year, then the capital will not flow. In practice, investors require a risk premium, so that the interest-rate differential needs to be somewhat higher than the contrary exchange-rate movement expected. If it is thought that the pound will fall by more than 5 per cent against the D-mark, then a 5 per cent interest-rate differential will not be sufficient to stop a reverse flow out of sterling into D-mark assets. The relevant time-period may not be a year: in fast-moving foreign-exchange markets, it can be measured in days, hours or even minutes.

In spite of the enormous amount of research that has been done, the UK trade and balance-of-payments figures are highly unpredictable. Erratic movements occur from one month to the next. Financial markets seldom heed the official warning that not too much should be read into one month's figures in isolation. If the key variables determining the balance of payments cannot themselves be predicted, then any explanation in which they are used, however well it fits the past, is not much use in foretelling the future. Exchange rates and interest rates are both highly unpredictable. If the capital account is the key to all else, the more's the pity, since its constituents are so hard to forecast.

Current-account variables are not quite so difficult to predict. Domestic and foreign demand can be forecast with some plausibility. Labour costs in the UK may rise too fast, but they are fairly predictable. Productivity is more difficult, because it depends in the short run on the demand for output, but this itself can be forecast. It is again the vagaries of the exchange rate which make it so hard to predict competitiveness, and thus the behaviour of exports and imports, as well as the sterling value of invisible earnings. Greater stability in the UK's exchange rate, such as full membership of the European Monetary System would provide, would make it less difficult to predict the growth of export earnings. This in its turn would help to promote industrial confidence, and encourage long-term investment.

7

Money, Banking and Finance

'Bank lending record fuels overheating economy fears.'
Steve Levinson, *Independent*, 21 July 1987

The money supply, bank and building-society lending, and public borrowing are closely linked, both by statistical definitions, and by the way in which British governments have chosen to run their monetary and fiscal policies during the last decade. Monetarism as a theory is centuries old. As applied to policy in the UK, it goes back to 1976, when the first monetary target was set under the influence of the IMF. From then on, the publication of the monthly money-supply figures began to displace the trade figures as the key indicator. The theory was that the money supply – the rate of growth of the stock of money – determined the rate of inflation, after a time-lag. At first it was hoped that targets for monetary growth would determine people's expectations about the future rate of inflation. As in the Federal Republic of Germany, trade unions would build a floor into their wage demands as low as the government's monetary targets, which would be taken as determining future inflation. This view was never accepted by the British trade unions. They were sceptical both about the government's ability to achieve the monetary targets, and about the influence of monetary growth on inflation. They were proved right on both counts.

It was the Bank of England's task to control the money supply in order to reduce inflation. During the early 1980s, the practical difficulties of applying the monetarist theory set out in the government's medium-term financial strategy (MTFS) – first unveiled in 1980 – came to seem insuperable. The money supply was being determined by bank and building-society lending. Since the government wanted to encourage free-market competition in lending, it could not at the same time limit its growth, and thus the money supply, except by short-term subterfuges. The emphasis was therefore gradually switched to the public sector borrowing requirement (PSBR), rather than the monetary targets, as the main instrument of the medium-term financial strategy (MTFS). This had always been foreseen by Sir Keith Joseph, the monetarist guru in Mrs Thatcher's inner circle, and a member of her Cabinet in 1979–86. In 1976, he gave the Stockton Lecture (ironically, named after one of monetarism's leading critics, Lord Stockton, formerly Harold Macmillan). It was called 'Monetarism is Not Enough'. His conclusion was that 'we must also have substantial cuts in tax and public spending'.

The message was more fully spelt out by Professor Sir Alan Walters, Mrs Thatcher's special economic adviser in 1981–3, in his book *Britain's Economic Renaissance*. He set out to stand Keynes's supposed support for government deficits on its head by arguing that a lower rather than a higher PSBR caused the economy to grow faster. His critics pointed out that it was the abandonment of the monetary targets and not the achievement of the PSBR targets which made the economy grow, because the supply of money and credit was able to increase freely. At any rate, the PSBR as an indicator came to rank as at least equal in importance to the money and banking figures.

Because the PSBR is financed mainly by the issue of gilt-edged government stocks, its monthly size is taken by financial markets as a clue to the yields, or interest rates, on these stocks. On the other hand, the money and banking figures are seen as a guide to short-term interest rates in the money markets, and to the Bank of England's operations designed to influence them. With the downgrading of the monetary targets during 1986, the exchange rate has become a more important determinant of interest rates. If it falls, interest rates may rise, and vice versa.

The meaning of money

'When I use a word it means just what I choose it to mean – neither more nor less,' said Humpty Dumpty. The various official definitions of money, bank lending, and public borrowing have been carefully chosen to reflect both changes in the financial system and official policy objectives. The Oxford philosophy school of linguistic analysis maintains that to study the meaning of a word you must see how it is used. Oxford philosophy is as relevant as economics to an understanding of UK monetary policy. (Mr Nigel Lawson's success as Chancellor of the Exchequer may be due to the fact that he studied both subjects at Christ Church, Oxford.) One feature common to all definitions of money is that they exclude holdings by banks of each other's deposits, known as inter-bank deposits. They are generally restricted to holdings by the non-bank private sector, in other words households and businesses. In the UK at the present time, money held by the public sector or by foreigners is excluded from the definition, with the minor exception of notes and coin.

Definitions of money can be roughly divided into two categories. 'Narrow' money is notes and coins, and may include deposits used as a means of payment. 'Broad' money generally includes narrow money, and in addition interest-bearing deposits used by savers as a store of value. They are all known as the 'monetary aggregates'.

The narrowest kind of money is M0 ('M-nought'), the 'wide monetary base', which was introduced only in 1982. About 90 per cent of it is notes and coins in circulation. The rest is nearly all notes and coins held in bank tills. Only about $1\frac{1}{2}$ per cent of it is the banks' operational deposits with the Bank of England. It cannot easily be defined as part of any other monetary aggregate, because it is a monthly average, not an end-period, figure, and includes holdings of money by banks. M0 was introduced after a public debate as to whether the Bank of England should try to control broad money by its influence on narrow money, or the monetary base. The Bank of England can influence the banks'

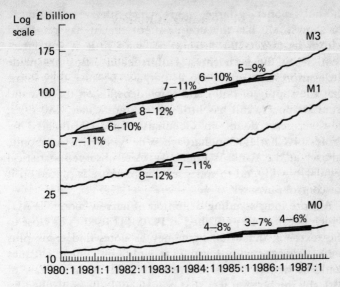

26. M0, M1 and M3: monthly levels and targets

operational deposits, but it cannot directly determine the amount of notes and coins in circulation. If it tried to, it would cause a run on the banks. Notes and coins are determined mainly by consumer spending and by interest rates. The Bank of England has some say in interest rates, but not consumer spending. So M0 is quite difficult to control in its own right. It is even more difficult to use as a lever with which to control broad money, because of changes in the ratio of notes and coins to bank deposits.

Monetary-base control was never adopted as an instrument to regulate broad money. But M0 was adopted as a target in its own right. It had the advantage that it grew rather slowly, because people tend to use notes and coins less as credit cards and other means of payment gain ground, and because interest rates have been high in real terms. Over the five years from its inception in June 1982 it increased by only 4.7 per cent a year, which was very close to the RPI inflation rate of 4.5 per cent. Targets have been set for it since 1984/5. In 1987/8, the 2–6 per cent target for M0 is the only monetary target figure which survives. As Figure 26 shows, M0 has the unique merit that it has remained within its targets for three years, with little if any intervention by the authorities. Unfortunately, this has made little impression on financial markets, because they know that the supply of notes and coins depends on the demand from shoppers, and has little wider significance. M0 does, however, cast doubt on Goodhart's Law (formulated by Professor Charles Goodhart when he was a chief economic adviser at the Bank of England): 'Any observed statistical regularity will tend to collapse once pressure is placed on it for control purposes.'

A more long-standing definition of narrow money is M1, which began to be published in 1970. M1 used to be close to the textbook definition of money as notes and coins plus bank deposits, withdrawable at sight, on which cheques could be written but no interest was paid. As in the case of M0, the implication was that money could be controlled by raising interest rates, because this would make it more expensive to keep money in non-interest-bearing bank current accounts. Unfortunately, M1 includes sight deposits on which interest is paid. At first these were large overnight deposits in the wholesale money markets, but more recently banks have begun to pay interest on some retail sight deposits. Interest-bearing sight deposits have been increasing faster than any other kind of money. They have multiplied eight times in the seven years to the end of 1986, rising from 14 to 45 per cent of M1. Non-interest-bearing current accounts in banks increased by only 75 per cent during the same period. The effect was that M1 multiplied by 2.5 times, rising by 13 per cent a year, or over 5 per cent faster than the RPI.

M1 was used as a target in 1982/3 and 1983/4, but was subsequently dropped. The rapid growth of interest-bearing sight deposits, a by-product of heightened financial activity in the City, caused M1 to grow faster than any credible target numbers. It was suggested by some analysts that it should be redefined as 'retail M1', without the interest-bearing wholesale sight deposits. Any such idea would have been overtaken by the trend among banks and building societies to start paying interest on certain kinds of retail sight deposit. The Bank of England does, however, now publish figures for non-interest-bearing M1.

A new narrow monetary aggregate called M2 was announced in 1982. It was differently defined from the old M2, which was published in the early 1970s. This consisted of M1 plus time deposits in 'deposit banks' – mainly clearing banks – and discount houses. The new M2 was the two non-interest-bearing components of M1, plus retail time deposits in all banks. Retail deposits were those on which cheques could be drawn or payment made in other ways, and all other deposits of less than £100,000 and less than one month's maturity or notice of withdrawal. M2, also known as 'transactions balances', has never been used as a target, although it was originally hoped that it might be used in conjunction with monetary base control. When building-society deposits were added to the definition of M2 in 1983, it roughly doubled in size, and became larger than the broad aggregate M3. It also became useless for control purposes, because it was artificially swelled as building societies offered almost as high interest rates on deposits of less than a month as on those of longer maturities. It increased by 11.3 per cent a year over the five years to June 1987.

The longest-surviving definition of broad money is M3, known until May 1987 as Sterling M3 (written £M3). It consists of M1 plus all private-sector time deposits with the monetary sector (banks and discount houses). It excludes foreign-currency deposits, because their sterling value varies with the exchange rate and with large swings in overseas transactions. Confusingly, M3 plus foreign-currency deposits is now called M3c, but was until May 1987 called M3. The old M3, including foreign currency, was the monetary aggregate used when targets began in 1976. £M3, now called M3, was substituted in 1977/8. Public-sector deposits were excluded from M3 in April 1984.

Targets were set for £M3 as the centre-piece of the MTFS from 1980/81 onwards. The aim was to reduce inflation by setting the targets one percentage point lower each year, with a 4 per cent range by the end of a year. The

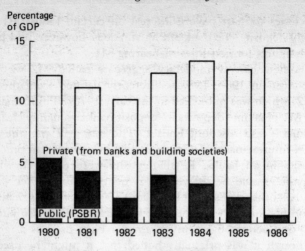

Percentage of GDP

27. Private- and public-sector borrowing as percentage of GDP at market prices, 1980–86 (*source: Economic Trends*, September 1987, tables 56, 64; *Financial Statistics*, October 1987, tables 7.6, 7.7)

target of 7–11 per cent for 1980/81 was exceeded, as was the 6–10 per cent target for 1981/2. In the two following years the targets were achieved, but only because they were raised by 3 percentage points above the original level, to 8–12 per cent in 1982/3 and 7–11 per cent in 1983/4. This was done in order to accommodate changes in financial markets such as the entry of the clearing banks into the market for mortgages, which required a corresponding rise in their £M3 deposits.

In 1982, public sector borrowing was halved, but private sector borrowing offset the cut with an increase of over a quarter. The March 1982 Budget thus marks the first stage of the transition from monetarism to fiscalism – the primacy of the PSBR over the monetary targets. In 1984/5 and 1985/6, the £M3 targets continued to be notched down one percentage point each year, but were exceeded. As the PSBR came down as a percentage of GDP, private sector borrowing by banks and building societies rose (see Figure 27). Total borrowing fell from 12 to 10 per cent of GDP between 1980 and 1982, then rose back to 12–13 per cent of

GDP in 1983–5. It was in 1986 that total borrowing rose sharply, to nearly 15 per cent of GDP. The flow of private sector borrowing rose from £37 billion in 1985 to £52 billion in 1986. For 1986/7 the £M3 target ranges were once again notched up to accommodate financial markets, this time by a breathtaking 7 percentage points, to 11–15 per cent. They were overshot even so. In October 1986 the Governor of the Bank of England announced what was in effect the abandonment of the £M3 target. The financial markets, which were by then assuming that the exchange rate had become the main influence on interest rates, reacted with indifference.

The £M3 target was abandoned because the authorities had given up the futile attempt to control it by raising interest rates, for four main reasons:

1. By the end of 1986, nearly three-quarters of £M3 consisted of interest-bearing deposits. A rise in bank interest rates was therefore more likely to raise than to lower £M3.

2. It was possible to control £M3 none the less by selling more gilt-edged stocks and National Savings than required to fund the PSBR. This 'overfunding' raised the interest yield on gilt-edged relative to that on bank deposits, and persuaded people to switch from the latter to the former. But the result was that the Bank of England was piling up a 'bill mountain' of commercial bills – short-term credit to business – funded by the excess sales of gilt-edged. The apparent control of £M3 was to some extent cosmetic, since bank credit, including the bill mountain, was unchanged. The overfunding ceased and was partly unwound during 1987; hence the rapid increase in £M3, as the banks took back on to their books some of the credit formerly granted by the Bank of England.

3. Interest rates were ineffective in controlling bank lending, which in its turn determined £M3. Personal and corporate borrowers alike borrowed more in order to pay the higher interest charges, knowing that interest rates were

variable, and could come down as quickly as they had gone up. Financial innovations such as variable-term mortgages and interest-rate futures also helped borrowers to hedge the risk of higher interest rates.

4. The UK authorities could gain only imperfect and short-run control over interest rates, which were strongly influenced by the increasingly de-restricted money and foreign-exchange markets. The abolition of exchange controls in October 1979, followed by the termination of the 'corset' control on the banks in July 1980, removed in advance the two policy instruments which alone could have made monetarism effective.

The drawback of narrow aggregates and even the broader £M3 is that financial market changes cause liquid assets to move across the frontiers between them. For example, if bank interest rates rise higher than building-society rates, an increase in £M3 is caused purely by a switch from a market which happens to be outside the definition of money to one that happens to come inside it. To overcome this, the authorities introduced in 1979 two wider aggregates, PSL1 and PSL2. (PSL stands for private-sector liquidity.) We can now forget PSL1. Its main function was to pick up distortions caused by the banking 'corset', by adding to the main part of £M3 commercial bills held outside the banking system. The broadest aggregate was PSL2, which added shorter-term building-society and National Savings deposits to PSL1 and £M3. It was thus unaffected by switching between bank and building-society deposits, and likely to be steadier and more predictable in its growth.

PSL2 was adopted as a monetary target, alongside M1 and £M3, for the two years 1982/3 and 1983/4. It was then dropped, partly because of the rapid growth in shorter-term building-society deposits due to the switch out of term shares, which caused it to overshoot the 6–10 per cent target in 1983/4. This defect was remedied in 1986, when building-society term deposits were included in PSL2. In May 1987 it was rescued from obscurity, and rechristened M5, with the confusing maturity cut-off removed so that it included all building-society shares and deposits. Alongside it was unveiled the new M4, leaving out money-market instruments such as commercial bills, and National Savings deposits. Since building societies are gradually coming to resemble banks more closely, particularly in the usefulness of their deposits as means of payment, M4 seems destined to become the main broad aggregate. The authorities have wisely refrained from using it as a target, although they are likely still to publish forecasts for the ranges within which its growth is expected to lie.

It can be seen from Table 37 that over the seven years to 1986 M1, M3 (formerly £M3), M4 and M5 (formerly PSL2) have all grown at 13–14 per cent a year on average, or about 6 per cent in real inflation-adjusted terms. However, the variability of M5 is less from month to month and from year to year than that of the other Ms. The income velocity of these aggregates has therefore fallen. This means that depositors are turning over their money balances less often, and using them more as a form of relatively liquid savings. However, notes and coin have fallen in real terms while non-interest-bearing sight deposits have just kept up with inflation. With hindsight non-interest-bearing M1, the sum of these two components, might have been the best indicator of inflation. Table 38 shows the indifferent achievement of successive Labour and Conservative governments in monetary targetry, from 1976 to 1987. Of eighteen targets set, eight have been hit, ten missed. Only M0 has been within target in all three years since it came into use. Both M1 targets were missed. Of the eleven M3 targets, four were hit, seven missed. PSL2 was used only twice, with one success and one failure.

The publication of money and banking statistics

The money and banking statistics are compiled by the Bank of England by means of frequent and detailed statistical returns from the commercial banks. Every few years, there are important changes. In May 1975, a new and more uniform system of statistics was introduced. As new banks are

Table 37. The components of M1, M3, M4 and M5, 1979–86 (not seasonally adjusted)[1]

	End-1979		Annual percentage change[2]		End-1986	
	£ billion	Percentage of M5	Nominal	Real[3]	£ billion	Percentage of M5
1. Notes and coin	9.5	8.3	4.9	−2.2	13.3	4.8
2. Non-interest sight deposits[4]	16.0	13.9	7.7	0.4	28.1	10.2
3. Interest-bearing sight deposits	4.3	3.7	30.5	21.6	33.8	12.2
4. Total M1[5]	29.8	25.9	13.2	5.5	75.2	27.2
5. Bank time deposits	27.4	23.8	13.8	6.1	76.5	27.7
6. Total M3[6]	57.2	49.7	13.4	5.7	151.7	54.9
7. Building-society deposits[7]	41.5	36.1	14.9	7.1	109.7	39.7
8. Total M4[8]	98.7	85.8	14.1	6.3	261.4	94.6
9. Money-market instruments and short-term National Savings	16.4	14.2	6.6	−0.6	14.9	5.4
10. Total M5[9]	115.1	100.0	13.3	5.6	276.3	100.0

1. *Notes and coins* and *deposits* are those held by the UK non-bank private sector. M0 equals 1 + banks' till money and their deposits with the Bank of England. M2 equals 1 + 2 + retail interest-bearing bank, building-society, and National Savings Bank ordinary accounts.
2. Adjusted for the inclusion of the Trustee Savings Banks in the monetary sector in 1981. Not adjusted for the inclusion of smaller banks from time to time, nor for that of privatized companies.
3. Deflated by RPI.
4. Adjusted for transit items.
5. 1 + 2 + 3 = 4.
6. 4 + 5 = 6.
7. Net of building-society holdings of M3, including shares.
8. 6 + 7 = 8.
9. 8 + 9 = 10.

Source: *Bank of England banking statistics, June 1987; Financial statistics.*

Table 38. Monetary targets and results, 1976–88

Year	Months	Aggregate[1]	Target (%)	Result (%)	Success
1976/7	Financial year	£M3	9–13	7.7	Yes
1977/8	Financial year	£M3	9–13	15.5	No
1978/9	Financial year	£M3	8–12	10.8	Yes
	October–October	£M3	8–12	13.1	No
1979/80	June–October	£M3	7–11	16.2	No
1980/81	February–April	£M3	7–11	18.4	No
1981/2	February–April	£M3	6–10	12.8	No
1982/3	February–April	M1	8–12	12.3	No
	February–April	£M3	8–12	11.1	Yes
	February–April	PSL2	8–12	11.5	Yes
1983/4	February–April	M1	7–11	14.0	No
	February–April	£M3	7–11	9.5	Yes
	February–April	PSL2	7–11	12.4	No
1984/5	February–April	M0	4–8	5.6	Yes
	February–April	£M3	6–10	11.9	No
1985/6	March–March	M0	3–7	3.6	Yes
	March–March	£M3	5–9	16.3	No
1986/7	March–March	M0	4–6	4.1	Yes
1987/8	March–March	M0	2–6	—	—

1. £M3 is now called M3, PSL2 M5.
Source: Bank of England.

created or non-banks are reclassified as banks, the money-stock figures grow. The main example was in November 1981, when the old banking sector was broadened to become the monetary sector, including licensed deposit-takers as well as authorized banks. This caused an increase of £7 billion, or about 8 per cent, in £M3, mainly because of the inclusion of the Trustee Savings Banks. The privatization of public corporations also adds to the private-sector deposits in the monetary aggregates. Thus Telecom added £500 million to M3 in 1984, and British Gas £800 million in 1986.

For the first five years of the MTFS, the growth of money was measured against targets from February of each year. This meant that if the month-to-month growth of money was relatively high early in the target period, the target was being exceeded, and the pressure on the Bank of England was greater to take action rather than to wait for the next month's figures, and hope that they would be better. This design defect was remedied only from 1985–6, when target ranges were substituted for target cones (see Figure 26). This meant that the rate of monetary growth was measured not from each February, but over the previous year. Another important change was made from October 1986. The banking month, which used to end in the middle of each calendar month, was changed to make it the same as the calendar month. This made it possible to add up bank and building-society deposits on the same day of the month, and to put money and banking figures on all fours with other economic and financial statistics. (This change resulted from a recommendation made by the author as long ago as September 1977.)

The most recent change is the renaming and redefinition of the monetary aggregates announced in May 1987. From June 1987 onwards, eight different aggregates are being measured; M0, non-interest-bearing M1, M1, M2, M3, M3c, M4 and M5. It might have been less confusing to have a composite broad aggregate, in which each component was given a weight in inverse proportion to the rate of interest on it. This kind of aggregate, named after a monetary economist called Divisia, was examined but not adopted by the Bank of England. With eight aggregates, it is usually possible for the authorities to direct the attention of markets to those which are increasing less rapidly. The markets now pay little attention to any of these aggregates, and are likely only to be confused by the sheer profusion of the statistics, even if it merely reflects the increasing complexity of the financial-services industry.

The provisional estimates of the monetary aggregates for the previous month are published by the Bank of England about three weeks after the end of the month. They show only M0, M3, M4 and M5, giving monthly rates of growth unadjusted and seasonally adjusted, and rates of growth over the previous year. Fuller figures are published about ten days later, about a month after the previous month-end. The London and Scottish banks (formerly the London clearing banks) also publish figures about their lending, deposits and balance-sheets on the same day as the Bank of England's provisional estimates. These figures are all arranged so as to lay

Table 39. The credit counterparts of changes to M4, 1983, 1986

	1983		1986	
	£ billion	Percentage of M4	£ billion	Percentage of M4
1. Public sector borrowing requirement	11.6	58.3	2.2	6.4
2. Private sector purchases of public sector debt	−9.8	−49.2	−5.8	−16.9
3. External finance to public sector	−1.6	−8.0	−2.1	−6.1
4. Public sector contribution	0.2	1.0	−5.7	−16.6
Sterling lending to UK private sector:				
5. Banks	12.1	60.8	29.1	84.8
6. Building societies	10.9	54.8	19.2	56.0
7. External finance to monetary sector	−0.7	−3.5	−0.9	−2.6
8. Net non-deposit liabilities	−2.6	−13.1	−7.4	−21.6
9. M4	19.9	100.0	34.3	100.0

Source: Bank of England banking statistics.

stress on the credit counterparts of the monetary aggregates, since they are widely used to explain and predict the changes in money supply (see Table 39). These counterparts have traditionally been related to £M3, which was in fact chosen as a target because it was relatively easy to link it with the PSBR and bank lending to the private sector. It is now possible to relate them also to M4 (as shown in the table) and to M5.

The PSBR was once regarded as an important source of money creation. In recent years it has been fully funded, and indeed overfunded, by issues of public sector debt to the UK private sector, such as gilt-edged stocks and National Savings. It is also sometimes funded by public borrowing from abroad, or the sale of official foreign-exchange reserves, termed external finance, to the public sector. As a result the public sector's contribution to the growth of M4 was roughly zero in 1983, and negative by over £5 billion in 1986. Overfunding reduces the monetary aggregates, but 'crowds in' credit to the private sector so that it can both increase and replace the cut in credit to the public sector.

A negative contribution is always made to monetary growth by the non-deposit liabilities of the banks. These consist of additions to retained profits or new issues of shares or bonds which increase bank capital. Increases in bank lending are matched by extra capital as well as by the growth of monetary deposits. Banks can also raise deposits from abroad to finance lending to the UK private sector – another negative contribution to monetary growth, because overseas deposits fall outside any UK definition of money. Bank lending has thus been able to grow more rapidly than the monetary aggregates. In 1986, for example, additional bank lending of £29 billion to the UK private sector accounted for 85 per cent of M4 growth, and building-society net mortgage increases accounted for another 56 per cent. Total sterling lending to the UK private sector was thus able to outrun monetary growth by 41 per cent. How much this matters depends on whether the growth of money is important in its own right or as a determinant of the growth of credit. In either case, spending power is created.

An important defect of the UK figures is that they express money growth in terms of the percentage of flows to stocks, but credit in terms of money flows and stocks, without any indication of percentages. This makes it considerably more difficult to judge the importance of any given credit flow compared with an increase in the monetary aggregates. Thus the £29 billion bank credit growth in 1986 was a 23 per cent increase in the end-1985 stock of bank credit, and the £19 billion building-society credit flow was a 20 per cent rise in outstandings at the end of 1985. Such percentages make the growth of even M3 look sedate by comparison.

The figures for bank lending to the private sector, which appear each month, are difficult to interpret (see Table 40). Instead of eight definitions of money, we show eight columns of different types of bank lending. The broadest, in column 7, is that which provides the counterpart of the monetary aggregates. However, it includes, sometimes as the biggest component (positive or negative), purchases or sales of commercial bills by the Bank of England Issue Department.

Table 40. Banks' sterling lending to the UK private sector, October 1986 to June 1987 (unadjusted, £ billion)

	(1) CLSB groups	(2) Other banks	(3) Discount houses	(4) BoE Banking	(5)[1] Monetary sector	(6) BoE Issue	(7)[2] Banking total	(8)[3] BoE total
1986 O	61	1,049	451	156	1,717	1,598	3,315	1,754
N	325	2,128	−350	−162	1,941	1,311	3,252	1,149
D	1,778	391	−187	90	2,072	1,969	4,041	2,059
1987 J	813	425	329	2,025	3,592	−2,229	1,363	−204
F	1,310	2,361	−619	−842	2,210	397	2,607	−445
M	3,502	2,639	2,305	−2,224	6,222	−2,842	3,380	−5,066
A	844	1,903	−491	1,078	3,334	−2,187	1,147	−1,109
M	2,769	2,053	229	−171	4,880	−2,614	2,266	−2,785
J	3,776	283	−934	−47	3,078	1,607	4,685	1,560

1. (1) + (2) + (3) + (4) = (5).
2. (5) + (6) = (7).
3. (4) + (6) = (8).

Source: Banking statistics; Bank of England Press notice; Monthly statement of the London and Scottish banks; Banking Information Service.

(Commercial bills are IOUs issued by one company to another and usually 'accepted' (guaranteed) by a bank, so that they are often called acceptances. When a bank, or the Bank of England, buys a commercial bill, then it has acquired a loan to the issuing company.) Bank of England commercial-bill transactions are due either to short-term money-market operations or to the overfunding of the PSBR. Taking away the Issue Department, which is part of the public sector, we get sterling lending by the monetary sector (in column 5). This, however, includes the Bank of England Banking Department, which also carries out money-market operations, sometimes offsetting, sometimes augmenting, those of the Issue Department.

The monetary sector also includes the discount houses, which carry out large operations in commercial bills – counted as bank lending – in close cooperation with the Bank of England. The only true banks which figure in 'bank lending' are the City of London and Scottish bank groups and the other commercial banks (in columns 1 and 2). The CLSB figures cannot be matched with those of the Bank of England, because they include subsidiaries as well as the parent banks. The Bank of England has a category called 'retail banks', which comprises CLSB parents, some other banks such as the Trustees Savings Banks, and the Bank of England Banking Department. The exclusion of the CLSB subsidiaries and the inclusion of the Banking Department make the 'retail banks' a concept of limited use. Some of the CLSB retail parent banks have merged with their wholesale subsidiaries, so they are no longer only retail. A definition by ownership rather than by function would be more useful. The figures for March 1987 show how complex the true position can be. The CLSB groups lent £3.5 billion, and total bank lending to the private sector was £3.4 billion (see columns 1 and 7). The closeness of the two figures is mere coincidence. The other banks lent £2.6 billion, and the discount houses lent £2.3 billion, mainly purchases of commercial bills. So the monetary sector apart from the Bank of England Banking Department lent £8.4 billion in one month. The Banking Department sold £2.2 billion in bills, so the monetary sector lent £6.2 billion. But the Bank of England Issue Department sold another £2.8 billion bills, making a total reduction of £5 billion in the bill mountain. This reduced the bank lending total to £3.4 billion.

The reduction in the bill mountain was the counterpart of an underfunding of the PSBR, which came to £3.3 billion in March; taking other transactions into account, the public-sector contribution to the growth of M3 was £4.4 billion. As the Bank of England was ceasing to give credit to the private sector by holding commercial bills, they had to be replaced by commercial bank credit, with a corresponding rise in monetary deposits. Funding the PSBR would have absorbed the extra deposits and squeezed private credit.

The Building Societies Association publishes its monthly figures for shares and deposits and mortgage lending about two weeks after the end of each month. These figures are beginning to be more closely integrated into the Bank of England's money and banking statistics, in view of the importance given to M4 and M5 from May 1987. Table 41 shows how the building societies' flows of funds have changed between 1982 and 1986. In 1982, the building societies' funds were nearly all from their retail network. The main source was 'net receipts'. Unlike the banks, the building societies show gross receipts of shares and deposits (a share is little more than the most common kind of deposit), and withdrawals. Their net receipts are the difference between the two. The building societies used to arouse public concern at their lack of adequate funds by stressing 'net receipts', which was always less than their increase in mortgage lending net of repayments. This left out interest credited to accounts, which by 1986 had grown to be as much as 'net receipts'. Most building-society interest is credited to accounts, and is thus an increase in shares and deposits just as much as 'net receipts'. The two together, termed 'increase in savings', are the equivalent in banking terms of an increase in deposits.

Table 41. Building societies' flow of funds, 1982 and 1986

| | 1982 | | | 1986 | | |
	£ billion	Percentage of stock	total	£ billion	Percentage of stock	total
Changes in liabilities						
Net receipts	6.5		58.6	6.6		34.9
Interest credited	4.0		36.0	6.1		32.3
Increase in shares and deposits	10.5	18.4	94.6	12.7	12.1	67.2
Wholesale funds, etc.	0.6	8.8	5.4	6.2	37.8	32.8
Total	11.1	17.5	100.0	18.9	15.6	100.0
Changes in assets						
Mortgages	8.1	16.6	73.0	19.1	16.4	101.1
Financial assets, etc.	3.0	20.5	27.0	−0.2	−0.6	−1.1
Total	11.1	17.5	100.0	18.9	15.6	100.0

Note: The liquidity ratio of financial assets to total assets/liabilities fell from 20.5 per cent in 1982 to 16.4 per cent in 1986, seasonally adjusted. Total assets/liabilities grew from £63 billion at end-1981 to £140.2 billion at end-1986, a compound growth rate of 17.2 per cent.
Source: Building Societies Association Press notice, July 1987; *Financial Statistics*, June 1987, tables 7.6, 7.7.

By 1986 the building societies' increase in savings was no longer sufficient to fund the rise in net mortgage lending. One-third of their funds came from non-retail sources, mainly wholesale funds such as certificates of deposit and bond issues. They also ran down their short-term financial assets, so that their net increase in mortgages came to slightly more than the whole rise in their balance-sheet. Their increase in retail savings funded only two-thirds of the net mortgage lending. During the five years to end-1986, their balance-sheets multiplied 2.2 times, and their liquidity ratio had fallen 4 percentage points to 16½ per cent.

In spite of the shortage of retail funds in relation to mortgages, the building societies have been gaining share in the

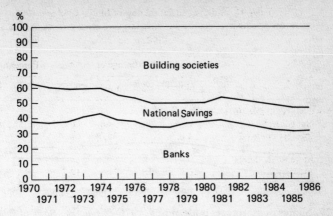

28. Shares in personal-sector liquid assets, 1976–86 (*source: Bank of England Quarterly Bulletin*, May 1987)

market for personal sector liquid deposits for most of the time since 1970, at least until 1986, when closer competition on deposit interest rates helped the monetary sector (banks) to stem the tide (see Figure 28). The banks have tended to lose market share, except at periods of high interest rates, but not as rapidly as National Savings. The building societies' share increase from 38 to 53 per cent has been even more at the expense of National Savings, with a fall from 25 to 15 per cent, than at the expense of the banks, with a fall from 38 to 32 per cent. The banks have, however, won one-sixth of the mortgage market, from only 5 per cent in 1980 (see Figure 29). Their gain has been mainly at the expense of other lenders, notably local authorities, whose share has fallen from 13 to 6 per cent as they have withdrawn from the market, while that of the building societies has fallen from 83 to 77 per cent. The CLSB now publishes monthly figures on housing loans, but without the same detail as those of the building societies.

Bank lending can be studied in more detail from the quarterly analyses of advances published by the CLSB about two weeks after the end of the quarter for the London and

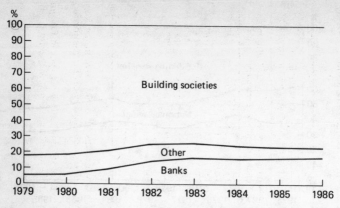

29. Shares of mortgages outstanding, 1979–86 (*source: Bank of England Quarterly Bulletin*, May 1987)

Scottish banks, and by the Bank of England about six weeks after the end of the quarter for all banks. These are divided up according to the standard industrial classification of 1980 (see Figure 2), which was applied to bank advances from November 1983 onwards. It is therefore difficult to compare advances in detail before and after this date. Table 42 shows how they have risen in the three and a half years from November 1983. Bank advances rose by £100 billion in this period, from £114 billion to £214 billion, an annual rate of increase of 20 per cent, or 15 per cent in real terms after allowing for inflation. The share of the London and Scottish banks fell from 61 to 58 per cent, with an annual rate of increase of 18 per cent. This expansion of credit was heavily skewed towards the financial and household sectors. Lending to manufacturing rose at an annual rate of only 9 per cent, and fell from 16 to 11½ per cent of total loans and advances. However, some of the 27 per cent a year increase in lending to financial companies was to the banks' leasing subsidiaries, which fund manufacturing investment (see Table 15). Lending to business services rose even more rapidly, by 37 per cent a year, from 13 to 21 per cent of all loans and advances. The most rapid growth in credit – from November 1986 – was to securities dealers, as a result of the

Table 42. Analysis of loans and advances to UK residents, 1983–7 (sterling and foreign currency): London and Scottish (clearing) banks and all banks in the UK

	November 1983				May 1987				All banks' increase, November 1983 to May 1987 [1]		
	LSB groups		All banks		LSB groups		All banks				
	£ billion	Percentage of all	£ billion	Percentage of total	£ billion	Percentage of all	£ billion	Percentage of total	£ billion	Percentage	Percentage p.a.
1. Agriculture	4.8	93.1	5.1	4.5	5.7	95.8	6.0	2.8	0.8	16.0	4.3
2. Energy and water	1.3	31.9	4.1	3.6	1.7	32.3	5.2	2.5	1.1	26.8	7.0
3. Manufacturing	11.2	60.9	18.3	16.1	15.6	63.1	24.7	11.6	6.4	34.8	8.9
4. Construction	2.9	77.0	3.8	3.7	5.0	77.9	6.4	3.0	2.6	67.0	15.8
5. Services	11.6	61.6	18.9	16.5	16.5	60.8	27.1	12.7	8.2	43.4	10.8
6. Financial	7.0	35.2	19.8	17.3	15.6[2]	33.9	46.1[2]	21.6	26.3	132.9	27.3
7. Business services	8.0	54.8	14.5	12.8	17.9[2]	40.4	44.2[2]	20.7	29.7	204.0	37.4
8. Persons: housing	12.3	87.4	14.0	12.3	24.8	86.6	28.6	13.4	14.6	104.0	22.6
9. Persons: other	10.7	71.1	15.0	13.2	20.4	80.8	25.3	11.8	10.3	68.6	16.1
10. Total	69.7	61.3	113.7	100.0	123.1	57.6	213.6	100.0	99.9	87.9	19.7

1. RPI increase during period: 14.6 per cent, 4.0 per cent p.a.

2. £1.4 billion of advances by LSB groups to securities dealers, and £16.7 billion of such advances by all banks, have in the May 1987 figures been reallocated from business to financial services, but are here still shown under business services for comparison with November 1983.

Note: Total assets of UK banks in May 1987 were £921.1 billion, of which 35 per cent were in sterling and 65 per cent in foreign currency; £422.6 billion were claims on the overseas sector, and £173.5 billion claims on the monetary sector, including inter-bank. Columns do not always sum exactly owing to rounding.

Source: Bank of England and CLSB Press notices.

City 'Big Bang'. Lending to property companies also rose very sharply.

As the footnote to Table 42 shows, advances of loans to UK residents were only 23 per cent of total assets of banks in the UK, including foreign banks in the Euromarkets. Claims on the overseas and inter-bank sectors made up 46 and 19 per cent of the total.

Consumer credit is the subject of a monthly DTI Press notice, *Credit Business*, which appears six weeks after the end of the month covered. From the June 1987 issue, this Press notice was changed so as to widen its coverage, and make it a more useful guide to credit trends. It has also become more comparable with the consumer credit figures published on a quarterly basis in *Financial Statistics*, although there are still superficially puzzling differences (see Table 43). From the end of 1986, the DTI Press notice has begun to include bank loans other than credit cards, thus widening the coverage by over 50 per cent. It has also switched the emphasis from gross new credit advanced to new credit net of repayments, or changes in amounts outstanding. The gross credit figures, which are still given, overstate the level of credit, particularly with regard to bank credit cards, which are often used as a means of payment within the interest-free grace period rather than as a form of credit. Gross advances and monthly figures can be given only for credit cards, finance houses and retailers, because banks do not publish monthly figures, nor do they keep track of gross loans and repayments separately – hardly a feasible procedure when personal overdrafts fluctuate from day to day. The most comprehensive figures, including the banks', are published only on a quarterly basis.

The DTI quarterly figures have since June 1987 become more meaningful than those in *Financial Statistics*, because they classify credit according to the type of institution granting it, rather than the financial sector within which it falls. *Financial Statistics* lumps together all monetary-sector lending to the personal sector, other than credit-card and house-purchase lending, including bank loans and credit granted by finance houses that are in the monetary sector because

Table 43. Consumer credit, 1986

| | Outstanding, end-1986 | | | | Net new credit, first quarter 1987 | |
| | *FS* (nsa) | | *DTI* (sa) | | *FS* (nsa), £ million | *DTI* (sa), £ million |
	£ million	%	£ million	%		
1. Bank loans	18,612	60.7	11,228	36.1	613	212
2. Bank credit cards	5,215	17.0	4,681	15.1	−52	248
3. Credit companies	3,758	12.2	12,151	39.1	180	637
4. Retailers	2,296	7.5	2,231	7.2	2	67
5. Insurance companies	804	2.6	804	2.6	8	8
Total	30,685	100.0	31,095	100.0	751	1,172
					(1,131 sa)	

Note:
FS = *Financial Statistics*, August 1987, table 9.3.
DTI = DTI *Credit Business* in August 1987 Press notice, 3 October 1987, table 2.
nsa = not seasonally adjusted.
sa = seasonally adjusted.
Line 1. FS bank loans are all monetary-sector loans to the personal sector other than for house purchase, including some by finance houses. DTI bank loans are bank loans on personal accounts not exceeding £15,000, other than for house purchase.
Line 3. FS credit companies are those outside the monetary sector. DTI credit companies are finance houses, including those in the monetary sector, other specialist credit grantors and building societies.
Lines 2, 3 and 4. Figures published on a monthly basis in the DTI *Credit Business* Press notice. Lines 1–5 are published on a quarterly basis by the same source. The *Credit Business* Press notice also gives gross new credit advanced for lines 2, 3 and 4, without netting off repayments.

they have the status of authorized banks or licensed deposit-takers. The DTI Press notice separates personal bank loans of under £15,000 from loans by finance houses and other credit companies, whether they are in the monetary sector or not. It may eventually split off from this category consumer loans by building societies, which they were able to start making only in 1986 under the new Act widening their powers. The DTI Press notice also gives seasonal adjustments for each category, while *Financial Statistics* seasonally adjusts only the quarterly total.

Market shares in consumer credit look very different according to which method of classification is chosen. Both agree roughly on the total outstanding, and on the seasonally adjusted quarterly change. They concur in giving credit cards about 16 per cent of the market, retailers about $7\frac{1}{2}$ per cent, and insurance companies about $2\frac{1}{2}$ per cent. *Financial Statistics* gives the monetary sector – banks in the broadest definition – 60 per cent, or 77 per cent including bank credit cards. The DTI gives bank loans only 36 per cent, or just over half including bank credit cards, and finance houses and other credit grantors 39 per cent. The biggest finance houses are in fact subsidiaries of the clearing banks, and are inside the monetary sector, so the *Financial Statistics* definition is helpful on an ownership basis and the DTI on an institutional basis. To put matters in perspective, we note that house-purchase loans at the end of 1986 were £153 billion, or five times consumer credit outstanding. A small proportion of these housing loans were being used to finance consumer spending.

The public sector borrowing requirement (PSBR)

The PSBR figures are published in a monthly CSO/ Treasury Press notice, about two weeks after the end of the month. The PSBR as a concept was first used as recently as 1969. Before that, the central government borrowing requirement (CGBR) was commonly referred to. The

PSBR consolidates the local authority borrowing requirement (LABR) and the public corporations' borrowing requirement (PCBR) with the CGBR on the central government's own account, to show how much the whole public sector is borrowing from outside itself, excluding transactions within the public sector, notably on-lending by the central government to the local authorities and the public corporations.

The PSBR was first calculated on a quarterly basis. Monthly figures exist only from January 1981 and began to be published for calendar months in November 1983, with some changes in definition. Financial markets became confused because often markedly different figures for the monthly PSBR were published for banking months (mid-point to mid-point of calendar months) as one of the counterparts of the money and banking statistics. The move from banking to calendar months for these statistics in October 1986 ended the anomaly. The PSBR figures still suffer from being annualized on the basis of the financial year, from April to March, and are thus difficult to relate to other variables for calendar years. PSBR figures are also published on a calendar-year basis, but they do not have the status of targets as do the financial-year figures.

The PSBR is notoriously difficult to predict or even measure. It is subject to huge month-to-month variations, and frequent subsequent revisions. It is also defined in a peculiar way. All these factors call into question its usefulness as a precise target for the medium-term financial strategy (MTFS).

The PSBR is the difference between two much larger amounts, public expenditure and public revenue. The central government borrowing requirement (CGBR) component is relatively easy to calculate. It is the balances of the Consolidated Fund and of the National Loans Fund kept at the Bank of England by the government, together with a small balance on other government funds. The Consolidated Fund receives mainly tax revenues, and pays out supply expenditures voted by the House of Commons to government departments and local authorities. The National Loans Fund lends to the rest of the public sector, pays interest on the national debt, and receives the interest on its loans. In 1986/7, the revenue of these two funds was £127 billion, and their expenditure £137 billion. The negative balance of about £10 billion was financed by the CGBR of £10.5 billion. A 1 per cent shortfall in revenue and a 1 per cent overrun in expenditure could thus have increased the CGBR by about 25 per cent.

The local-authority and public-corporation components of the PSBR are more difficult to calculate, although the Treasury has improved the accuracy and timeliness of the information which it has to obtain from hundreds of borrowing entities within the public sector. The relationship between the borrowing of the three subsectors of the public sector is shown in Table 44. In 1986/7 the CGBR consisted of £6 billion for on-lending to local authorities and public corporations, and £4.5 billion for the use of central government itself. The on-lending is shown on the same line as a part of the LABR and the PCBR, which cover borrowing both from central government and from the public. In 1986/7 the borrowing of local authorities and public corporations from the public is shown as negative, because they repaid debts to the public, while borrowing from the central government. Central government was thus substituting its own debt in the hands of the public for that of the other parts of the public sector. The PSBR can be expressed either (reading across the page) as the sum of the CGBR for the own use of central government, plus total LABR and PCBR, also for the own use of local authorities and public corporations; or it can be expressed (reading down the right-hand column) as the whole of the CGBR, plus the local authorities' and public corporations' borrowing from, or minus repayment to, the public. The latter concept is somewhat easier to grasp, since it covers simply all borrowing by each part of the public sector from outside the sector.

The PSBR is an unsatisfactory concept, because of the way in which it treats the government's sales of assets in

Table 44. The public-sector borrowing requirement, 1986/7 (£ billion)

Central-government borrowing requirement (CGBR)		Local-authority borrowing requirement (LABR)		Public-corporation borrowing requirement (PCBR)		Public-sector borrowing requirement (PSBR)	
On-lending to local authorities	5.8	From central government	5.8	Repayment to public	−1.6	CGBR	10.5
On-lending to public corporations	0.2	Repayment to public	−5.6	From central government	0.2	Public-corporation repayment to public	−1.6
CGBR for own use	4.5	LABR (for own use)	0.2	PCBR (for own use)	−1.4	Local-authority repayment to public	−5.6
Total CGBR	10.5					PSBR for own use	3.3
						Privatization proceeds	4.4
						Miscellaneous transactions and accruals	2.3
						Public-sector financial deficit	10.0

Note: Percentages of GDP: PSBR 0.9 per cent, PSFD 2.6 per cent. General: government borrowing requirement (GGBR) = CGBR + local-authority repayment to/borrowing from public = 10.5 − 5.6 = 4.9.

Source: CSO/Treasury Press notice; CSO (87)67, 16 July 1987; Financial Statistics, June 1987, table 1.2.

public corporations when they are privatized. These privatization proceeds, amounting to £4.4 billion in 1986/7 from sources such as British Gas, are treated as negative public expenditure. They are therefore subtracted from public expenditure and treated as reducing the PSBR. This results in an underestimation of what is being spent by the public sector. It is not even consistent with the accounts of the Consolidated Fund, where privatization proceeds are treated as a positive revenue item. This is at least more in accord with common sense. As the Treasury Select Committee of the House of Commons has pointed out, it would be better to treat privatization proceeds as financing the PSBR, rather than as reducing it. Otherwise, when they are increasing, a rise in public expenditure is being concealed. This would have given a PSBR of £7.7 billion in 1986/7. The government's indefensible accounting procedure has the sole merit of reducing overt public-sector borrowing to only about 40 per cent of its actual figure, to take the case of 1986/7. It is not even as if financial markets are particularly impressed, since they are generally takers of privatization shares, and could hardly object to their being shown as part of the PSBR to be financed.

The actual financial deficit of the public sector is the difference between its surplus on current account ('above the line') and its deficit on capital account ('below the line'). It does not take account of transactions in financial assets and liabilities, such as privatizations, and may be more or less than the PSBR in any particular year. In 1986/7 it amounted to £10 billion, three times as much as the PSBR, but still only a moderate $2\frac{1}{2}$ per cent of GDP. Many commentators believe that the public-sector financial deficit (PSFD) would be a better measure of the public sector's fiscal stance than the PSBR. However, PSFD figures do not become available until some time after those for the PSBR.

Another unsatisfactory feature of the PSBR is that, unlike the money supply, it is never expressed as a percentage increase in an outstanding stock of debt. The liabilities of the consolidated public sector were £210.7 billion at the end of 1985 – the latest figure published in mid-1987 – so the

PSBR of £2.2 billion in 1986 was an increase of only 1 per cent. The liabilities of the public sector need to be computed on a more up-to-date basis, so that the PSBR can be expressed as a percentage increase in them as soon as it is published. If the PSBR could be presented as a change in a known outstanding stock of debt, then financial strategy could be formulated more easily in terms of a ratio of public debt to national income. Present policies aim to reduce this debt-to-income ratio. Opposition spokesmen have argued that if it were merely held constant, the PSBR could rise to finance faster expansion of the economy.

The PSBR is particularly difficult to assess on a monthly basis in relation to target. The pattern of tax revenues is bunched into the first quarter of the calendar year (the last quarter of the financial year). It is also disrupted from time to time by strikes among tax and rate collectors and post-office workers. This can never be fully allowed for by seasonal adjustment, which is in any case not applied to the monthly Press notice figures. The result is that the PSBR tends to reach an annual peak in the last quarter of the calendar year, and then falls on a cumulative basis, with net repayments of public debt each month. The uneven sequence of privatization adds further volatility to the figures, although this is easy enough to measure once dates and share prices are known.

The year 1986/7 was a remarkable one for the PSBR. The target of £7 billion set in March 1986 looked hard to achieve, given the halving of North Sea oil revenues by the fall in the oil price. By September the PSBR for the first half of the financial year was £5.7 billion, approaching the target for the whole year. However, by February, the cumulative PSBR had fallen back to zero, thanks to £2.6 billion in privatization sales and £3.1 billion in surpluses of revenue over expenditure. Yet the PSBR in the single month of March 1987 was £3.3 billion, which thus became the outcome for the whole year. This was due mainly to a surge of over £2 billion in government spending, as departments rushed to use their allocations before the end of the financial year or risk losing them.

As Table 39 and Figure 27 show, the PSBR's contribution to monetary growth, and thus to short-term interest rate determination, has become minimal. It was much greater, for example, in 1975/6, when the PSBR was nearly 10 per cent of GDP, and one-third of it had to be financed by bank lending to the public sector, which creates monetary deposits on the liabilities side of the banks' balance-sheets.

Interest rates

Interest rates are not published in any Press notice, but daily in the Press itself, and for longer periods in the *Bank of England Quarterly Bulletin* and *Financial Statistics*. The PSBR has become more important as a target of financial policy than the monetary aggregates, but it is less of a help than in previous years in judging the trend of interest rates. Although issues of government debt have gone down with the PSBR, this has not noticeably brought down yields on gilt-edged stocks. These remain under the influence of inflation and exchange-rate expectations, with foreign investors playing an increasingly large part in what has become a global financial market. It is to the short-term money markets that we must look for the main influences on interest rates.

Financial Statistics publishes yields on gilt-edged stocks and company securities. It carries short-term interest rates on Treasury bills, commercial bills, inter-bank loans and deposits, certificates of deposit, and local-authority loans. It shows retail banks' base rates and seven-day deposit rates. For building societies it shows both basic and average rates for mortgages and shares; average rates are over two percentage points higher than basic rates on shares, because of the proliferation of shares at longer maturities and higher rates than the basic. No figures are available, however, for average rates paid by retail banks on deposits, including those at higher than seven-day rates. Nor are there official figures for the spreads above base rates charged by retail banks for different types of loan. These can be discovered from advertisements and specialist publications, but it is difficult

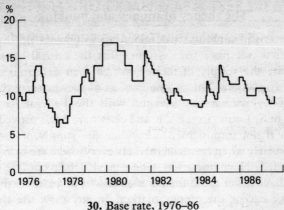

30. Base rate, 1976–86

to use announced rates to work out the average interest charged on various types of lending over periods of time. Such figures would improve understanding of the banking system, but the banks are reluctant to provide them, on grounds of cost of compilation and commercial secrecy.

Figure 30 shows changes in the London clearing banks' base rates over the last ten years. They reached a peak of 17 per cent, which was maintained from November 1979 to July 1980, and a low point of 8.5 per cent, which lasted two months, from mid-March to mid-May 1984. The sharpest ever rise in base rates then occurred, from 9.5 per cent in November 1984 to 14 per cent in January 1985, when the pound fell to just above one dollar. Interest rates invariably come down at around the time of the Budget in March. Indeed, the Budget has generally been worked out so as to achieve the anticipated interest-rate cut. This is perhaps the only time in the year when the PSBR influences interest rates, more by the announcement of an unexpectedly low figure for the year than by the outcome in any particular month. Interest rates then tend to rise in the last quarter of the year, or early in the following year. This is more often the result of pressure on the pound than because of an over-run of monetary targets, on which interest rates, as we have seen, may have a perverse effect.

The theory of money and banking

Monetarism contains two main cross-currents of theory. The first (see page 162) assumes that the central bank can regulate the supply of money, which then determines the rate of inflation. This is one version of the quantity theory of money, which is associated with the Federal Reserve Bank of St Louis. In the UK and elsewhere it has proved difficult, if not impossible, to regulate the supply of money, particularly when financial markets everywhere are being deregulated. The monetarists, who tend also to favour free markets, have never faced the paradox of why all markets should be free except the money market. In any case, the theory that the money supply determines prices has failed most of the tests to which it has been put, except in some developing countries with simple financial and economic systems.

The other main theory is that which sets out to explain the demand for money as a function of real incomes, prices and interest rates. Here the causal chain runs from prices to money rather than from money to prices. The Bank of England sought for many years to discover a stable demand-for-money function, hoping that it could then control the supply of money by determining the demand through interest rates. The demand for money, on any definition, proved to be unstable, for reasons of the kind explained in this chapter. Goodhart's Law (page 166) expressed the despair of the Bank of England at its inability to carry out Mrs Thatcher's orders to keep money under control. Since the authorities had from 1979 renounced prices and incomes policy, they could not regulate the demand for money by limiting increases in inflation and in real national income. Their only weapon was short-term interest rates. By May 1987, the Governor of the Bank of England had to confess in the Mais Lecture: 'Our ability to determine interest rates is limited . . . Our understanding of the precise effects of interest rates on the economy is limited.' The rise in interest rates brought about by the Bank in 1979–80 cut inflation more by raising the exchange rate and plunging the economy into recession than by limiting the rise in £M3.

By the early 1980s, it was the Treasury rather than the

Bank of England which was attempting to build economic models of the demand for money. It was found that, while short-term interest rates could have a perverse effect on the demand for interest-bearing money, the differential between money-market rates and gilt-edged yields could have a beneficial influence. This led to the dead-end of seeking to raise the yield on gilts relative to that on money, and thus reduce the money supply, by overfunding the PSBR (page 169). This was an example of portfolio theory, in which the demand for money was derived almost as the residual element after the demand for other financial assets had been explained by relative interest rates, among other factors. There were two main complications. First, different financial assets, such as bank and building-society deposits, were becoming closer substitutes for each other; financial markets were becoming integrated. Second, financial innovation was spawning new kinds of financial asset, such as banks' high-interest cheque accounts, which could not be studied because they had no track record. Since many of the components of the various monetary aggregates were themselves subject to the twin processes of integration and innovation, a study of recent financial history became a better way of explaining monetary trends than economic theory as applied through econometric modelling.

At one stage the UK authorities hoped that they could contain the demand for money either by controlling the supply of bank lending to the private sector, or at least by acting on the demand for it. When the 'corset' control on bank lending was removed in July 1980, moral suasion by the Bank of England on the clearing banks, backed by rules of 'guidance', proved ineffective. The rules were gradually abandoned, so as to allow the clearing banks a free rein in competing in the personal lending market against rivals who were impervious to central-bank guidance. The banks argued, with some success, that it had been necessary to increase their lending to industry to rescue it from the worst rigours of the 1980–81 recession, and that the free supply of credit to persons and to the service industries was essential to the economic recovery which followed.

The demand for borrowing by industry has been explained by reference to such obvious factors as stockbuilding, capital investment, rising costs of labour and materials inputs, and expansion of the business. As in the case of the demand for money, inflation and real incomes appeared to be determining bank lending, rather than the other way round. As a rule of thumb, it is sometimes assumed that bank lending rises in line with GDP in current-money terms. Table 39 shows that it has been rising very much faster than that. Lending to persons, especially for mortgages, has risen partly in line with the rise in house prices, which has also outpaced GDP. There is also a major increase in activity in the financial-services sector. Both banks and their borrowers have been building up financial assets and liabilities on both sides of their balance-sheets. The amount of credit, like the amount of money, required for each unit of GDP has risen rapidly. To put it a different way, the velocity of money and credit has fallen. GDP was 2.7 times M3 at the end of 1986, compared with 3.3 times four years earlier.

The demand for bank loans, like the demand for money, needs a portfolio approach, in which banks can be seen as one among a number of different sources of finance. When less lending is done by the banks, and more through holdings of commercial bills or commercial paper by non-banks, 'disintermediation' is said to occur, because a bank is no longer acting as intermediary. In recent years the Eurobond and UK equity markets have become as important as traditional bank lending to industry and commerce as sources of finance (see page 71). In spite of this, bank lending has grown rapidly, but to sectors other than the major corporations, who are the main users of alternative sources of finance.

In addition to theories about the financial system as a whole, there are theories to explain the behaviour of particular types of institution, such as banks or building societies. Such theories build in supervisory constraints, such as capital and liquidity ratios, and assume that financial institutions seek to maximize profits by widening the margin between interest income and interest expense. They can help to explain how it is that banks in the UK have been able to increase lending so much faster than deposits, notably by reducing holdings of public debt, drawing in funds from abroad, and increasing capital, or liabilities other than monetary deposits.

The PSBR can best be studied by looking at the two much larger magnitudes between which it is the difference: tax revenue and public expenditure. Tax revenue generally rises faster than GDP; in other words it has an elasticity of more than one. The exact value of the elasticity differs from one tax to another, as the Institute for Fiscal Studies has pointed out. Even if the elasticities are known, tax revenue cannot be precisely predicted, because the income components of GDP, notably pay and profits, can be forecast even less reliably than current-money GDP itself. In 1986/7, the Treasury secured a windfall gain by having underpredicted tax revenue. The Treasury can itself influence tax revenue by raising or lowering tax rates, but this can normally be done only once a year, in the Finance Bill, and the results of such changes can be unpredictable (because tax changes lead to changes in economic behaviour).

Public expenditure, unlike taxation, tends if anything to rise more slowly as GDP rises faster, and vice versa. Rapid GDP growth reduces unemployment, and the enormous social-security costs entailed by it. On the other hand, if personal incomes are rising, people may expect higher standards of public health and education to keep pace with their standard of private consumption. Public expenditure, according to the present government, should, however, be determined by revenue, rather than by the public's demand for it. Mrs Thatcher's original aim was to reduce or at least stabilize public expenditure in real terms. This has been modified to reducing it as a proportion of GDP. It can rise in real terms, but more slowly than GDP. Such an aim can be achieved if economic growth is fairly rapid, even if it means that public-expenditure targets are exceeded. Thus GDP can rise by 3 per cent in real terms, and public expenditure by 2 per cent, with a target increase of 1 per cent.

In the absence of government action, the combined effect

of taxation and public-expenditure trends is that the PSBR tends to fall when GDP is rising rapidly, and to rise when GDP is increasing slowly or falling, thanks to the so-called 'automatic stabilizers'. Governments are sometimes tempted to take discretionary action to override the stabilizers. Thus in 1982/3, when the recovery had hardly begun, the government increased taxation so as to cut the PSBR. In 1987/8, there is a temptation to cut taxes and increase public expenditure because the strength of the recovery is tending to reduce the PSBR to vanishing-point. Such measures are pro-cyclical, in that they tend to exaggerate the fluctuations of the economic cycle, rather than damping them down by allowing the counter-cyclical mechanism of the automatic stabilizers to take its course.

The Thatcher government has departed from tradition by seeking steadily to reduce the PSBR, like public expenditure and taxation, as a proportion of GDP, as part of the MTFS to curb inflation (see page 163). The PSBR has been reduced because taxation has risen or remained static as a proportion of GDP, while public expenditure has fallen, thanks mainly to the economic recovery. The reduction in tax rates should not be confused with a cut in the burden of taxation, because taxpayers pay tax on a higher proportion of their incomes as real incomes rise – whether they are persons or corporations.

Private and public sector finance cannot be seen in isolation from each other. The Thatcher government's MTFS has been a story of public restraint and private freedom, leading in the real economy to what J. K. Galbraith condemned in the 1950s as 'private affluence and public squalor'. This is the real-world counterpart of the statistical linkages between money, bank lending and public borrowing.

Conclusions

> 'Economists are like boring bedroom scenes on television.
> The only way to rid ourselves of them is to switch
> them off – but we don't because there is always the
> faint chance that we might miss something good.'
> Councillor T. Geraghty, Letters to the Editor, *Financial Times*, 22 August 1987

Some of the points made in each chapter are summarized
here, followed by some concluding remarks arising out of
the book.

Introduction

The economic and financial statistics which the government
releases to the Press are often difficult to interpret. They
can have a big influence on business expectations and on
financial markets. Government departments have the power
to control official statistics, which is sometimes used for political
ends. When a statistic becomes a political objective, there
is a temptation to change its definition so as to make the
objective easier to achieve. This could be avoided if the Central
Statistical Office was given more independence within
Whitehall, and more centralized authority over statistics.

1 Economic growth

There are three different ways of measuring economic
growth, by output, income, and expenditure, which should

give identical results, but do not do so in practice. This makes nominal GDP a poor instrument of government economic policy. Since 1945, each political party's period of office has been marked by a lower rate of economic growth than in the preceding period. The lowest rate of growth, 1.4 per cent, has been during the Conservative period of office since 1979. This rises to 2.7 per cent only if the 1980–81 recession is omitted.

Manufacturing output was at an all-time peak in 1973. It peaked again in 1979, 5 per cent below the 1973 peak. After the 1980–81 recession, manufacturing output took until 1987 to reach the 1979 level, and was still below the 1973 level.

2 Personal income and saving

Discretionary saving by households is only just over 2 per cent of their disposable income. The much higher personal sector saving ratio is misleading, because it includes saving through life insurance and pension funds, unincorporated businesses and private non-profit-making bodies. Consumer spending has for some years been rising faster than post-tax incomes, and retail sales even faster, as the saving ratio has fallen as inflation has come down.

Higher interest rates appear to increase the savings ratio because people substitute financial assets for consumer goods.

3 Industry and commerce

The profits of non-North Sea industrial and commercial companies rose by 15 per cent a year in real terms in 1983–6, so their share of GDP increased. The profits of North Sea oil companies have moved in the opposite direction, rising sharply in the 1980–81 recession, and slumping in 1986.

Industrial and commercial companies have been in financial surplus in the 1980s, but have still had to borrow to finance take-overs and overseas investment. They have come to rely less on bank loans, and more on equity and Eurobond issues.

Fixed capital expenditure is highly cyclical, and has risen by only 1 per cent a year in real terms in 1980–86. The stockbuilding cycle contributed to both the recession and the recovery in the early 1980s, but stocks are tending to fall in relation to output over the years.

4 Labour statistics

The UK official definition of unemployment is based on the number of benefit claimants, and differs substantially from the UK Labour Force Survey definition of unemployment. If the two definitions are merged, unemployment is shown to be 800,000 higher than the official definition in 1986, reaching 4 million in that year.

The UK unemployment figures have been reduced by over 400,000 by a series of statistical redefinitions, and by nearly 400,000 by special job-creation measures. While the statistical changes can be justified on grounds of accuracy, there may also have been political motives at work.

Earnings in manufacturing rose by 9 per cent a year in 1982–6, but productivity rose by 5 per cent a year, so unit-labour-cost increases were only 4 per cent. But productivity growth (including the 1980–81 recession) was only $3\frac{1}{2}$ per cent a year up to 1986 in manufacturing, and only $1\frac{1}{4}$ per cent a year in the much larger services sector.

5 Inflation

The Retail Prices Index was brought up to date in 1987, but the opportunity was missed to remove mortgage costs, which cause it to be unnecessarily volatile because of interest-rate movements.

Prices, as measured by the RPI, have multiplied by ten since 1950, by five since 1970, and by two since 1978. Zero inflation has come to have a low priority among even the present government's objectives.

The Tax and Price Index has been rising more slowly than the RPI in recent years, because it allows for income-tax cuts. However, the government has failed to promote its use in pay bargaining.

6 The balance of payments

The UK has always had a deficit in non-oil primary products and a surplus in invisible income from abroad. In the 1970s, there was still a surplus in manufacturing. In the early 1980s, the traditional oil deficit turned into surplus, giving a large surplus on the current account as a whole. During the 1980s, manufacturing has moved into deficit, and the oil surplus has shrunk, so that the current account has moved into deficit.

The UK balance of payments could be healthier than is shown by the figures, because of unrecorded items. The invisibles account is unreliable, and constantly being revised, and the capital outflow has been larger than can be explained by the published current-account position.

Both exports and imports have increased faster than GDP, and export prices have tended to rise faster than import prices. But exports and imports of services have risen less rapidly than those of goods. The good performance of the City of London has been offset by the decline of the shipping industry.

7 Money, banking and finance

The government has seldom been able to achieve its monetary targets, in spite of periodically changing the definition of the monetary aggregates and raising the target numbers.

Monetarism has been replaced by fiscalism, and the monetary targets by the exchange rate and the public sector borrowing requirement (PSBR) as instruments of government policy. Privatization has greatly reduced the size of the PSBR, because of its debatable statistical treatment, and the objective of a low PSBR has thus been rather easily achieved.

Private sector borrowing has risen even faster than public sector borrowing has fallen. Free competition in lending between banks and building societies, and financial innovation in the City, have rendered monetary control impossible. The monetary authorities admit that they have limited power over interest rates, and limited understanding of their effects on the economy.

Concluding remarks

Increasing weight is being placed on economic indicators, by financial markets, by the Press, and by politicians. They have the advantage that they provide monthly or quarterly snapshots of continuous processes of change which may be too imperceptible or too tedious to observe day by day. The danger is that the balance of payments, for example, becomes a 'story', to be dramatized if possible, on a particular day in each month, and is of little interest at other times. This gives the financial markets a spasmodic and feverish character, particularly since there is often a high degree of consensus as to which direction they should move in in response to a given divergence between the actual and the expected value of an indicator. Matters are not much improved when, in a week bereft of important indicators, unimportant ones are blown up in significance in order to provide some movement in asset prices from which market-makers stand to benefit thanks to higher turnover.

It is fruitless to remind the users of indicators how inaccurate, approximate and subject to later revision many of them are. They are usually the best estimate that can be made at the time. In any case, month-to-month changes are often greater than the alterations made to earlier figures as later data become available. So even if greater accuracy and precision could be achieved, it would in many instances make little difference. It is arguable that some indicators are wide of the mark not because they are not being measured expertly enough, but because they have been wrongly defined; unemployment is one example (see Chapter 4). A change in the definition of an indicator could thus make more of an impact on the reactions to it than any improvement in data collection. The government has, for example, damped down the effect of the monetary indicators by persuading the markets to pay as much attention to M0 as to M3 (see Chapter 7).

There is always a time-lag between the occurrence of the phenomenon to which an indicator refers and the date at which the figures on it are published. The exceptions are market prices such as interest rates and exchange rates; they have the double merit of being open to immediate inspection, and not requiring the time and expense of subsequent data collection and collation by official statisticians. In other cases, indicators are subject to the 'double-take'. For example, the bad trade figures for one month are published during the next month, when the trade figures may be good – but observers will discover this only in the following month. A manic-depressive reaction cycle can be avoided either by attempting to forecast the current month's figures while interpreting the previous month's, or by averaging out the last three months' figures. The latter procedure is used by the official statisticians for volatile series such as the trade figures. It is possible to imagine, but would be expensive to implement, a system of real-time statistical measurement; the value of goods going through the Customs would be fed into a computer as they went through, and the total could be read day by day like a tape of stock-exchange dealings.

In practice, it is becoming harder all the time to carry out accurate statistical measurements, just as more importance is being attached to them. The first reason is that deregulation of economic activity removes the direct access which officials have to the private sector's figures in a more controlled system; the removal of exchange control in 1979 is a case in point, because it made it more difficult to measure cross-frontier capital movements. The right not to fill in statistical returns is in itself a form of deregulation. Many smaller companies, and all those operating in Enterprise Zones, have been absolved from doing so. Freedom of a kind has been obtained at the cost of statistical accuracy. At the limit, an economy free from any taint of interference by official statisticians might achieve a record rate of growth without ever being able to find out that it had done so. (People's subjective impressions of rates of growth and inflation, revealed by public-opinion polls, are notoriously inaccurate.)

The second reason why it is harder to measure indicators accurately is economic and financial innovation. Privatization is continuously changing the boundaries between the public and private sectors. The concept of the public-sector borrowing requirement may not change, but the reality to which it refers changes. (Since privatized companies tend to be those which repay debt, the shrinkage of the public sector expands the PSBR.) Similarly, the size of the industrial and commercial company sector is growing, making it more difficult to measure its profits (see Chapter 3). The constant changes among the monetary indicators are also a reflection of the rapid pace of innovation in banking (see Chapter 7).

It is becoming more difficult to know whether a trend in an economic indicator is a true sign that what is being measured is rising or falling, or the result of a change in behaviour due to either the start-up of a new form of private enterprise, or the opening of a once forbidden field by the public authorities. Innovation may itself be one form of deregulation. For example, commercial paper in the City, which was permitted in 1986, was an innovation in the sense that it had previously been banned, but it did not have to be invented, since it had flourished for years in the USA.

Government economic policy, far from playing down the importance of the economic indicators in view of such limitations, has tended to emphasize it. Although the Thatcher government has never believed in planning objectives, in the sense of precise targets, it has become more and more committed to maximizing such indicators as economic growth and company profits, and to minimizing, for example, money stock, public borrowing, and unemployment. The economic indicators have become performance criteria by which the government's record of economic management is judged. As a general election approaches, they take on an extra dimension, and become political indicators of whether the government is likely to be re-elected, which in turn feed back into such financial variables as the exchange rate and stock-market prices.

Politicians, whether in government or in opposition, have become adept at extolling indicators when it suits their case, and rubbishing them when they do not. When the unemployment figures rise, the Conservatives explain how much they are spending on benefits, and how fast productivity is rising for those in jobs, while Labour points to the human misery and waste of economic resources. When the unemployment figures fall, the Conservatives claim the credit for their wise expansionary policies, while Labour casts doubt on the accuracy of the figures by reminders of how many people in need of jobs are not defined as unemployed, and not receiving benefit. All these arguments have some validity. Fortunately, uncommitted economic commentators can steer a middle course in their interpretations. Unfortunately, they are often obliged to pronounce on how financial markets will react, rightly or wrongly, to the figures, rather than on how they should be reacting, if only they understood them properly.

Sometimes the very existence of an economic indicator, or the decision to make it the subject of a Press notice, reflects some theory of official economic policy. The budget deficit – later to be known as the PSBR – became important in the heyday of Keynesian theories after the Second World War. The monetary aggregates hardly existed before the 1960s, and proliferated into prominence only in the mid-1970s, with the rise of monetarism. One indicator, domestic credit expansion, was used in the UK only because the IMF insisted on it as a performance criterion when making loans to the UK in the late 1960s and mid-1970s. Once the markets have 'bought' an indicator as a result of official espousal of it, it may be difficult to wean them off it on to an alternative. One way of reducing the market effects of indicators would be to issue them after the close of the London markets – but markets in other time zones would be open – or at weekends. This would at least give time for economists to provide market-makers with more mature interpretations.

The British government has sometimes defined or redefined indicators to suit its book. Unemployment, monetary aggregates and public-sector borrowing are examples of those which have been manipulated for political reasons. There are mitigating factors. No British government manipulates statistics to the extent that some foreign governments have done – even democratic governments of industrial countries. The manipulations are generally backed by respectable academic statistical arguments, even if such arguments can also be advanced against them. Nor have financial markets been excessively concerned with the definition of indicators. Because their horizons are so short-term, they easily forget that unemployment was differently defined five years ago. Because they prefer good news to bad, they readily accept a minimalist concept of public borrowing such as the PSBR rather than craving a wider indicator such as the public-sector financial deficit, which might suddenly make it look as if the government was borrowing three times the number first thought of.

The ultimate mitigation of the charge that the government manipulates statistics is that it has so consistently failed to carry out a number of obvious manipulations for which there is an overwhelmingly sound case. For example, the opportunity has been missed to revise all the latest economic-growth figures upwards by $\frac{3}{4}$ per cent (see page 34), to improve the current account of the balance of payments by £2 billion a year (see page 155), and to iron out the fluctuations in the inflation rate caused by the inclusion of mortgage costs (see page 118). Politicians are amateurs in the art of manipulating statistics, and official statisticians do not see it as their role to show them how they could present the figures in a more favourable light. For example, few attempts have been made by anyone in government to show why monthly trade deficits of a few hundred million pounds – even if they were not exaggerated – would not be any particular cause for concern, given the UK's huge surplus of foreign assets over liabilities.

In a democratic society, everyone has access to statistics. There are hardly any leaks of economic indicators before publication, and no one has become rich by insider trading based on foreknowledge of them. The wider diffusion of Press notices by facsimile would, however, dilute some of the advantage now accruing to those within messenger distance of Whitehall. This apart, anyone who has read this book should be able to derive some enlightenment from a study of Press notices of economic indicators and the statistical publications which incorporate them. A do-it-yourself approach is the best antidote to the danger of being carried away by the epidemics of misinterpretation which are caused by over-hasty over-reaction to official statistics. Anyone who can grasp the changing monthly and quarterly trends is well on the way to understanding the working of the economy, and fleshing out their theories with reality, warts and all.

Appendix: Main official macro-economic Press notices and publication days

Monthly. Monthly Press notices appear during the month after that covered, except where stated otherwise.

Chapter	Title	Issuing department	Month and week of publication
6	UK official reserves	HMT	2nd working day (ex-Friday)
3	Capital issues and redemptions	BoE	2nd working day (ex-Friday)
7	Credit business	DTI	1st or 2nd Monday, following month
5	Producer prices	DTI	2nd Friday
5	Retail Prices Index	DE	2nd or 3rd Friday
5	Tax and Price Index	CSO	2nd or 3rd Friday
1	Output of the production industries	CSO	13th–19th, following month
1	Retail sales [1]	DTI	3rd Monday
7	Public sector borrowing requirement	HMT/CSO	16th–19th
4	Labour market statistics	DE	2nd or 3rd Thursday
7	Monetary aggregates [2]	BoE	18th–22nd
7	Building societies	BSA	12th–22nd
1	Cyclical indicators	CSO	15th–23rd
6	Balance of payments	DTI/CSO	23rd–31st

Quarterly. Quarterly Press notices appear during the quarter after that covered, except where stated otherwise.

Chapter	Title	Issuing department	Month and week of publication
2	Institutional investment	BoE	Jan., Apr., July, Oct., third, following quarter
2	Consumers' expenditure	CSO	Jan., Apr., July, Oct., fourth
1	GDP (output-based)	CSO	Feb., May, Aug., Nov., third
3	Capital expenditure [3]	DTI	Feb., May, Aug., Nov., third
3	Stocks [4]	DTI	Same day as above
6	Balance of payments	CSO	Mar., June, Sept., Dec., first
7	Analysis of bank lending	BoE	Mar., June, Sept., Dec., second [5]
1	GDP	CSO	Mar., June, Sept., Dec., third
2	Personal income, expenditure and saving	CSO	Mar., June, Sept., fourth [6]
3	Industrial and commercial companies	CSO	Mar., June, Sept., fourth [6]

Occasional

3	Investment intentions	DTI	June, Dec., first half
6	Overseas earnings of City	CSO	July, end of month

1. Provisional: a final notice is published two or three weeks later. 2. Provisional: a final notice is published nine to thirteen days later. The monthly statement of the London and Scottish Banks is published on the same day by the Banking Information Service. 3. Provisional: a revised notice is published four weeks later. 4. Provisional: a revised notice is published five weeks later. 5. The quarters covered end in February, May, August and November. 6. The fourth publication date is the first week in January rather than the fourth week in December.

References

Note. The time-period given after each Press notice is the time between the end of the period covered and the date of publication.

Introduction

General

Financial Statistics Conference Proceedings, Statistics Users Council/Bank of England, (1) November 1977, (2) November 1985.

Financial Statistics Explanatory Handbook, 1987 edn, CSO/HMSO, February 1987.

Government Statistical Services, HMSO, April 1981 (Cmnd 8236).

Guide to Official Statistics, no. 5, 1986 (HMSO).

Harris, Anthony, 'Putting the headlines in perspective', *Financial Times*, 25 July 1987.

Rayner, Sir Derek, *Review of Government Statistical Services*: pt 1, *Report on the Central Statistical Office*; pt 2, *Report to the Prime Minister*, CSO, October and December 1980.

United Kingdom National Accounts: Sources and Methods, 3rd edn, CSO/HMSO, 1985.

Statistical

Annual Abstract of Statistics, HMSO.

Bank of England Quarterly Bulletin, Bank of England.

The British Economy, Key Statistics 1900–1966, Times Newspapers, 1968.

Economic Progress Report, HM Treasury. Monthly.

Economic Trends, H M S O. Monthly and annual supplement.

Feinstein, C. H., *Statistical Tables of National Income, Expenditure and Output of the U K, 1855–1965*, Cambridge University Press, 1972.

Financial Statistics, H M S O. Monthly.

Monthly Digest of Statistics, H M S O.

Release Dates of Economic Statistics, C S O. Monthly.

U K National Accounts, H M S O. Annual.

Chapter 1. Economic Growth

Press Notices (all from C S O)

Cyclical Indicators of the U K Economy. Monthly. Seven weeks.

Gross Domestic Product (output-based). Quarterly. Seven weeks.

Gross Domestic Product. Quarterly. Twelve weeks.

Index of Output of the Production Industries. Monthly. Seven weeks.

General

C S O, 'Introduction of the revised standard industrial classification 1980', *Economic Trends*, March 1983.

Industry Statistics, C S O, March 1987 (Occasional paper no. 20, 2nd edn).

Kavanagh, T. J., and Clary, M. J., 'The effects of rebasing on the estimates of gross domestic product', *Economic Trends*, December 1983.

Kenny, P. B., 'Revisions to quarterly estimates of G D P', *Economic Trends*, July 1985, August 1987.

Lloyds Bank Economic Bulletin, nos. 35, 38, 51, 96, 100.

Lockyer, M. J. G., 'Rebasing and reclassifying the national accounts: the reasons and the likely effects', *Economic Trends*, March 1983.

Lomas, Eric, 'Cyclical indicators: some developments and an assessment of performance', *Economic Trends*, November 1983.

Macafee, Kerrick, 'A glimpse of the hidden economy in the national accounts', *Economic Trends*, February 1980.

Melliss, C. L., *H M Treasury Macroeconomic Model 1986*, 1986 (Treasury working paper no. 43).

Output Measures, C S O, October 1983 (Occasional paper no. 16 (revised)).

Perry, John, 'Index of Industrial Production – rebasing and reclassification', *Economic Trends*, March 1983.
Perry, John, 'The rebased estimates of the output of the production industries', *Economic Trends*, November 1983.

Statistical

Economic Trends, tables 6, 8, 26, 28, 68–71. Special section January, April, July and October.
Monthly Digest of Statistics, tables 1.1, 1.2, 1.3, 7.1.
UK National Accounts, sections 1, 2, 3.

Chapter 2. Personal Income and Saving

Press Notices

CSO:
Personal Income and Expenditure. Quarterly. Twelve weeks.
Preliminary Estimate of Consumers' Expenditure. Quarterly. Four weeks.

DTI:
Retail Sales: Provisional Estimate. Monthly. Two weeks.
Retail Sales. Monthly. Five weeks.

Bank of England:
Institutional Investment. Quarterly. Fifteen weeks.

Confederation of British Industry:
Distributive Trades Survey. Monthly. Four weeks.

General

Davis, E. P., *A Recursive Model of Personal Sector Expenditure and Accumulation*, February 1984 (Bank of England discussion paper no. 6).
Friedman, M., *A Theory of the Consumption Function*, Princeton University Press, 1957.
Jones, Tim, 'A note on the personal sector saving ratio', *Economic Trends*, September 1984.
Keynes, J. M., *The General Theory of Employment, Interest and Money*, Macmillan, 1936.

Lloyds Bank Economic Bulletin, nos. 54, 71.
Pareto, V., *Manuale d'economia politica*, 1906.
Ramsey, Frank, 'On saving', *Economic Journal*, 1927.

Statistical

Economic Trends, tables 10, 12, 14.
Financial Statistics, section 9.
Monthly Digest of Statistics, tables 1.5, 14.1, 14.2.
UK National Accounts, section 4.

Chapter 3. Industry and Commerce

Press Notices

CSO:
Industrial and Commercial Companies. Quarterly. Thirteen weeks.

DTI:
Capital Expenditure (Provisional). Quarterly. Seven weeks.
Capital Expenditure (Revised). Quarterly. Eleven weeks.
Industry's Investment Intentions. Twice yearly. June and December.
Stockbuilding. Quarterly. Twelve weeks.

Bank of England:
Capital Issues and Redemptions in the UK. Monthly. Six days.

General

'Company profitability and finance', *Bank of England Quarterly Bulletin*. Annual article (latest in) August 1987.
'Estimating companies' rate of return on capital employed', *Economic Trends*, November 1974.
'Financial balances of industrial and commercial companies', *Economic Trends*, December 1978.
Lloyds Bank Economic Bulletin, nos. 33, 61, 78, 91, 104.
'The rate of return', *British Business*, 10 October 1986.
Twenty-five Years of 'Ups' and 'Downs', Confederation of British Industry, October 1983.

Statistical

Business Monitor MA3, Business Statistics Office. Annual.
Economic Trends, tables 16, 18, 22, 60, 62.
Financial Statistics, section 8.
Monthly Digest of Statistics, tables 1.7–1.9.
UK National Accounts, section 5.

Chapter 4. Labour Statistics

Press Notices (Department of Employment)

Labour Market Statistics. Monthly. Two weeks.

General

Employment Gazette (Department of Employment):
'Underlying movements in the average earnings index', April 1981.
'Payment of benefits to unemployed people', April 1981.
'Compilation of the unemployment statistics', September 1982.
'Revised employment estimates', July 1984.
'Unemployment adjusted for discontinuities and seasonality', July 1985.
'Changes in average earnings', June 1986.
'Changes affecting the unemployment count', October 1986.
'1984 Census of Employment and revised employment estimates', January 1987.
'Unemployment benefit – the availability for work condition', March 1987.
'Preliminary results of the 1986 Labour Force Survey', April 1987.
'Labour force outlook for Great Britain', May 1987.

Unemployment Unit:
'The jobs gap: measuring hidden unemployment', *Unemployment Unit Briefing*, no. 10, March 1986.
Unemployment Bulletin: issue 20, summer 1986, 'Seventeen statistical sleights'; issue 23, spring 1987, 'Forceful arguments' (by David Taylor).

Centre for Labour Economics, London School of Economics, Discussion paper series.

'Declining unemployment: a statistical illusion?' *Charter for Jobs Economic Report*, vol. 2, no. 7, May 1987.

'Employment in the public and private sectors 1980–86', *Economic Trends*, December 1986.

Employment Institute, Pamphlet series.

'High-tech campaign over fraud hopes to save £50m', *The Times*, September 1987.

'How to fix unemployment rates', *Economist*, 27 June 1987.

Shields, J., 'The official figures which conceal more than they reveal', *Independent*, 16 July 1987.

Trade Union Research Unit, 'A million new jobs since 1983?' *Labour Market Issues*, no. 8, February 1987.

Wood, J. B., *How Little Unemployment*, Institute of Economic Affairs, 1975 (Hobart paper 65).

Lloyds Bank Economic Bulletin, nos. 27, 77, 86, 97.

Lloyds Bank Review:

'North Sea oil – a chance to tackle unemployment' (by D. Basnett), October 1978.

'Unemployment in the 1980's' (by M. Timbrell), April 1980.

'Long term recovery: a return to full employment' (by T. Barker), January 1982.

'A new Keynesian approach to full employment' (by J. Meade), October 1983.

'The UK labour market: Equilibrium or disequilibrium?' (by S. Hall, S. G. B. Henry, A. Markandya and M. Pemberton), July 1987.

Statistical

Economic Trends, tables 34, 36, 38, 40.

Employment Gazette. Labour market data. Historical supplement no. 1, February 1987, *Employment Statistics*.

Monthly Digest of Statistics, section 3.

Chapter 5. Inflation

Press Notices

Index of Retail Prices. Department of Employment. Monthly. Two weeks.

Producer Prices. D T I. Monthly. Two weeks.
Tax and Price Index. C S O. Monthly. Two weeks.

General

Barnett, John, *A History of the Cost of Living*, Penguin Books, 1969.

Beckerman, W., 'How the battle against inflation was really won', *Lloyds Bank Review*, January 1985.

Employment Gazette: 'Retail prices in 1986', March 1987. 'Retail prices index: revision of weights', April 1987. 'A short guide to the retail prices index', August 1987.

Fry, Vanessa, and Pashardes, Panos, *The RPI and the Cost of Living*, Institute for Fiscal Studies, 1986.

Kay, J. A., and Morris, C. N., 'Adjusting price indices for tax changes', *Fiscal Studies*, vol. 1, no. 1, November 1979.

Lloyds Bank Economic Bulletin, nos. 8, 24, 37, 86, 103.

Marris, R., 'Does Britain really have a wages problem?', *Lloyds Bank Review*, April 1987.

Methodological Issues Affecting the RPI, Retail Prices Index Advisory Committee, H M S O, July 1986 (Cmnd 9848).

'Purge R P I of mortgage costs', *Lloyds Bank Economic Bulletin*, July 1987.

'Retail and consumer prices: an explanatory note', *National Institute Economic Review*, no. 94, November 1980.

'The tax and price index – sources and methods', *Economic Trends*, August 1979.

'Wholesale price index to be rebased', *British Business*, 15–21 April 1983.

Statistical

Economic Trends, tables 5, 42.

Employment Gazette, tables 6.1–6.7.

Family Expenditure Survey (annual), Department of Employment, H M S O.

Monthly Digest of Statistics, tables 18.1–18.6.

United Kingdom National Accounts, 1986, table 1.16.

Chapter 6. The Balance of Payments

Press Notices

The Current Account of the Balance of Payments. D T I. Monthly. Four weeks. With standard notes.
The Reserves. H M Treasury. Monthly. Two days.
UK Balance of Payments. CSO. Quarterly. Nine weeks.
UK Balance of Payments: Overseas Earnings of the City. CSO. Annual (July).

General

Bank of England:
Trade in Manufactures (by A. C. Hotson and K. L. Gardiner) (Discussion paper no. 5).
'Services in the UK economy', *Quarterly Bulletin*. September 1985.

Treasury working papers:
30. *Measuring Import Penetration in the UK* (by Hugh Bredenkamp), June 1984.
41. *Modelling imports of manufactures* (by Richard Gleed), May 1986.

Economic Trends, February 1981:
'Exports and imports of services analysed by industry' (by Alwyn Pritchard).
'Seasonal adjustment of the overseas trade figures' (by David Ellis Williams).

Lloyds Bank Economic Bulletin, nos. 69, 82, 85.

Brech, Michael, and Sharp, Margaret, *Inward Investment: Policy Options for the UK*, Royal Institute of International Affairs, 1983.
Congdon, Tim, 'A new approach to the balance of payments', *Lloyds Bank Review*, October 1982.
Cuthbertson, Keith, 'The behaviour of UK imports of manufactured goods', *National Institute Economic Review*, no. 113, August 1985.

Leake, Andrew, *International Trade*, Economist, 1985.

'Rebasing the visible trade figures', *British Business*, 23 September 1983.

Report from the Select Committee on Overseas Trade, House of Lords, session 1984–5, HMSO, 30 July 1985 (HL 238).

Report on the World Current Account Discrepancy, International Monetary Fund, 1987.

UK National Study of Trade in Services, DTI, May 1984.

Statistical

Bank of England Quarterly Bulletin, statistical annex, sections 14–18, 'External balance sheet of the UK', annual article, September or August issue.

British Council for Invisible Exports. *Annual Report*.

Economic Trends, tables 46, 48, 50, and quarterly balance-of-payments article in March, June, September and December issues.

Financial Statistics, section 10, and tables 13.1–13.3.

Monthly Review of External Trade Statistics, and *Annual Supplement*. DTI.

The Overseas Trade Statistics of the United Kingdom. CSO. Monthly.

Overseas Transactions. Business Monitor MA4. Business Statistics Office.

The United Kingdom Balance of Payments (Pink Book). CSO Annual.

Chapter 7. Money, Banking and Finance

Press Notices

Bank of England:

Provisional Estimates of Monetary Aggregates. Monthly. Three weeks.

Monetary Aggregates and Banking Statistics. Monthly. Four weeks.

Analysis of Bank Lending to UK Residents. Quarterly. Six weeks.

Institutional Investment. Quarterly. Fifteen weeks.

Capital Issues and Redemptions. Monthly. One week.

Committee of London and Scottish Bankers:
Monthly Statement of the London and Scottish Bankers (with Balances). Monthly. Three weeks.
Analysis of Advances to UK Residents by the London and Scottish Banks. Quarterly. Three weeks.
House Purchase Finance. Quarterly. Four weeks.

Building Societies Association:
Building Societies Monthly Figures. Monthly. Two weeks.

DTI:
Credit Business. Monthly. Six weeks.

CSO/Treasury:
Public Sector Borrowing Requirement. Monthly. Two weeks.

General

Treasury Working Papers:
18. *The Role of Money in Determining Prices: A Reduced Form Approach* (by Simon Wren-Lewis), March 1981.
20. *The Demand for Sterling M3 and Other Aggregates in the UK* (by Joe Grice and Adam Bennett), August 1981.
28. *The Demand for Non-interest-bearing Money in the UK* (by R. B. Johnston), February 1984.

Economic Trends:
'Measuring the public sector borrowing requirement' (by John Alexander and Susan Toland), CSO, no. 322, August 1980.
'Monthly estimates of the public sector borrowing requirement' (by Paul Luke), CSO, no. 361, November 1983.

The Treasury:
Financial Statement and Budget Report ('Red Book'). Annual. March.
The Government's Expenditure Plans. Annual, 2 vols. (*1987–88 to 1989–90*, January 1987: Cm 56.)
The Government's Expenditure Plans. Annual. Report from the Treasury and Civil Service Committee. (*1987–88 to 1989–90*, February 1987: HC 153.)

The Next Ten Years: Public Expenditure and Taxation into the 1990s, March 1984. (Cmnd 9189.)

Building Societies: A New Framework, July 1984. (Cmnd 9316.)

Bank of England:

Competition and Credit Control, 1975.

Bank Lending, Monetary Control and Funding Policy (by A. D. Bain), July 1982 (Panel paper no. 19).

Composite Monetary Indicators for the U K (by T. C. Mills), May 1983 (Discussion paper no. 3).

Monetary Trends in the UK (by A. J. Brown, D. F. Hendry and N. R. Ericsson), October 1983 (Panel paper no. 22).

The Development and Operation of Monetary Policy 1960–1983, Oxford, 1984.

A Model of the Building Society Sector (by J. B. Wilcox), August 1985 (Discussion paper no. 23).

'Changes in the banking and monetary system – the statistical response' (by P. Bull), paper to Financial Statistics Conference, 13 November 1985.

Bank of England Quarterly Bulletin:

'Purposes of banking statistics', September 1981.

'Money and banking figures: forthcoming changes', December 1981.

'Transactions balance – new monetary aggregate', June 1982.

'Monetary statistics', December 1982.

'Review of banking statistics', March 1983.

'Funding the public sector borrowing requirement: 1952–83', December 1984.

'Financial change and broad money', December 1986.

'Measures of broad money', May 1987.

'The instruments of monetary policy', August 1987.

'Building societies: a changing role', August 1987.

Lloyds Bank Review:

'A new view of money', (by R. Coghlan), July 1978.

'Managing the money supply' (by R. Coghlan and C. Sykes), January 1980.

'Rethinking monetary policy' (by M. Lewis), July 1980.

'The case against monetary activism' (by K. Brunner), January 1981.

'A Keynesian perspective on money' (by N. Kaldor and J. Trevithick), January 1981.

'The integration of monetary, fiscal and incomes policy' (by M. Peston), July 1981.

'Monetarism in an open economy' (by M. Panic), July 1982.

'Is government borrowing now too low?' (by D. Glynn), January 1983.

'Origins of the monetarist fallacy – the legacy of gold' (by R. Bootle), July 1984.

Lloyds Bank Economic Bulletin, nos. 13, 23, 29, 40, 44, 50, 59, 68, 79, 80, 86, 98.

Artis, M. J., and Lewis, M. K., *Monetary Control in the UK*, Philip Allan, 1981.

Ashworth, M., Hills, J., and Morris, N., *Public Finances in Perspective*, Institute for Fiscal Studies, 1984.

Brittan, Samuel, *How to End the 'Monetarist' Controversy*, Institute of Economic Affairs, 1981 (Hobart Paper 90).

Brown, Roger, *A Guide to Monetary Policy*, Banking Information Service.

Brown, Roger, *A Guide to the British Financial System*, Banking Information Service.

Congdon, Tim, *Monetary Control in Britain*, Macmillan, 1982.

Dow, J. C. R., *A Critique of Monetary Policy*, Oxford University Press, 1988.

Goodhart, C. A. E., *Money, Information and Uncertainty*, Macmillan, 1975.

Goodhart, C. A. E., *Monetary Theory and Practice: The UK Experience*, Macmillan, 1984.

Johnson, Christopher, *The Failure of Monetarism*, Manchester Statistical Society, 1982.

Joseph, Sir Keith, *Monetarism is Not Enough*, Centre for Policy Studies, 1976.

Monetary Control, HMSO, March 1980 (Cmnd 7858).

Monetary Policy, Third Report for the Treasury and Civil Service Committee, Session 1980–81, HMSO, 24 February 1981 (HC 162).

Robinson, W., 'How buoyant is public revenue?', *Fiscal Studies*, May 1987.

Smith, David, *The Rise and Fall of Monetarism*, Penguin Books, 1987.

Walters, Alan, *Britain's Economic Renaissance*, Oxford University Press, 1986.

Statistical

Abstract of Banking Statistics. C L S B. Annual.
Bank of England Quarterly Bulletin, statistical annex.
Economic Trends, tables 52, 54, 56, 64, 66.
Financial Statistics, sections 3, 6, 7, 11.

Index

Page references in bold type indicate Tables; those in italics Figures.

accounting 66, **67**, 107
agricultural growth 24

balance of payments 202
  capital account 138, 151, **152**,
    158: flows 160; reserves
    in *153*, 154
  current account 136–8, **145**,
    157–8: changing composition
    140–2, *141*, **148**; predictability
    of variables 161; revisions
    142–3, **144**; *see also* trade
    figures
  deficits 138–41, 151, 154, 202,
    207
  dramatization 203
  economics 157–61
  Press notices 137
  surpluses 138–40, 202
  unpredictable 160–61
  world deficit 155
bank deposits 166–7
Bank of England 159
  Banking and Issue Departments
    176, 178–9
  commercial bill transactions 178
  exchange intervention 154
  guidance to clearing banks 195
  money-supply control 162,
    164–5, 167, 169, 173, 194
  Press notices 48, 71
  publications 171, 174, 182
  statistics 171, 174–5, 177–9
  trade survey 145

banking 196
  innovations 205
banks
  acceptances 178
  clearance rules of guidance
    for 195
  commercial bills 177–8
  'corset' control 170, 195
  credit 179, 184–6, *185*:
    cards 184, 186; growth 182,
    195–6
  inter-bank deposits 164
  interest rates 169–70, 192–3
  liquid assets market share 181
  loans 178–9, 181–2, **185**, 186,
    195: by types **174**, 176;
    demand for 196;
    disintermediation 196;
    increase in 176, 182–4, **183**,
    196–7; mortgages 181;
    non-deposit liabilities 176;
    overseas investment 153; to
    public sector 192;
    retail 178; short-term
    deposits 153; sight deposits,
    non-interest bearing 171
base rate *193*
base-year selection 25, 35–6
black economy 10, 20, 154
borrowing
  central government requirement
    (CGBR) 186–8, **189**
  government 138
  higher interest rates
    increasing 169–70

borrowing–*contd.*
  local-authority
    requirement 187–8, **189**
  net requirement (NBR) 69, *70*
  private *168*, 169, 203
  public corporations'
    requirement 187–8, **189**
  public debt-to-income ratio 191
  public sector *168*
  see also public sector borrowing
    requirement
Bretton Woods era 139
British Gas 173
British Telecom 65, 173
Budget 193, 206
building societies
  deposits 167, 170–71, 179, 192
  flow of funds 170, **180**
  liquidity ratio 180
  market share growth 181
  mortgage increases 176
Building Societies Association
  124, 179

capex 72–4
capital
  expenditure, personal 49
  exports 140
  formation, gross domestic fixed
    (GDFCF) 68–9, 72, 75
  gains, owner-occupiers' tax-
    free 121
  investment 32
Central Statistical Office
  (CSO) 7–9, 49, 53, 136
  cyclical indicators 36–9
  Press notices 41, 49, 62, 69, 75,
    152
central government borrowing
  requirement (CGBR) 186–8,
  189
chemicals output 28
City of London
  banks 178
  overseas earnings 146
  and Scottish banks 178, 181–2
coal
  contribution to GDP growth
    29, 30
  strike 29–30, 76
commercial bills 178, 196, 205

commodity
  analysis of overseas trade *147*
  prices 79
Community Programme 93
competitiveness 159–60
Confederation of British Industries
  (CBI) 28, 55, 77–8, 82
Consolidated Fund 187–8, 190
construction industry output
  indices 28
consume, propensity to 57
consumer credit 184–6, **185**
consumer goods, price increase
  58–9
consumers' expenditure 40, 49–
  51, 200
  deflator (CED) 105, **130**, 133–5
  forecasting 51
  prices and *125*, 126
  retail sales and **52**, 53, **54**
consumption
  components 49
  income elasticity 57
  per head 15
  private and public 32, **33**
  saving and 56–9, **54**
corporation tax 62
credit
  consumer 184, **185**
  domestic, expansion of 206
  flows 176
  growth 176, 195–6, 203, 206
  M4 changes and **175**
  per unit of GDP 196
  'securitization' of 71
  see also banks, credit; banks,
    loans
Credit Business 184

data sources 10
definition, changes in 10–11
deflators 133
  see also consumers' expenditure;
    gross domestic product; Retail
    Prices Index
demand 102, 161
  elasticity, of imports 158–9
  price and income elasticity 125–
    6
deregulation
  of economic activity 204
  innovation as 205

devaluation 102, 139, 159–60
discount houses 178
distributive-trades survey 55
Divisia 174
domestic credit expansion 206
domestic expenditure, total
   (TDE) 33
dwelling purchases 120–21

earnings 98–9, **101**, 201
  prices and 99, **100**
econometric models 13, 35–6
economic cycle, damping
   down 198
Economic Trends 31, 36, 75, 78
education, measuring output 22
Edwardes, Sir Michael 104
employment 33, 81, *92*, 94, *95*
Employment Department
  Family Expenditure Survey
   (FES) 111
  Press notices 81, 98–9
Employment Institute 90
energy industries 24
engineering growth 29
Enterprise Zones 204
equity withdrawal 122
Eurodollar market 153
European Economic Community
   (EEC) 148
  Common Agricultural Policy
   (CAP) 24, 147
European Monetary System, UK
  membership 161
exchange rate 27, **156**, *157*, 204
  control 154, 170
  determinant of interest
   rates 163
  effect of change in 157
  effective 155–6
  fixed and floating 139
  government policy 25–6
  indicators 155
  influence on profits 79
  unemployment and 102, 103–4
  unpredictable 161
excise duties 126
expenditure 17
  total domestic (TDE) 32, **33**
  total final (TFE) 32, **33**
  see also capital, consumers',
   personal *and* public
   expenditure
export–import price ratio 31
exports 142–3, 148, 151, 159

factor income distribution *33*
Family Expenditure Survey
   (FES) 111, 115–16, 119, 122
Finance Bill 197
finance houses 186
financial
  assets, net acquisition of
   (NAFA) 43
  companies 61–2, 72: income
   sources and allocation 66, **67**,
   68;
  deficit, public-sector
   (PSFD) 190
  innovation 195, 203, 205
  institutions other than monetary
   (OFIs) 61
  markets, integration 195
   periods 14
  strategy, Government's medium
   term (MTFS) 163, 167,
   172, 173–6, 198, 204
Financial Statistics 184, 186, 193
Financial Times 60
financing, official 138
Fiscal Studies Institute 115, 121,
   130, 197
fiscalism 168, 202
food prices, seasonal
   variations 13
forecasting 12–14
  by quarterly cyclical
   indicators 36–9
  capital expenditure 78
  consumers' expenditure 51
  with econometric models 13,
   35–6

Galbraith, J. K. 198
German Federal Republic, wage
  demands 162
Goodhart's Law 166, 194
Government Statistical Service 7,
  9
gross domestic fixed capital
  formation (GDFCF) 68–9,
  72, 75

gross domestic product (GDP)
18, *19*
average (A) 17, 19, 34–5
changes in 17
definition 16–17
deflator **130**, 133, 134–6
disparity between measures **21**, 27
domestic demand growth and 32
expenditure-based (E) 17, 20, 31–2, **33**, 36, 40
forecasting 35–6: by quarterly cyclical indicators 36–9
growth of 197
income-based (I) 17, 20, 32–5, *33*, 40
money 16
output-based (O) 16–17, 21–7: coal strike and 76; forecasting 36; press releases on 21; production industries in 28; revisions of 21–2; sectoral shares 23–9, *23*, **25**, *26*, **30**; sectoral weighting 26–7
pre-1939 estimates 18
public sector borrowing requirement (PSBR) relationship to 198
publication of 18, 31–2
Gross Earnings Deflator 130–31
gross national product (GNP) 18
gross trading profits (GTPs) 62–6, *65*, **67**, 68
growth, economic 15
average 19
fall in, political parties and 200
government attitude 15–16
per head 15–16
revision of figures 207
sectoral disparity 24, **25**
UK record 18–21

Hattersley, Roy 152
health, measuring output 22
home improvement 49, 122
house prices 120–21
household costs 135
household sector 41
accounts **45**
consumers' expenditure 50

income, components *46*
saving 44, *48*, 200

import prices 135–6, 151
imports 142, 158–9
income 15, 17
personal, *see* personal income
real national disposable (RNDI) 31
tax 41, 56, 129
undeclared, measure of 20
indicators, economic 203–4
announcement of 5
cyclical 36–9
departments publishing 8
forecasting 12–14
government use 205, 206–7
lagging 37–8
market effects 206
measuring 204–5
misleading 9–12
political use 205–6
Press notices, wider circulation desirable 207–8
psychological 37
redefinition of 206–7
revisions 9–10, 12
seasonality 9
industrial and commercial companies (ICCs) 60
appropriation account 66, **67**
borrowing 200–201
capital account 68, 71–5, *72–3*, **74**, 201
constant purchasing power (CPP) accounting 107
financial surplus 68–9
functions 61–2
income sources and allocation 66, **67**
investments 70–71
net borrowing requirement (NBR) 69, *70*
Press notices 64–5
profits 61–2, **63**, 79, 200: gross trading (GTPs) 62–6, *65*, **67**, 68; measuring 205
statistics 60–61
stocks 68–9, 75, **76**
industrial sectors
capital expenditure analysis by 72, *73*, 74

shares of GDP   *23*, 24
industrial trends quarterly survey
    77–8
industries
    classification   22
    weighting   22, *23*
industry, demand for money
    by   196
inflation   201–2
    accounting   107
    causes of   136
    control   16, 167, 194
    definition   104
    economic influences   135
    government policy   106
    gross trading profits and   64
    income increase needed to
        compensate for   129–31
    indices   **130**, 131–5
    money supply and   162, 171
    personal savings ratio and   58
    rapid changes in   35
    rate   113–14, 127, 207
    Retail Prices Index criterion
        of   106, 126–7
    trade figures and   150
Inland Revenue *Survey of Personal
    Income*   128
institutional investment   48
interest rates   192–3, 204
    balance of payments and   139
    bank and building society   170
    base rate   *193*
    control   194
    effect on GDP   37
    futures   170
    guide to   163
    income and substitution ef-
        fects   59
    increase in   194
    inflation and   59
    influences on   192–3
    money demand and   195
    money-supply control through
        169–70
    publication of   192
    Retail Prices Index and   106
    unpredictable   161
interest as transfer payment   24
International Monetary Fund
    (IMF)   154–5, 162, 206
investment   70–75, *72–3*, **74**

accelerator theory   79
    direct   152
    industrial and commercial
        companies   70–75, *72–3*, **74**
    institutional, quarterly Press
        notice   48
    intentions survey   78
    portfolio   152–3
    risk premium   160
    theory of profits and   78–80

job creation   96, 201
job vacancies   98
Joseph, Sir Keith   163

Keynes, J. M.   56, 58
Keynesian models   36

labour
    costs, predictability   161
    inputs, as proxy for outputs   22
    productivity   81–2, 99–100, **101**
    unit costs, rise in   99–100
Labour Force Survey   97–8
Lawson, Nigel   106, 117, 164
leaks by ministers   13
leased assets   73–4
life assurance and pensions funds
    (LAPFs)   41–2, 44, 50
    flow of personal sector
        saving   46, *47–8*
Lloyds Bank   60
local authorities
    borrowing requirement (LABR)
        187–8, **189**
    mortgage market share   181

manufacturing
    decline in   200
    earnings increase in   201
    growth in   99–100
    investment   75
    output cycles   24–5, *96*
    overseas trade   160
    price index   131
    productivity   80, 100, **101**, 201
    terms of trade   132–3
measuring the economy,
    methods   16–17
minerals production   29
monetarism   136, 163, 168, 194,
    202

monetarist models 36
monetary sector 61
money
  broad 164–5, 167
  demand for 194–7
  GDP, increase in 161
  markets, interest in 166
  meaning of 162–71
  narrow 164
  per unit of GDP 196
  quantity theory 194
  statistics 171
  stock, growth 173, 176
money supply 162
  aggregates 164, 195: credit
    counterparts 174–5, **175**;
    MTFS 163, 167, **172**, 173–6,
    198, 204
  control 139, 154, 162–7, *165*,
    194: by interest rates 169–70
  growth 173–6
  prices and 194
  publications 174
  statistical problems 174, 176,
    178–9
money supply targets 202
  components 171, **172**
  M0 164–6, *165*, 171, 204
  M1 166–7, 171
  M2 167
  M3 167–71, 171, 175–6, 194,
    204
  M3c 167
  M4 170–71, **175**, 176, 179
  M5 170–71, 175
  PSL1 and 2 170–71
  results 171, **173**
Monthly Digest of Statistics 29,
  133
mortgage costs 110, 116, **117**, *118*,
  127, **130**
  measuring 122–4
mortgages 168, 170, *182*, 186,
  196
Moser, Claus 7

National Food Survey 53
National Loans Fund 187–8
National Savings 169–71, 175,
  181
national insurance contributions
  44, 56

net borrowing requirement
  (NBR) 69, *70*
North America, exports to 148
North Sea oil 24–5, 27, 31, 62
  balance of payments and 140–
    41
  prices 74–5
  profits 34, 62, 64–5, 200
  revenue decline 191
  surpluses 145
  unemployment caused by 103–4
  US investment in 152
Northern Ireland, unemployed
  in 9

oil and gas, contribution to GDP
  growth 29, **30**, 31
oil prices 140, 151, 160
  fall in 26, 34, 133, 135
Organization of Petroleum
  Exporting Countries (OPEC),
  trade with 148
overseas trade, commodity
  analysis *147*
Overseas Trade Statistics 142, 147
Overseas Transactions 152
owner-occupation
  cost of **117**, **120**
  imputed rent 24, 44, 50, 119–
    20, 134
  mortgages for 116, **117**
  Retail Prices Index and 116–24,
    117, *118*
  tax-free capital gains from 121
  user cost 121–2

Pareto, Vilfredo 59
pay bargaining, Retail Prices Index
  and 107
pension funds, contributions
  to 46, 48–9
pensioners, retail prices index
  for 115
periods in years, indication of 14
personal expenditure, growth
  of 41, **42**
personal income 40
  components *46–7*
  disposable (PDI) 40, 42, 44, 49,
    57: components 56; real
    (RPDI) 40

personal saving 40, 43–5, *47*, 49
  changing shares in *48*
  consumption and 54, 56–9
  derivations 43
  ratio 56, 58, 200
personal sector 41
  accounts 45
  financial surplus 43–4
  liquid assets 180, *181*
  statistics, reliability 49, *50*
petrol prices 127
political use of statistics 7–9, 199–
  200
population
  growth 15–16
  inactive *94*, 96, 97
  working age *94*, 96
portfolio investment 152–3
portfolio theory 195
Press notices 5–6, 199
prices 79, 108, 151, 201
  see also Retail Prices Index; Tax
  and Price Index
prices and incomes policy 194
Prime Minister, power of 8
private non-profit-making bodies
  (PNBs) 41, 45–7, 50
private sector liquidity (PSL) 170
privatization 65, 188–91, **189**, 202,
  205
producer prices 105, **130**, 131–5
production industries
  disparities in growth rates 28
  output index 27–31
productivity 100–101, 135, 161,
  201
  see also labour productivity
profits 79, 200
  gross trading (GTPs) 62–6, *63*,
  65, 68
  theory of investment and 78–80
psychological indicators 37
public corporations
  borrowing requirement 187–8,
  189
  privatization 188, **189**, 190–91
public debt-to-income ratio 191
public expenditure, increase 197
public limited companies
  (PLCs) 61
public sector borrowing, reduced
  168

public sector borrowing
  requirement (PSBR) 163,
  168, 186–92, 197
  by components 188, **189**
  as debt increase
  percentage 190–91
  financing 192
  GDP relationship to 198
  increase in 205
  influence on interest rates 193
  monetary growth contribution
  192
  monthly figures 186–7
  overfunding 175, 178, 195
  privatization and 188, **189**, 190–
  91, 202
  reduction in 202
  target achievement 191
public sector financial deficit
  (PSFD) 190, 207
purchasing power, constant
  accounting (CPP) 107

quality, Retail Prices Index
  and 115

Ramsey, Frank 58
rates 110, 116, 126
Rayner, Sir Derek 9, 84
rent 110, 116, 126
  imputed 24, 44, 50, 119–20,
  134
reserves, official 137–8, *153*, 154
Restart scheme 93, 97
Retail Prices Index (RPI) 105–7,
  201
  Advisory Committee
  (RPIAC) 108–10, 118–19,
  122–4
  averaging **114**
  components **112**, 124–6
  deflators **130**, 134–6
  economic influences 135–6
  history 107, *108*, 109–10
  home improvement loans in 122
  house prices in 120–21
  import prices in 136
  income weighting 114–15, 122
  increases in 111, **112**
  inflation indicator 136
  interest rates related to 123–4

Retail Prices Index–*cont*.
  methods of compiling   111–14,
    113, 115–16
  mortgage costs in   110, 116, **117**,
    118, 127, **130**: measuring
    122–4
  owner-occupation and   110,
    116–24, **117**, *118*
  pay bargaining and   107
  petrol prices in   127
  quality and   115
  rents and rates in   126
  short-term movements   126–7
  strengths and weaknesses   114–
    16
  Tax and Price Index compared
    with   128–30
  taxation in   126, 130
  US   113
  weighting changes   109, **110**,
    116
retail sales   51, 53
  consumers' expenditure and   52,
    53, **54**
revenue surplus   191
RNDI, *see* income, real national
  disposable
Royal Economic Society   139
RPDI, *see* personal income,
  disposable, real

saving, *see* personal saving
saving ratio   49, 200
school-leavers, unemployed   86–7
securities, index-linked   107
self-employment   20, 41–2, 94, 96
  unemployment figures and   86–
    7, 91
services sector   24, 26, 100–101,
  103
share valuation ratio   80
shipping industry decline   202
short-term changes   6
social security   41–2, 106
stabilizers, automatic   198
Standard Industrial Classification
  (SIC)   22
statistical measurement   204
statistical returns   204
statistics
  comparisons of   11–12

  manipulation   207
  out-of-date publications   6
  political use   7–9, 199–200
  reliability   7–8, 10–12
  revision   9–10
  seasonality   9
  sources   10, 14
  turning points   11–12
Sterling M3 (£M3)   167–71
stockbuilding   75, **76**
stocks, gilt-edged   169, 175
Stockton, Lord   163
supply-side models   36

take-overs   79–80
tax
  allowances   76, 106
  cuts   198
  evasion, allowance for   20
  revenue   191, 197
Tax and Price Index (TPI)   127–
  31, 201–2
TDE, *see* expenditure, domestic
technological progress,
  unemployment from   103
terms of trade   151, 157
TFE, *see* expenditure, final   127
Thatcher Government   198
  attitude to economic
    growth   15–16
  economic indicators and   205
  first Budget   128
  medium-term financial strategy
    (MTFS)   163, 167, 172–6,
    198, 204
  money-supply control and   194
  public expenditure control
    by   197–8
trade
  competitiveness   159–60
  increase in world   158
trade figures   137–47, 202
  changing composition of   140–
    42, *141*
  computerization   204
  deficits   138–41
  inflation and   150
  interest, profits and dividends
    (IPD) surplus   145–6
  invisibles   140, 143, **144**, 146–7,
    155

manic-depressive reaction cycle
204
as percentage of GDP   150
services   145
surpluses   138–40
unpredictable   160–61
visibles: area analysis   *148*;
    changing pattern of   147–51,
    148, **149**; commodity an-
    alysis   *147*; re-weighting   150;
    revisions of   142–3, **144**
Trade and Industry Department
    (DTI)   51–2, 54–5
    investment-intentions
        survey   78
    Press notices   71, 74–5, 137, 184,
        186
    producer prices indices   131
trading profits, gross (GTP)   34
transfer payments
    excluded from GDP   20
    in personal income   40
Treasury   137, 154, 186–8, 194–
    5
Trustee Savings Banks   173

UK Balance of Payments   152
UK National Accounts   133
unemployment   203
    benefit, fraudulent claims   84–5

by age and sex   **84**, 91
causes of   102–4
criteria for   82, **83**
definition   8, 11, 82–7, **83**, 201
fall in   97, 197
increase in   96–7
Labour Force Survey   85–6
long-term   89
minimizing   83–4, 87–93, **92**
monthly Press notice   81
pay bargaining and   81
percentage   86, **87**, 90–91, *92*
political use of figures   206
remedies   102–3
school-leavers   86–7
statistics   87–9, *89*, **90**, *94*, **95**
UK and GB figures   97–8
Unemployment Unit   88–9
unincorporated businesses
    (UIBs)   41, 46–7, 72

value added   16, 22, 116

wages   81–2, 103
    see also earnings
Walters, Sir Alan   163
wholesale-price indices   105, 132
Wilson, Harold   7

Youth Training Scheme   93, 97

FOR THE BEST IN PAPERBACKS, LOOK FOR THE

In every corner of the world, on every subject under the sun, Penguin represents quality and variety – the very best in publishing today.

For complete information about books available from Penguin – including Puffins, Penguin Classics and Arkana – and how to order them, write to us at the appropriate address below. Please note that for copyright reasons the selection of books varies from country to country.

In the United Kingdom: Please write to *Dept E.P., Penguin Books Ltd, Harmondsworth, Middlesex, UB7 0DA.*

If you have any difficulty in obtaining a title, please send your order with the correct money, plus ten per cent for postage and packaging, to *PO Box No 11, West Drayton, Middlesex*

In the United States: Please write to *Dept BA, Penguin, 299 Murray Hill Parkway, East Rutherford, New Jersey 07073*

In Canada: Please write to *Penguin Books Canada Ltd, 2801 John Street, Markham, Ontario L3R 1B4*

In Australia: Please write to the *Marketing Department, Penguin Books Australia Ltd, P.O. Box 257, Ringwood, Victoria 3134*

In New Zealand: Please write to the *Marketing Department, Penguin Books (NZ) Ltd, Private Bag, Takapuna, Auckland 9*

In India: Please write to *Penguin Overseas Ltd, 706 Eros Apartments, 56 Nehru Place, New Delhi, 110019*

In the Netherlands: Please write to *Penguin Books Netherlands B.V., Postbus 195, NL–1380AD Weesp*

In West Germany: Please write to *Penguin Books Ltd, Friedrichstrasse 10–12, D–6000 Frankfurt/Main 1*

In Spain: Please write to *Longman Penguin España, Calle San Nicolas 15, E–28013 Madrid*

In Italy: Please write to *Penguin Italia s.r.l., Via Como 4, I-20096 Pioltello (Milano)*

In France: Please write to *Penguin Books Ltd, 39 Rue de Montmorency, F-75003 Paris*

In Japan: Please write to *Longman Penguin Japan Co Ltd, Yamaguchi Building, 2-12-9 Kanda Jimbocho, Chiyoda-Ku, Tokyo 101*

FOR THE BEST IN PAPERBACKS, LOOK FOR THE 🐧

PENGUIN BUSINESS

Great management classics of enduring relevance, business texts with a
proven track record, and exciting new titles – books for all the diverse needs
of today's businesses.

Management and Motivation   Victor H. Vroom and Edward L. Deci

The Art of Japanese Management
   Richard Tanner Pascale and Anthony Athos

The Penguin Management Handbook   Thomas Kempner (ed.)

Introducing Management   Peter Lawrence and Ken Elliott (eds.)

The Entrepreneurial Manager   A. L. Minkes

An Insight into Management Accounting   John Sizer

Too Good to be True   Fraud in the City   Rowan Bosworth-Davies

Understanding Company Financial Statements   R. H. Parker

The Social Psychology of Industry   J. A. C. Brown

The Human Side of Enterprise   Douglas McGregor

Successful Interviewing   Jack Gratus

Working in Organizations
   Andrew Kakabadse, Ron Ludlow and Susan Vinnicombe

Offensive Marketing   J. H. Davidson

Corporate Recovery   Stuart Slatter

Corporate Strategy   Igor Ansoff

The Mind of the Strategist   Kenichi Ohmae

FOR THE BEST IN PAPERBACKS, LOOK FOR THE 🐧

PENGUIN POLITICS AND SOCIAL SCIENCES

Political Ideas David Thomson (ed.)

From Machiavelli to Marx – a stimulating and informative introduction to the last 500 years of European political thinkers and political thought.

On Revolution Hannah Arendt

Arendt's classic analysis of a relatively recent political phenomenon examines the underlying principles common to all revolutions, and the evolution of revolutionary theory and practice. 'Never dull, enormously erudite, always imaginative' – *Sunday Times*

The Apartheid Handbook Roger Omond

The facts behind the headlines: the essential hard information about how apartheid actually works from day to day.

The Social Construction of Reality Peter Berger and Thomas Luckmann

Concerned with the sociology of 'everything that passes for knowledge in society' and particularly with that which passes for common sense, this is 'a serious, open-minded book, upon a serious subject' – *Listener*

The Care of the Self Michel Foucault
The History of Sexuality Vol 3

Foucault examines the transformation of sexual discourse from the Hellenistic to the Roman world in an inquiry which 'bristles with provocative insights into the tangled liaison of sex and self' – *The Times Higher Educational Supplement*

A Fate Worse than Debt Susan George

How did Third World countries accumulate a staggering trillion dollars' worth of debt? Who really shoulders the burden of reimbursement? How should we deal with the debt crisis? Susan George answers these questions with the solid evidence and verve familiar to readers of *How the Other Half Dies*.

FOR THE BEST IN PAPERBACKS, LOOK FOR THE 🐧

PENGUIN BUSINESS AND ECONOMICS

Almost Everyone's Guide to Economics
J. K. Galbraith and Nicole Salinger

This instructive and entertaining dialogue provides a step-by-step explanation of 'the state of economics in general and the reasons for its present failure in particular in simple, accurate language that everyone could understand and that a perverse few might conceivably enjoy'.

The Rise and Fall of Monetarism   David Smith

Now that even Conservatives have consigned monetarism to the scrapheap of history, David Smith draws out the unhappy lessons of a fundamentally flawed economic experiment, driven by a doctrine that for years had been regarded as outmoded and irrelevant.

Atlas of Management Thinking   Edward de Bono

This fascinating book provides a vital repertoire of non-verbal images that will help activate the right side of any manager's brain.

The Economist Economics   Rupert Pennant-Rea and Clive Crook

Based on a series of 'briefs' published in *The Economist*, this is a clear and accessible guide to the key issues of today's economics for the general reader.

Understanding Organizations   Charles B. Handy

Of practical as well as theoretical interest, this book shows how general concepts can help solve specific organizational problems.

The Winning Streak   Walter Goldsmith and David Clutterbuck

A brilliant analysis of what Britain's best-run and most successful companies have in common – a must for all managers.

Lateral Thinking for Management   Edward de Bono

Creativity and lateral thinking can work together for managers in developing new products or ideas; Edward de Bono shows how.

Understanding the British Economy   Peter Donaldson and John Farquhar

A comprehensive and well signposted tour of the British economy today; a sound introduction to elements of economic theory; and a balanced account of recent policies are provided by this bestselling text.

A Question of Economics   Peter Donaldson

Twenty key issues – the City, trade unions, 'free market forces' and many others – are presented clearly and fully in this major book based on a television series.

The Economics of the Common Market   Dennis Swann

From the CAP to the EMS, this internationally recognized book on the Common Market – now substantially revised – is essential reading in the run-up to 1992.

The Money Machine   How the City Works   Philip Coggan

How are the big deals made? Which are the institutions that really matter? What causes the pound to rise or interest rates to fall? This book provides clear and concise answers to these and many other money-related questions.

Parkinson's Law   C. Northcote Parkinson

'Work expands so as to fill the time available for its completion': that law underlies this 'extraordinarily funny and witty book' (Stephen Potter in the *Sunday Times*) which also makes some painfully serious points about those in business or the Civil Service.